STUDY GUIDE

Abnormal Psychology

Fourth Edition

Abnormal Psychology

FOURTH EDITION

David L. Rosenhan, Elaine Walker,
and Martin E. P. Seligman

Kieran T. Sullivan

SANTA CLARA UNIVERSITY

 W • W • NORTON & COMPANY • NEW YORK • LONDON

Copyright © 2001 by W. W. Norton & Company, Inc.

Printed in the United States of America

Composition and layout by Roberta Flechner Graphics

ISBN 0-393-97704-8 (pbk.)

W. W. Norton & Company, Inc., 500 Fifth Avenue, New York, NY 10110
www.wwnorton.com

W. W. Norton & Company Ltd., Castle House, 75/76 Wells Street, London W1T 3QT

1 2 3 4 5 6 7 8 9 0

CONTENTS

Abnormal Psychology

Fourth Edition

CHAPTER 1 | Abnormality: Past and Present

A GUIDE TO THE READING

This chapter introduces four themes and challenges that recur throughout the book: the relationship between biological and psychological factors; the importance of development; the decision regarding treatment of choice; and the contributions of science and practice. Be sure to become very familiar with these, as they will help you structure your reading for all subsequent chapters. The remainder of the chapter provides a historical overview of the field, discussing early approaches to abnormality, the treatment of the insane, and the establishment of criteria for defining abnormality.

Themes and Challenges

Biological and psychological levels of analysis were traditionally separate, but now are often integrated in explanations of the causes of psychological abnormality. These two traditions (biological and psychological) are described on p. 5. Two terms that illustrate the interaction between biological and psychological levels of analysis are *bottom-up causation* (when a biological state causes a psychological state) and *top-down causation* (when a psychological state causes a biological state). The text provides examples of both (on p. 7) in determining the causes of depression. Social and cultural factors have also been implicated in many psychological disorders, but these factors typically influence, rather than cause, the onset of disorders. Sociocultural variables are therefore viewed as *moderators* of abnormality; the sociocultural approach is not used as a separate level of analysis.

Development: A person's vulnerability to psychological problems varies over his or her lifespan due to changes in societal expectations, developmental changes in the brain, the cumulative effects of experience, and the interplay between nature and nurture. See p. 9 for a detailed explanation of these factors.

Treatment of Choice: Outcome studies, in which new treatments are rigorously compared to control treatments, are yielding more and more information about the treatments of choice for many psychological disorders. The treatment of choice depends on the type of disorder and may include medications, psychotherapy, or a combination of the two. Keep in mind that medications often relieve symptoms without treating the underlying disorder, and thus discontinuance of medications may lead to a relapse.

Science and Practice: Scientists test causes and treatments for any number of similar people with similar problems. Practitioners focus on treating a particular person with a particular problem. Integrating these two approaches is challenging but fruitful; thus, the contributions of both will be emphasized throughout the text.

Early Approaches to Abnormality

This section outlines the history of beliefs about the causes of abnormality. Common explanations for madness included possession by evil spirits (in premodern and medieval societies), physical causes (in premodern, ancient Greek, and modern societies), and psychogenic origins (in ancient Greek and modern societies). Pay special attention to the discussion of the modern development of the psychological levels of analysis found on pp. 15–17. This section also describes some of the important figures who advanced psychological analysis, including Mesmer, who practiced early forms of hypnosis; Charcot, who further developed hypnosis and used it to distinguish symptoms with psychological causes from symptoms with physical causes; Breuer, who used hypnosis to treat patients by inducing an emotional catharsis; and Freud, who developed psychoanalysis.

Treatment of the Insane

This section traces the history of treatment of the mentally ill, from the opening of the first psychiatric hospital in France in the seventeenth century to the present day. Note especially the loss of personal liberty and the often brutal conditions resulting from *animalism* (the belief that the insane had lost their ability to reason and were essentially like animals). The growth of humane treatment began at the end of the eighteenth century (see pp. 18–19 for a description of these changes). Patients in many countries were unshackled and provided with better living conditions; note particularly Pinel's contributions in France, the religious cures implemented in Belgium and England, and the use of "moral treatment" in the United States.

Defining Abnormality Today

Defining abnormality is complex, and definitions are often hotly debated. Be sure to know the seven elements that are used in deciding whether a person's behavior is abnormal: suffering, maladaptiveness, irrationality, unpredictability and loss of control, rareness and unconventionality, observer discomfort, and violation of standards. *Suffering* implies that the behavior and/or feelings are distressing to the person experiencing them. *Maladaptiveness* refers to behaviors that interfere with the person's functioning in social environments, such as work or school, or in interpersonal relationships. *Irrationality* concerns behaviors that have no rational meaning, such as absurd or bizarre beliefs. *Unpredictability and loss of control* refer to behaviors that do not follow ordinary guidelines and that seem to have no rational cause, for example, extreme rage for no apparent reason. *Rareness and unconventionality* suggest behaviors that are unusual or are perceived to be unusual. *Observer discomfort* refers to behavior that makes others feel uncomfortable, for example, (in Western culture) placing your face two inches away from someone else's face. *Violation of standards* alludes to behaviors that are against the moral standards and norms of the majority of people. Note that many of the elements represent a necessary but not sufficient cause (for example, maladaptiveness), and several represent neither a necessary nor a sufficient cause (for example, suffering). Instead, to identify most clearly whether someone is abnormal, a family resemblance approach is used.

The *family resemblance approach* is used to determine whether the person, behavior, or thought bears a resemblance to the clearest examples of people, behaviors, and thoughts we would all recognize as abnormal. An excellent example of how to apply this approach to an actual case can be found on pp. 23–24. However, you should also keep in mind that there are some hazards to using this approach. First, several of these elements involve social judgments that may not be constant over time and between cultures, such as observer discomfort, maladaptiveness, unconventionality, and violation of standards. Second, two observers using this approach may come up with two different conclusions about whether someone is abnormal. In other words, the criteria are not precise and, ultimately, the conclusion is subjective. Third, people who are judged as abnormal by others may not see themselves as abnormal. This may be due to the increased amount of information available to them, the changing nature of their distress, or the fact that people tend to perceive themselves more favorably than others perceive them.

TESTING YOUR UNDERSTANDING

Test your understanding of what you have read by working through the following tasks with a classmate.

1. A friend is very upset because his sister was just diagnosed with Major Depressive Disorder. His mother mentioned that both his aunt and his maternal grandfather were depressed at several times throughout their lives. Your friend wants to know if his sister inherited the disorder or if something happened after she was born to cause it. Having taken an abnormal psychology class, you are able to explain that the question is not "nature *versus* nurture," but rather "nature *and* nurture." Explain this further. What are some causes for depression at the biological and psychological levels of analysis?

2. How do both research psychologists and practicing psychologists contribute to the understanding and treatment of abnormality?

3. We have learned that developmental changes can affect the onset of abnormal behavior. What happens over the course of our lives that makes us more vulnerable to certain disorders at specific times?

4. A friend is wondering whether his sister should take antidepressants or go to therapy to treat her disorder. How would a research psychologist determine the treatment of choice for her depression?

5. A friend is very worried about the stigma attached to receiving psychological treatment. To give your friend some perspective, describe how mental illness has been viewed historically, and what effect these views have had on the treatment of the mentally ill.

6. Knowing that depression runs in families, your friend worries about whether he may have Major Depressive Disorder. He mentions that he does feel depressed sometimes and wonders whether his depression is normal or abnormal. Using the family resemblance approach, provide criteria he can use to determine whether his behaviors and emotions are normal or abnormal.

Multiple-Choice Questions

1. In any given year, _____ of Americans suffer from mental illness.
   a. 1 percent
   b. 5 percent
   c. 20 percent
   d. 30 percent

2. The direct cost per year of psychological disorders in America is estimated at:
   a. $50 million.
   b. $100 million.
   c. $50 billion.
   d. $100 billion.

3. Which of the following is NOT one of the themes and challenges addressed in the book?
   a. Modern health-care delivery
   b. Biological and psychological levels of analysis
   c. Treatment of choice
   d. Science and practice

4. In the case presented in the text, Celia experienced panic attacks during which she felt dread, dizziness, and shakiness. She thought she was going crazy or was going to die. Her heart rate doubled, her blood pressure soared, and she broke into a flop sweat. What is the most likely explanation for her panic?
   a. Her thoughts (that she would die or go crazy) and her feelings (dread, dizziness, and shakiness) caused her to experience physical symptoms (increases in heart rate, blood pressure, and flop sweat).
   b. Her physical symptoms caused her to experience distressing thoughts and feelings.
   c. Her panic was a natural response to an environmental danger.
   d. Celia's bodily and cognitive symptoms influenced each other, leading to a state of spiraling, out-of-control panic.

5. Celia experienced panic attacks during which she felt dread, dizziness, and shakiness. She thought she was going crazy or was going to die. Her heart rate doubled, her blood pressure soared, and she broke into a flop sweat. In explaining her symptoms, a "bottom-up" explanation is that _____, and a "top-down" explanation is that _____
   a. her thoughts (that she would die or go crazy) and her feelings (dread, dizziness, and shakiness) caused her to experience her physical symptoms (increases in heart rate, blood pressure, and flop sweat); her physical symptoms caused her to experience the distressing thoughts and feelings.
   b. her physical symptoms caused her to experience the distressing thoughts and feelings; her thoughts and feelings caused her to experience the physical symptoms.
   c. her physical symptoms caused her to experience distressing thoughts and feelings; her panic was a natural response to an environmental danger.
   d. her panic was a natural response to an environmental danger; her physical symptoms caused her to experience distressing thoughts and feelings.

6. Researchers have found that for depression:
   a. bottom-up explanations are most consistently supported.
   b. top-down explanations are most consistently supported.
   c. studies indicate that it is mainly a physical disease.
   d. both bottom-up and top-down explanations are supported.

7. Women are much more likely to experience anxiety disorders, while men are more likely to experience substance abuse disorders. Poor people have a higher rate of schizophrenia than their wealthier counterparts. Such findings indicate that:
   a. sociocultural factors are an important level of analysis when considering mental disorders.
   b. sociocultural factors moderate the effect of mental disorders.
   c. sociocultural factors cause mental disorders.
   d. sociocultural factors mediate the effect of mental disorders.

8. The study of the effects of development on the onset of mental disorders has yielded many important findings. Which of the following is NOT one of those findings?
   a. Depression is much more frequent in girls than boys before puberty; after puberty, it evens out.
   b. Preoccupation with weight gain is commonplace in teens, but few elderly patients are seriously concerned with their weight.
   c. Fear of separation from parents can be a serious problem for young children, but rarely occurs among adults.
   d. Between 1 and 2 percent of people aged twenty to forty have experienced a hallucination, but hallucinations rarely occur among children.

9. The textbook lists several reasons why our vulnerability to different psychological problems changes as we age. Which of the following is NOT one of those reasons?
   a. developmental changes in the brain
   b. increased willingness to break with social norms as we age

    c. different expectations from society

    d. cumulative effects of experience

10. When psychologists use a developmental approach to the understanding of mental disorders, they focus on three key issues. Which of the following is NOT one of those issues?
    a. Developmental stage of emergence
    b. Evidence of vulnerability in advance of major symptoms
    c. Best treatments at various stages of development
    d. Developmental changes as clues to the causes of the disorder

11. The treatment of choice theme is the corollary of which other theme?
    a. development
    b. biological and psychological levels of analysis
    c. modern health-care delivery
    d. science and practice

12. According to your text, how many disorders can now be treated successfully?
    a. four
    b. fourteen
    c. twenty-two
    d. twenty-eight

13. Dr. Miles treated Celia successfully with cognitive therapy. There are many reasons why this was the treatment of choice for Celia's panic disorder. Which of the following is NOT one of those reasons?
    a. Research suggests that cognitive therapy works for 80 percent of patients with panic disorder.
    b. Medications, such as Xanax, treat the symptoms but do not prevent relapse.
    c. This approach took advantage of one of Celia's strengths, her rationality and ability to think clearly under stress.
    d. Panic is a disorder that is clearly psychological, with no major physical component.

14. According to the textbook, all of the following can be treated quite easily EXCEPT:
    a. alcoholism.
    b. sexual dysfunction.
    c. depression.
    d. panic.

15. A psychologist conducted a research study to determine how well a new treatment for obsessive-compulsive disorder worked at her HMO. This type of study is BEST described as an:
    a. outcome study.
    b. effectiveness study.
    c. efficacy study.
    d. analogue study.

16. The prevention of mental disorders is a burgeoning field in psychology today. The prevention of disorders falls under which theme?
    a. biological and psychological levels of analysis
    b. modern delivery of health care services
    c. treatment of choice
    d. science and practice

17. A patient described in your text experienced voices being transmitted to her and believed that she was being watched twenty-four hours a day. She attributes this to punishment at "the hands of God's servants for deeds I had committed earlier in my life." During which period(s) of history would her symptoms most likely be viewed as supernatural in nature?
    a. premodern society
    b. medieval society
    c. premodern and medieval society
    d. premodern society and society in the 1800s

18. Purges, bleeding, and trephining (drilling holes through the skull) were all early remedies consistent with:
    a. the belief that "mad" people were possessed.
    b. the medical approach.
    c. the psychogenic approach.
    d. mesmerism.

19. Galen, a physician in the second century A.D., concluded that one of his patients was either suffering from melancholy, which was thought to be an imbalance of one of the four bodily "humors," or from "something she was unwilling to confess." This second explanation is consistent with the _____ approach.
    a. psychogenic
    b. medical
    c. supernatural
    d. sociocultural

20. Mesmer believed that many diseases, from epilepsy to hysteria, were caused by a disruption of the flow of the "universal magnetic fluid." He treated patients by putting them in a large tub, playing gentle music, and touching them with an iron rod. He was dismissed by his colleagues as a charlatan, despite his considerable therapeutic success. We now know that his success was probably due to:
    a. the placebo effect.
    b. his patients' self-deception.
    c. the use of magnets.
    d. hypnotism.

21. The establishment of psychiatric hospitals in the seventeenth century marks an important shift in treatment of the mentally ill. These hospitals were:
    a. an improvement in the conditions of the mentally ill.
    b. still inhumane in their treatment of the mentally ill.
    c. quite successful in treating the mentally ill.
    d. both a and b

22. The treatment of the mentally ill in early psychiatric hospitals is best explained by
    a. animism.
    b. animalism.
    c. the medical approach.
    d. the psychogenic approach.

23. Which of the following is NOT true about the development of humane treatment of the mentally ill?
    a. It was spearheaded by groups of dissatisfied patients.
    b. Charugi in Italy, and Dacquin and Pinel in France were important figures in this movement.
    c. Religious communities were responsible for improving the conditions of many of the mentally ill.
    d. Moral treatment, although not especially effective in treating mental disorders, did much to improve conditions for the mentally ill in the United States.

24. Which of the following is NOT one of the seven elements for evaluating abnormality as discussed in the text?
    a. irrationality
    b. observer discomfort
    c. violence toward others
    d. rareness

25. Which of the following BEST fits the family resemblance approach to defining abnormality?
    a. Disorders run in families, so people from families with disorders are more likely to be abnormal.
    b. People must meet strict criteria in order to be seen as abnormal.
    c. All people must agree that a person is abnormal for that person to be defined as abnormal.
    d. If a person is similar to the paradigm cases of abnormality, he or she is probably abnormal.

26. In the case of Ralph, the book suggests that the following two elements alone qualify his behavior as abnormal:
    a. maladaptive and irrational
    b. unpredictable and violates standards

c. maladaptive and unconventional
d. violates standards and creates discomfort in observers

27. The hazards of using the family resemblance approach include all of the following EXCEPT:
    a. societal norms are subjective.
    b. it is a normative rather than a descriptive approach.
    c. observers may disagree.
    d. the actor and observer may disagree.

28. A person is less likely than outside observers to view him- or herself as abnormal. This is due to all of the following EXCEPT:
    a. observers are more accurate at rating behavior.
    b. the person has more information available to him- or herself than the observers have.
    c. distress comes and goes.
    d. people are inclined to see themselves in a more favorable light than that in which observers see them.

29. Humans are capable of changing some things about themselves but other things are very difficult to change. This fact can be difficult to accept for those who live in the United States in the twenty-first century because:
    a. new findings in the field of genetics make us believe we can't change anything.
    b. we believe that we can improve in almost every way, if we work at it.
    c. we believe that how we were raised dictates our future mental health.
    d. both a and b

30. Most people who suffer from psychological disorders never seek treatment. According to the book, all of the following are reasons why people do not seek treatment EXCEPT:
    a. the stigma of having a mental disorder.
    b. the belief that they cannot change.
    c. lack of knowledge about therapy.
    d. lack of money.

Fill in the Blank

1. In understanding abnormality, the biological and the psychological _____ _____ _____ have begun to be integrated.

    levels
    of analysis

2. _____-_____ explanations for abnormality say that a biological state causes a psychological state, whereas _____-_____ explanations say that a psychological state causes a biological state.

    Bottom-up
    top-down

3. _____ _____ is a new field that focuses on how developmental changes affect the onset and progress of psychological disorders.

   Developmental psychopathology

4. _____ studies are outcome studies under controlled laboratory conditions, whereas _____ studies test treatments as they are actually administered in the field.

   Efficacy

   effectiveness

5. _____ is the belief that everyone and everything has a soul.

   Animism

6. _____ are holes found in the skulls of Paleolithic cave dwellers; they were probably performed to provide an exit for demons trapped within the skull.

   Trephines

7. _____ _____ is a hallucinogenic condition thought to have affected the children who testified in the Salem witch trials.

   Ergot poisoning

8. _____, named after the Greek word for uterus, is a psychological disorder that arises from physical causes.

   Hysteria

9. _____ was the belief that mentally ill people were like animals, that they could not control themselves, that they were capable of violence, and that they could live without protest in miserable conditions.

   Animalism

10. _____, which means "originating in the soul," was the forerunner of the modern psychological level of analysis.

    Psychogenic

11. _____ _____, a term coined by Mesmer, refers to an invisible and impalpable entity that could cause disease if blocked.

    Animal magnetism

12. _____ is an emotional release; it was used by Breuer to treat patients with hysteria.

    Catharsis

13. _____ is the theory and therapeutic technique developed by Sigmund Freud.

    Psychoanalysis

14. A defining property of abnormality is termed a _____ condition for abnormality.

    necessary

15. A distinguishing element shared only by cases of abnormality and not by cases of normality is called a _____ condition.

    sufficient

16. The use of the family resemblance approach to describe abnormality can be hazardous because it is a _____ approach; that is, it describes how the phrase "mentally ill" is actually used, not how it should be used. On the other hand, _____ approaches dictate how the phrase "mental illness" ought to be used in an ideal world.

    descriptive

    normative

ANSWER KEY

MULTIPLE-CHOICE QUESTIONS

1 c. According to the surgeon general's report on mental illness (1999), 20 percent of Americans, more than 44 million people, have at least one mental illness in any given year.

2 d. The direct cost of psychological disorders in treatment and rehabilitation was estimated in 1996 at $100 billion for that year. Indirect costs are estimated at another $80 billion per year.

3. a. The four themes used throughout the book are: (1) biological and psychological levels of analysis, (2) development, (3) treatment of choice, and (4) science and practice. Issues regarding modern health-care delivery are important to the field of psychology, but are not one of the themes of the book.

4. d. It has become very clear in recent research that many disorders have both biological and psychological elements and that these two elements interact with one another to cause and maintain a disorder. Panic is clearly a disorder that fits this description. Patients typically experience mild physical symptoms, which they misinterpret catastrophically and which increase following the catastrophic interpretation.

5. b. According to bottom-up explanations, biological states cause physical states; According to top-down explanations, psychological states cause changes in biological states.

6. d. Depression, like panic disorder, is explained by both top-down and bottom-up explanations.

7. b. Sociocultural factors clearly influence mental illness; however, they do not offer a complete theory of the cause and treatment of mental illness. Therefore, they are best construed as moderators of mental illness, rather than as a separate level of analysis.

8. a. Depression appears in about the same proportion of boys and girls before puberty, but following puberty, women are twice as likely as men to suffer from depression. All the other answers are accurate statements of the effects of development on the onset of disorders.

9. b. Answers a, b, and c are all reasons for varying degrees of vulnerability to certain disorders over one's lifespan. There is no evidence that we are more willing to break with social norms as we age or that our level of willingness to comply with social norms affects our vulnerability to disorders.

10. c. Answers a, b, and c are the three key issues for the developmental approach. While there is some evidence in favor of using different treatment approaches based on age (e.g., play therapy for children), this is not one of the key issues.

11. b. Treatment of choice almost always involves either medication or psychotherapy. This treatment decision is the equivalent of biological and psychological levels of analysis.

12. b. The textbook asserts that we can now treat fourteen disorders successfully.

13. d. Panic, like most disorders, has both a psychological and physical component. All the other statements regarding the treatment of panic disorder are true.

14. a. According to your textbook, "No treatment is known to improve much on the natural course of recovery from alcoholism." Sexual dysfunction, depression, and panic are all disorders for which effective treatments have been developed.

15. b. Efficacy and effectiveness studies are both types of outcome studies, but an effectiveness study is the better answer because it is more specific. Effectiveness studies test a treatment as it is actually administered in the field. Efficacy studies test a treatment under controlled laboratory conditions. Analogue studies are similar to efficacy studies but are not mentioned in Chapter 1.

16. c. One of the key questions for the treatment of choice theme is "What interventions may prevent disorders from occurring in the first place?"

17. c. Both premodern and medieval societies attributed mental illness, among other things, to supernatural causes, such as possession by demons or pacts with Satan.

18. b. Although trephining is hypothesized to be related to the medical approach as well as to the supernatural belief that people were possessed, the link to the medical approach is consistent with all three remedies mentioned above.

19. a. The psychogenic approach is the forerunner of the psychological level of analysis. In this case, Galen is explaining his patient's symptoms as due to something psychological.

20. d. Mesmer's successful treatment of his patients was probably due to suggestion. In other words, they recovered because they were hypnotized by Mesmer.

21. d. While there is certainly plenty of evidence that the mentally ill were cruelly and inhumanely treated in hospitals in the seventeenth century, it also seems clear that being fed, clothed, and sheltered by the government was an improvement over earlier conditions.

22. b. The mentally ill were treated like animals due to the belief in animalism, that is, that patients could no longer reason like humans and were therefore similar to animals in many ways. Animism is the premodern belief that everyone and everything has a soul.

23. a. In most cases, the mentally ill did not even have their most basic needs met, leaving them very unlikely to improve their mental condition. Thus, the growth of the humane movement is attributed mainly to the reasons mentioned in the other responses.

24. c. Violence toward others is just one of many types of violation of standards; the other responses represent an entire element.

25. d. Option d is the response that best describes the family resemblance approach.

26. a. Maladaptive and irrational behavior are enough to qualify someone as abnormal. Violation of standards and unpredictability add further evidence for abnormality but are not sufficient by themselves.

27. b. The family resemblance approach is a descriptive, rather than a normative, approach.

28. a. There is no evidence that observers are more accurate. The observer's accuracy is impeded by a lack of information; the actor's accuracy is impeded because people tend to see themselves in a favorable light.

29. d. Both a and b are mentioned as aspects of the current culture in the United States that make it difficult to accept that some things can be changed while others cannot.

30. c. People's reluctance to seek therapy seems to be due to a perceived stigma, the belief that they cannot change, and lack of money. Generally, people are aware that psychotherapy exists and that it can be useful for treating mental and emotional problems.

CHAPTER 2

Assessment, Diagnosis, and Research Methods

A GUIDE TO THE READING

The overall goal of this chapter is to explain the methods that psychologists use to determine the nature of a patient's complaint, the cause of the complaint, and the best treatment or treatments for the patient. The chapter is divided into three sections: psychological assessment, diagnosis, and research methods. You will find this material manageable if you focus on one section at a time.

Psychological Assessment

Psychologists strive to make their assessments as systematic, thorough, and objective as possible. Assessments must also be reliable (that is, they must generate the same findings on repetition) and valid (they must measure what they are supposed to measure). Additional information and specific methods for assessing reliability and validity can be found on p. 34. The methods used to assess a patient's complaints include physical examinations, clinical interviews, self-reports, observations, and psychological testing. Physical examinations are often recommended because psychological problems are sometimes caused by physical problems (see p. 34 for some examples).

The clinical interview is the most common method of assessment and is discussed in detail on pp. 35–36. Keep in mind that interviews vary in terms of structure. *Structured interviews* are standardized (that is, the psychologist almost always asks the same questions in the same order), and they rely much less on clinical judgment; they are therefore used routinely in research to allow for replication and to make sure the results can be applied to individual patients. *Unstructured interviews* are more flexible and individualized, but they are less reliable and valid than structured interviews. Psychologists often use behavioral assessment, supplementing the interview with information gained from observing the patient during the interview and in other settings. As part of this process, the clinician, family members, and even the patients themselves are asked to keep accurate records of the patient's behaviors and thoughts. Behavioral assessment can help to define the problem, provide a record of what needs to be changed, and document progress.

Most of the section on assessment describes various psychological tests. You should become very familiar with the MMPI (pp. 42–44; Table 2-1 and Figure 2-2 are particularly helpful for an overview), the Rorschach Inkblot Test (see pp. 45–47 for an overview and be familiar with the controversy surrounding it; Box 2-1), the TAT (p. 48), the major intelligence tests (the Stanford-Binet and the Wechsler tests; pp. 49–50), and the most widely used tests for neuropsychological assessment (the Bender-Gestalt, p. 51; the Halstead-Reitan Battery, p. 53; and the Luria-Nebraska, p. 53). Be aware of the technological advances such as psychophysiological assessments of the autonomic nervous system, which can help in the assessment and treatment of patients, and advances in neuroimaging, which allows psychologists to observe both the structure and the function of the brain (see Figure 2-1 for a synopsis with visual images).

Diagnosis

Most diagnostic systems around the world use a categorical approach, which assigns a diagnostic label based on whether patients meet certain symptom criteria. The DSM-IV (the Diagnostic and Statistical Manual, used widely in the United States) and the ICD (the International Classification of Diseases, used widely in Europe) both employ categorical classification systems. Be familiar with the five reasons for making a diagnosis: (1) to communicate a lot of information very efficiently, (2) to understand etiology, (3) to guide treatment, (4) to aid scientific investigation, and (5) to allow clinicians to be paid for their services. You can find a more detailed explanation of these reasons on p. 55).

A description of the development of the DSM-IV appears on pp. 57–61. Be aware of the reasons for past revisions, the current content, and how a diagnosis is made. Criticisms of the DSM-IV include ongoing questions of reliability for personality disorders, diagnostic criteria that are too extreme, and failure to take into consideration the dimensional nature of many characteristics. Factors that limit the reliability of diagnoses are discussed in detail on pp. 61–64; they include the influence of context, expectations, and information from credible sources on the meanings people ascribe to behaviors.

Be aware that cultural considerations are an ongoing concern in the classification of mental disorders. Although there is evidence that much of the DSM-IV is not culturally biased, it appears that some of the disorders do not appear at the same rates in different cultures. The DSM-IV currently includes a section for "Culturally-Specific Disorders" such as *ataque de nervios, koro,* and *pibloktoq* (see Box 2-3 for a description), though some believe these are cultural variants of traditional disorders and do not warrant a separate diagnostic category. Remember that, despite their limitations, we need categorization and diagnosis to advance the science of abnormal psychology and to assist us in understanding the causes and best treatments for various disorders.

Research Methods

It is important to become familiar with the various research methods presented here, as they will be referred to throughout the book. Methods include the case study, the experiment, laboratory animal models, and nonexperimental research. Be familiar with the strengths and weaknesses of each method (see Table 2-4 for a summary of each model's strengths and weaknesses).

The case study is a detailed history of one or a few representative examples of a given disorder. It is very useful for documenting rare disorders and helps the psychologist generate causal hypotheses.

A scientific experiment is used to establish evidence for causality. This is the strongest method we have, so be sure to be familiar with it. Study both the excellent description on pp. 67–70 and Figure 2-6, which provides a useful synopsis. Considerable terminology is associated with experimental method, and you should become familiar with it. For instance, experimental variables are termed *independent* (IV) and *dependent* (DV). The *independent variable* is the variable that is manipulated by the experimenter; the *dependent variable* is the variable that is measured; an *operational def-*

inition is a set of clear-cut, measurable criteria; *experimental effect* is seen when the IV causes a change in the DV; a *confound* is a variable other than the IV that may cause changes in the DV; the *experimental group* receives the IV and the confounds; the *control group* receives only the confounds; *random assignment* ensures that each subject has an equal chance of being assigned to each group; *experimenter bias* is the subtle influence, either conscious or unconscious, by the experimenter on the results; *subject bias* describes the subject's inclination to alter a behavior based on what he or she thinks the experimenter expects; a *double-blind experiment* is one in which neither experimenter nor subject knows which group the subject is in; and *demand characteristics* are aspects of the research procedures that convey clues to the research participants.

The *laboratory animal model* is used to produce behavioral syndromes in animals that are analogous to naturally occurring mental disorders in humans. This model is useful for conducting research that would be unethical with human subjects and is helpful in increasing our understanding about the etiology and treatment of disorders.

Nonexperimental studies (comparative and correlational studies, experiments of nature, and epidemiological studies) are used when experimental research is practically or ethically impossible. Nonexperimental studies allow us to learn about the relationships between variables, which can be a useful first step for establishing causality. *Comparative studies* contrast two or more groups (for example, a group made up of people with a particular disorder compared to a group of people without the disorder). *Correlational studies* examine the relationships between two variables. Relationships may be positively correlated (as variable X increases, variable Y also increases), negatively correlated (as X increases, Y decreases), or uncorrelated (an increase in X has no effect on Y). Statistically, correlation coefficients range from -1.0 (perfect negative correlation) to 1.0 (perfect positive correlation) with 0 representing no correlation. Causality cannot be inferred by correlation, but *longitudinal studies* help us to infer causation (for example, if X comes first, it is more likely to have caused Y than Y is to have caused X).

Keep in mind that researchers use statistics to determine whether one variable has an effect on the other. There is a good summary of statistical inference on pp. 73–75. Remember that statistics are used to ensure that findings are significant and not just due to chance.

Experiments of nature involve studying the effects of natural disasters on survivors and investigating the factors that help people cope with stress. Experiments of nature are very useful for studying trauma without deliberately (and unethically) causing the trauma.

Finally, *epidemiological studies* are used to determine how common mental illness is by examining the lifetime prevalence (the proportion of people who have ever experienced a particular disorder), differences among groups (the odds of being diagnosed with a certain disorder based on one's gender, ethnicity, etc.), and the annual rates of disorders in different countries. Results of one of the largest epidemiological studies in the United States (the Epidemiologic Catchment Area, or ECA), indicate that about one-third of Americans suffer from at least one major disorder in their lifetime (see Table 2-2 for a summary of the prevalence of many major disorders). A second study, the National Comorbidity Study, indicates that the relative risks of having a disorder varies based on gender, ethnicity, and income level (see p. 82 for a summary), but a third study found few differences in rates of major mental disorders around the world.

TESTING YOUR UNDERSTANDING

Test your understanding of what you have read by working through the following tasks with a classmate.

1. Imagine you are a psychologist who is about to see a patient complaining of depression, lack of sleep, low appetite, and difficulty concentrating. What techniques would you use to determine if your patient is suffering from a mental disorder?

2. There is quite a bit of evidence that the brains of people with schizophrenia are structured differently than the brains of people without schizophrenia. For example, the brains of schizophrenics tend to have enlarged ventricles. In addition, the brains of people with schizophrenia seem to function differently through a lack of certain types of neurotransmitters in the brain. What psychological and neuroimaging tests would you use to test this evidence?

3. There is some debate about whether to use categorical approaches or dimensional approaches for classifying mental disorders. Which approach does the DSM-IV use? What are the advantages and disadvantages of using that approach?

4. A fellow student created a new scale to measure the levels of depression in college students. He knows you are a psychology major and therefore knowledgeable about assessment. He wants to know how to make sure his scale is a good one. Explain what makes a scale good, and how he can go about testing his scale.

5. One of the biggest problems encountered in the development of the DSM-IV was that different clinicians came up with different diagnoses for the same client. This may be due to some subtle bias in the clinicians' procedures. What are the conditions that can lead to bias in diagnosis?

6. A professor states in class that children need to hear certain sounds at certain critical periods in order to develop proper speech. She bases this on the story of Jeanie, a modern-day "wild child" who was locked in a closet for most of her childhood and who has since had difficulty developing language skills. What do you think of the professor's claims? What are the values and limitations of the evidence she presents? How would you go about collecting additional, more convincing evidence that the deprivation of hearing spoken language caused Jeanie's language difficulties? What are some ethical considerations you might encounter?

7. Why do scientists use nonexperimental methods? What are the advantages and disadvantages of these approaches?

Multiple-Choice Questions

1. Which of the following is an example of a psychological problem being secondary to a physical problem?
   a. A person's sleeping difficulties and loss of appetite seem to have no physical basis but are symptoms of depression.
   b. A person who has witnessed a gruesome car accident can no longer see, though nothing is wrong with her eyes.
   c. A person experiences visual hallucinations following a severe blow to the head.
   d. A person continually goes to her physician with multiple complaints, none of which seem to have any clear physical basis.

2. Which of the following is NOT a typical physical test used to assess people with psychological symptoms?
   a. blood tests to measure hormone levels
   b. an EKG
   c. an EEG
   d. a neurological examination

3. Structured interviews are used by psychologists because they have several important advantages over unstructured interviews. Which of the following is NOT an advantage of structured interviews?
   a. They allow the clinician flexibility in assessing clients.
   b. They are useful for research.
   c. They increase reliability.
   d. They reduce the amount of suggestive techniques used by interviewers.

4. Who can conduct a behavioral assessment?
   a. the psychologist only
   b. the patient only
   c. one of the patient's family members
   d. any of the above

5. Statements such as "I often have the sensation that I am floating in the air" and "I usually feel fine" appear on the:
   a. Rorschach Test.
   b. Thematic Apperception Test (TAT).
   c. Minnesota Multiphasic Personality Inventory (MMPI).
   d. Stanford-Binet.

6. There is some controversy about the use of projective tests because:
   a. they are based on Freudian theory, which, though historically important, isn't really used anymore.
   b. some studies have shown that they do not have adequate reliability.
   c. they do not appear to yield important information about patients.
   d. there are not adequate scoring systems for these tests.

7. The need for achievement is one of the personality characteristics captured by which test?
   a. Thematic Apperception Test (TAT)
   b. Rorschach Inkblot Test
   c. Minnesota Multiphasic Personality Inventory (MMPI)
   d. California Psychological Inventory (CPI)

8. There are a number of intelligence tests available to assess intelligence in people of all age ranges. The most commonly used intelligence test for adults (which provides an overall IQ score, a Verbal IQ score, and a Performance IQ score) is the:
   a. Stanford-Binet.
   b. KAB-C.
   c. WAIS-III.
   d. Flynn Intelligence Scale.

9. All of the following tests are used to diagnoses brain damage EXCEPT:
   a. the Luria-Nebraska Neurological Battery.
   b. the Wechsler Memory Scales (WMS).
   c. the Wisconsin Card Sorting Test (WCST).
   d. the Picture Arrangement Test.

10. Clinicians continue to use neuropsychological batteries despite advances in neuroimaging because:
    a. neuroimaging techniques do not measure brain function, only brain structure.
    b. neuropsychological assessment is needed is needed to document the nature and extent of functional impairment.
    c. clinicians are primarily concerned with the functional consequences of brain abnormality, not the brain abnormality itself.
    d. both b and c

11. In order for a person to be diagnosed with a mental disorder, he or she must:

    a. obtain a profile, based in ratings on several dimensions, that is consistent with an abnormal profile.
    b. meet the clinical criteria for a specific disorder, including a threshold for severity.
    c. have a chronic, rather than an acute, problem.
    d. have a continuous, rather than an episodic, problem.

12. There are many good reasons for diagnosis. All of the following are reasons EXCEPT:
    a. they allow psychologists to communicate a lot of information quickly to other providers.
    b. they generate some hypotheses about treatment.
    c. they allow psychologists to charge for their services.
    d. none of the above.

13. The _____ validity of the "bipolar disorder" diagnosis is quite high because certain medications are very effective in treating it.
    a. test-retest
    b. construct
    c. inter-rater
    d. predictive

14. All of the following are true of the DSM-IV EXCEPT:
    a. it provides specific and operational criteria for each mental disorder.
    b. it provides information about the causes of each disorder.
    c. it uses a multiaxial system.
    d. it is organized into classes, or clusters.

15. Which of the following is NOT part of a DSM-IV diagnosis?
    a. treatment plan
    b. psychosocial problems
    c. global assessment of functioning
    d. medical conditions

16. The committees that worked on the later editions of the DSM used many techniques to attempt to make it more reliable. All of the following are changes that were made to increase reliability EXCEPT:
    a. the categories were made more specific and precise.
    b. temporal criteria were established.
    c. fewer categories were included.
    d. behavioral criteria were established.

17. In the most recent edition of the DSM, the Axis II disorders have been criticized for all of the following reasons EXCEPT:
    a. test-retest reliabilities are especially low for Axis II disorders.
    b. the diagnostic categories are too conservative.
    c. the use of cutoffs rather than continuums to describe personality disorders.
    d. there is a lot of overlap between the disorders.

18. Research indicates that certain factors can bias diagnosis. These factors include all the of the following EXCEPT:
    a. expectation.
    b. source credibility.
    c. context.
    d. none of the above

19. All of the following are true regarding cultural factors and the DSM-IV EXCEPT:
    a. the DSM-IV pays more attention to cultural factors than its predecessors.
    b. there has been a great deal of research on the nature and extent of cultural influences on mental health.
    c. culturally-specific syndromes are now included in the DSM-IV.
    d. there is some evidence that national rates of certain disorders vary.

20. All of the following are nonexperimental research methods EXCEPT:
    a. epidemiological studies.
    b. comparative studies.
    c. laboratory animal models.
    d. correlational studies.

21. In order to establish causation (that is, that one variable actually causes a change in another variable), psychologists need to use:
    a. naturalistic studies.
    b. experiments.
    c. comparative studies.
    d. clinical case studies.

22. Dr. Shaftoe wants to determine whether her new cognitive-behavioral treatment for panic attacks is effective. She randomly assigns half of a group of thirty people who suffer from panic disorder to her new treatment and the other half to a wait-list control group. She administers a questionnaire assessing the nature and frequency of panic attacks to both groups and then begins treatment with the treatment group. After twelve weeks, she re-assesses both groups with the same questionnaire. In this experiment, the independent variable is _____, the dependent variable is _____, and _____ is a possible confound.
    a. the change in the nature and frequency of panic attacks; treatment vs. no treatment; the use of random assignment.
    b. treatment vs. no treatment; the change in the nature and frequency of panic attacks; the use of random assignment.
    c. the change in the nature and frequency of panic attacks; treatment vs. no treatment; the attention the treatment group receives from the therapist.
    d. treatment vs. no treatment; the change in the nature and frequency of panic attacks; the attention the treatment group receives from the therapist.

23. There are a number of common problems with experimental control, including nonrandom assignment, experimenter bias, subject bias, and demand characteristics. Self-fulfilling prophecies are involved in which of the following?
    a. nonrandom assignment
    b. experimenter bias
    c. subject bias
    d. demand characteristics

24. Why do researchers conduct statistical analysis on data?
    a. to ensure that the sample is representative of the population
    b. to be 95 percent sure that their experiments are valid
    c. to ensure that chance did not produce the result
    d. to avoid misses and false alarms

25. Researchers have more confidence in group designs than in clinical case studies because group designs involve repeatability (the experimental manipulation is repeated on several subjects) and generalizability (with several subjects, we can generalize our findings to the entire population). However, when carefully conducted, single case experiments can demonstrate:
    a. repeatability.
    b. generalizability.
    c. both
    d. neither

26. A psychologist was interested in studying the effects of trauma on people but could not ethically manipulate trauma. The psychologist decided to go to Bosnia during the war, to a town that was not yet involved in the war but was expected to become involved shortly. This is an example of:
    a. a case study.
    b. a retrospective experiment of nature.
    c. a prospective experiment of nature.
    d. an epidemiological study.

27. A researcher wants to investigate whether depressive thoughts are related to depressed mood. She collects data on a group of people who have been diagnosed with depression and on a group of people who are not depressed, and finds that those diagnosed with depression have significantly more depressed thoughts. Further, she notes that on days when the depressed subjects have more depressed thoughts, their mood is also more depressed. This is an example of a(n):
    a. comparative study.
    b. correlational study.
    c. epidemiological study.
    d. both a and b

28. A researcher found that as the temperature in a certain town increased, fewer people stayed at home during the day. The relationship between the temperature and staying at home is best expressed with which correlation coefficient?
    a. −.68
    b. 0
    c. .15
    d. .69

29. An experimenter would conduct a correlational study for all of the following reasons EXCEPT:
    a. to avoid the artificiality of laboratory studies.
    b. to avoid unethical experiments.
    c. when it is not practical to do an experiment.
    d. to establish causation.

30. Which figure is the best estimate of how many Americans experience a serious mental disorder in their lifetimes, according to the Epidemiological Catchment Area study?
    a. .05 percent
    b. 5 percent
    c. 33 percent
    d. 66 percent

Fill in the Blank Questions

1. _____ _____ is an evaluation of a person's mental functions and psychological health.   Psychological assessment

2. A test is _____ if it generates the same findings on repeated use.   reliable

3. A test is _____ if it measures what it is supposed to measure.   valid

4. The _____ _____ is the most commonly used approach to assessment.   clinical interview

5. A _____ interview involves asking every interviewee the same questions in roughly the same order.   structured or standardized

6. _____ _____ consists of keeping an accurate record of the behaviors and thoughts that are the focus of research or treatment.   Behavioral assessment

7. _____ _____ are highly structured psychological tests, containing statements that can be answered in a limited number of ways (such as true/false).   Psychological inventories

8. _____ tests utilize ambiguous stimuli, such as inkblots or pictures.   Projective

9. _____ _____ refers to the fact that successive generations seem to be scoring higher on intelligence tests.   Flynn effect

10. _____ _____ involves the measurement of one or more physiological processes that reflect autonomic nervous system activity.   Psychophysiological assessment

11. A _____ is a collection of symptoms that occur together.   syndrome

12. The _____ of a disorder is another word for the *cause* of the disorder.   etiology

13. According to the DSM-IV, a _____ _____ is a behavioral or psychological pattern that has either caused the individual distress or disabled the individual in one or more significant areas of functioning.   mental disorder

14. _____ refers to the co-occurrence of two or more diagnoses.   Comorbidity

15. _____ studies compare the effects of one treatment approach to another treatment or no treatment.

Treatment or outcome

16. A _____ _____ is the number of occurrences in each given class observed.

frequency distribution

17. A _____ _____ effect indicates that there is less than a 5 percent chance that the effect occurred by chance.

statistically significant

18. The strength of the relationship between two variables is expressed statistically as a _____ _____.

correlation coefficient

19. _____ _____ is the proportion of people in a sample who have ever experienced a particular disorder.

Lifetime prevalence

Matching

Match the following research methods terms and definitions.

_____ 1. IV

_____ 2. DV

_____ 3. Operational definition

_____ 4. Experimental effect

_____ 5. Confound

_____ 6. Control group

_____ 7. Experimental group

_____ 8. Random assignment

_____ 9. Experimenter bias

_____ 10. Allegiance effect

_____ 11. Self-fulfilling prophecies

_____ 12. Double-blind experiment

_____ 13. Random sample

a. obtained when manipulating the IV causes in changes in the DV

b. the group that receives the confounds, but not the IV

c. each subject has an equal chance of being assigned to each group

d. the tendency for people to conform to others' expectations for them

e. independent variable

f. treatment favored by the researcher is more likely to be the one that shows the greatest efficacy in an outcome study

g. dependent variable

h. an experimental design where the subject and the researcher do not know which condition the subject is receiving

i. a set of clear-cut, measurable criteria

j. all people in the population have an equal chance of being subjects in the experiment

k. occurs when an experimenter subtly influences the experiment to produce the results he or she wants, sometimes without being aware of it

l. factors other than the IV that might produce an experimental effect

m. the group that receives the confounds and the IV

Additional Exercise: Psychological Tests

For each acronym below, provide the full name of the test, and in the blank to the left of each acronym, give the construct that each of these tests is designed to assess. Use either D (Diagnosis of mental disorders), I (Intelligence), PI (Personality Inventory), PP (Projective test of Personality), N (Neuropsychological problems/brain damage).

Construct   *Name of Test*

1. _____ CDI or   _____

2. _____ Bender Visual-Motor Gestalt Test

3. _____ CPI or   _____

4. _____ WCST or   _____

5. _____ BDI or   _____

6. _____ Halstead-Reitan Battery

7. _____ SCID or   _____

8. _____ WISC-III or   _____

9. _____ Rorschach Inkblot Test

10. _____ WAIS-III or   _____

11. _____ TAT or   _____

12. _____ SCL-90-R or   _____

13. _____ DISC-C or   _____

14. _____ CBCL or   _____

15. _____ Trail Making Test

16. _____ MMPI or   _____

17. _____ WMS or   _____

18. _____ WPPSI or   _____

19. _____ Luria-Nebraska Battery

LEVELS OF ANALYSIS: EXAMINING CHAPTER THEMES

This chapter explicitly addresses two of our recurring themes: biological and psychological levels of analysis, and science and practice.

Biological and Psychological Levels of Analysis

A thorough assessment of an individual presenting psychological problems often includes a referral for a physical ex-

amination, especially if the symptoms are typically associated with a physical illness. When psychological symptoms are a consequence of physical conditions, they are said to be *secondary* to a physical condition. Examples of this include anxiety or depression secondary to thyroid hormone deficiency, psychotic symptoms being secondary to brain tumors, and the psychological side effects of some medications. When psychological symptoms are secondary to a physical condition, it is essential to diagnose and treat the physical condition in order to relieve the psychological symptoms. Keep in mind that physical symptoms can also be secondary to psychological problems. In these cases, physicians may refer the patient to a psychologist for an assessment. The DSM-IV multiaxial system includes a report of any relevant medical conditions (Axis III) when making a psychological diagnosis. See Box 2-3 for an example of the interaction between biological and psychological dysfunction in a young girl suffering from an eating disorder.

Science and Practice

This theme emerges in the discussion of assessment procedures, the utility of neuropsychological assessment, and in the controversy over the Rorschach Inkblot Test. Psychologists use highly structured procedures when assessing a client because the consequences of diagnosis can be quite serious (prescriptions for powerful medications, hospitalization, etc.) and because a standardized assessment allows clinicians to take advantage of research findings that shed light on a patient's particular pattern of symptoms. Regarding neuropsychological assessment, the increasing sophistication of neuroimaging (PET scans, fMRI) has caused some to question the utility of neuropsychological batteries (a series of tests of mental functioning that can help to identify the specific type of brain damage). While neuroimaging is extremely helpful, it is clear that neuropsychological assessment is still very important clinically. Neuropsychological assessment provides information to clinicians about the functional consequences of brain abnormality, which aids in constructing and implementing a rehabilitative program.

The controversy over the Rorschach Inkblot Test is another area where science and practice need to be integrated. Clinicians undergo extensive training in the use of the Rorschach and often find it very useful in the assessment and therapeutic process. Some psychologists, however, have been concerned about the reliability and validity of the test, and their concern has been corroborated by empirical studies that indicate that neither the reliability nor the validity of the test is particularly high. See Box 2-1 for a detailed discussion of the controversy surrounding the Rorschach.

ANSWER KEY

MULTIPLE-CHOICE QUESTIONS

1. c. When psychological problems are caused by physical conditions, the psychological problems are said to be secondary to the physical problems. Only c is an example of this; all the other responses represent a physical condition caused by a psychological problem.

2. b. Hormone levels, brain activity (measured using an EEG), and neurological problems may all be implicated in some psychological problems. An EKG measures heart activity, which is not typically assessed for psychological problems.

3. a. Structured interviews are standardized (the same questions are asked in more or less the same order for every interviewee), which makes them much more reliable and useful for research. They also reduce the use of suggestive techniques by the interviewer. They are not, however, very flexible; they cannot be changed based on the client or the client's specific problem.

4. d. A behavioral assessment is an accurate record of the behaviors or thoughts that are the focus of research or treatment. It does not matter who conducts the assessment; it only matters that the person who does conduct the assessment can observe the behaviors and record them carefully and accurately.

5. c. The Rorschach and the TAT are projective tests; they present ambiguous stimuli such as inkblots and pictures and contain no written statements. The MMPI, from which these items were derived, is a test of personality and psychopathology and contains hundred of true/false questions. The Stanford-Binet is a test of intelligence.

6. b. Projective tests, such as the Rorschach and the TAT have not always been shown to have adequate reliability. They do, however, often reveal valuable information about clients which, when used in conjunction with other assessment methods, can help generate hypotheses about clients. There are detailed scoring systems for these tests (for example, Exner's scoring system for the Rorschach). Finally, Freudian theory is used today by a number of clinicians.

7. a. The TAT assesses personality characteristics and motives, particularly the need for achievement.

8. c. The Wechsler Adult Intelligence Scale–III is the most commonly used test for adults and yields three scores: IQ (intelligence quotient), VIQ (based on subtests that measure language capacities) and PIQ (based on subtests that are less dependent upon verbal ability). The Stanford-Binet and the KAB-C are used primarily for children and they yield different scores. There is no Flynn Intelligence Scale. However, there is a Flynn effect, which refers to the unexplained rise in intelligence scores over the last century.

9. d. The Luria-Nebraska Neurological Battery, the WMS, and the WCST are all neuropsychological tests (or batteries) used to diagnose brain damage. Picture arrangement is one of the scales on the WAIS-III.

10. d. Both b and c are reasons why clinicians continue to use neuropsychological assessment. Neuroimaging techniques can measure both structure and function, but neuropsychological tests provide more information about the nature, extent, and consequences of brain dysfunction.

11. b. The dominant way of classifying mental disorders is the categorical approach (the approach used by the DSM-IV). Dimensional ratings are not widely used at this time. Chronic, acute, continuous, and episodic are qualifiers for diagnosis, not criteria themselves.

12. d. All of the reasons given above are reasons for diagnosis.

13. d. Predictive validity of diagnostic categories refers to their ability to predict the course and treatment outcome. Construct validity refers to the extent to which patients can be differentiated by using these categories. Test-retest and inter-rater both refer to reliability.

14. d. Answers a, b, and c are all true of the DSM-IV. The DSM-IV provides research findings about factors such as age of onset, predisposing conditions, and prevalence of each disorder, but does not provide information about the causes of the disorders.

15. a. Diagnoses are made using five axes: Axis I, Major Mental Disorders; Axis II, Personality Disorders; Axis III, General Medical Condition; Axis IV, Psychosocial and Environmental Problems; Axis V, Global Assessment of Functioning.

16. c. More, rather than fewer, categories were added as diagnoses became more specific. Both temporal and behavioral criteria were added to increase reliability.

17. b. The diagnostic categories have not been criticized for being too conservative. Rather, they have been criticized for being too extreme and for leaving out people with mild or moderate personality disorders. All of the other criticisms are accurate.

18. d. The context in which a diagnosis is made (for example, a hospital), the expectations of the diagnosticians, and the source credibility of the people who evaluate a patient's condition are all factors that can bias diagnosis.

19. b. While the DSM-IV does pay more attention to cultural factors, there is still very little research on the nature and extent of cultural influences on mental health.

20. c. Laboratory animal models are conducted under controlled conditions in a lab using the scientific method. The other three types of studies are nonexperimental.

21. b. True experiments, using a control group, random assignment, and controlled conditions, are the only way to establish causation.

22. d. Remember that the IV is the variable that is manipulated by the researcher, the DV is the variable that is measured, and confounds are variables other than the IV that might affect the DV. Random assignment helps to limit confounds by making sure that the two groups are roughly equivalent in terms of subject characteristics.

23. b. Self-fulfilling prophecies are the tendency for people to subtly influence the outcome of an experiment so that the results come out as they predicted. Self-fulfilling prophecies are a form of experimenter bias.

24. c. Inferential statistics are used to ensure that the result was due to the independent variable's effect on the dependent variable, and not due to chance. Researchers must first make sure that the sample is representative, in order to be confident that their results can be generalized to the entire population. Misses and false alarms are an unfortunate by-product of inferential statistics.

25. a. Single-subject experiments can demonstrate repeatability by establishing a baseline and then adding or removing treatments. Generalizability can only be demonstrated by performing the same experiment on several subjects.

26. c. A prospective experiment of nature is when an observation is made before the expected outcome occurs.

27. d. Comparative studies contrast two or more groups to find out how people with a particular disorder differ from individuals without the disorder. Correlational studies determine whether this is a relationship between two variables. In this particular case, both comparative and correlational analyses have been conducted.

28. a. Correlation coefficients range from −1.0 (a negative correlation; as one variable goes up, the other goes down) through 0 (no correlation) to 1.0 (a positive correlation; as one variable goes up, the other also goes up). In this case, as the temperature went up, staying-at-home behavior went down, indicating a negative relationship.

29. d. Always remember that correlation does not imply causation. All the other answers are legitimate reasons to use a correlational design.

30. c. Findings from the ECA study indicate that approximately one-third of Americans experience a serious mental disorder in their lifetime.

MATCHING

1. e
2. g
3. i
4. a
5. l
6. b
7. m
8. c
9. k

10. f

11. d

12. h

13. j

ADDITIONAL EXERCISE

1. D; Children's Depression

2. N

3. PI; California Psychological Inventory

4. N; Wisconsin Card Sorting Test

5. D; Beck Depression Inventory

6. N

7. D; Structured Clinical Interview for DSM

8. I; Wechsler Intelligence Scale for Children–III

9. PP

10. I; Wechsler Adult Intelligence Scale–III

11. PP; Thematic Apperception Test

12. D; Symptom Checklist-90-Revised

13. D; Diagnostic Interview Schedule for Children

14. D; Child Behavior Checklist

15. N

16. PI; Minnesota Multiphasic Personality Inventory

17. N; Wechsler Memory Scales

18. I; Wechsler Preschool and Primary Scale of Intelligence

19. N

| Psychological Approaches

A GUIDE TO THE READING

This chapter introduces four major psychological approaches to understanding and treating abnormality, each of which represents a distinct level of psychological analysis. The *psychodynamic approach* focuses on unconscious conflicts and early childhood experiences; the *existential and humanist approach* stresses taking responsibility and reaching your full potential; the *behavioral approach* examines behaviors and the contingencies that govern them; and the *cognitive approach* emphasizes thought processes. An illustration of how these approaches represent different levels of psychological analysis is given in the case of Angela, who was treated using each approach (pp. 98, 102, 111, 115–16, and 119).

Psychodynamic Approach

It is important to know Freud's theory of the structure of the mind, which is summarized in Table 3-1. Freud proposed that there are conflicts among the three basic processes of the mind: the *id,* which seeks pleasure; the *ego,* which deals with reality; and the *superego,* which serves as our conscience. Whether we are normal or abnormal depends on how well we cope with these conflicts and the resulting anxiety. The defense mechanisms that people use to cope with this anxiety include repression, projection, denial, displacement, and sublimation. *Repression,* in which the individual unconsciously forces unwanted thoughts out of the conscious mind, is the most fundamental defense mechanism. *Projection* consists of attributing to others the feelings that we repress in ourselves. *Displacement* is used when it is unsafe to show negative feelings (for instance, toward your boss) so instead, negative feelings are vented to another,

safer target. *Denial* occurs when we refuse to accept that something bad is happening or may happen. *Sublimation* is the rechanneling of psychic energy from socially unacceptable goals to socially desirable ones.

Neo-Freudians, the followers of Freud who modified and expanded his theories, emphasized the social, rather than sexual, aspects of personality development. Be familiar with the major neo-Freudians and what they added to Freud's theories, especially Carl Jung and his emphasis on archetypes and the collective unconscious; Alfred Adler and his focus on the self; and the neo-Freudians (Horney, Sullivan, Erikson, and Fromm) who emphasized the importance of early childhood relationships with caretakers (see p. 92 for more details). Modern psychodynamic theory focuses on the development of the self. Know the three aspects of the self and how they develop: the *core self,* the sense of separateness and identity (develops between the second and sixth months of life); the *subjective self,* the sense that we can empathize with other people (seven to nine months); and the verbal self, in which the self acts as a storehouse of knowledge and experience (fifteen to eighteen months).

See the treatment case on pages 94–96 for an example of treatment based on psychodynamic theory. Treatment seeks to alter thought and behavior by examining early conflicts and by making conscious what is repressed. Know the basic terms related to this type of treatment: *free association* means saying whatever comes to mind; *dream recall* is the examination of dreams; *processing resistance,* is a momentary block in dealing with an issue; *catharsis* means the uncovering and reliving of earlier traumas; and *transference* is the process by which clients transfer emotions, conflicts, and expectations from and about others onto the therapist. The strengths of psychodynamic theory include that its comprehensive description of human functioning explains both normal and abnormal behavior, and that it was the first method for treating psychological distress. Though much of Freud's original theory has not been supported by research, modern versions of psychodynamic therapy have been shown to be effective. Some shortcomings of psychodynamic theory are that it is difficult to prove or disprove, that its premises have generally not been supported by research, and that it emphasizes the person to the neglect of the situation. To review these strengths and shortcomings in more detail, see pages 96–97. Keep in mind that psychodynamic theory is consistent with the medical model, which holds that mental illness is a syndrome with underlying causes.

Existential and Humanistic Approaches

The existential and humanistic approaches represent philosophical ideas about human nature rather than a comprehensive theory of personality and abnormality. These approaches arose in reaction to Freudian theory, which humanists and existentialists viewed as overly deterministic. Therefore, humanistic and existential approaches emphasized freedom and choice, responsibility, willingness, and the fear of dying. These concepts are discussed in detail on pages 98–100. In brief, these approaches assert that people must make authentic choices based on their own desires, must take responsibility for their perceptions and actions, and must exercise will to achieve a goal. These approaches also assert that the ultimate anxiety is the fear of death, and that people cope with this fear both by cultivating the notion that they are special and by fusing with others. Treatment based on these approaches concentrates on developing independence, goal-directed behavior, and personal responsibility (see the case of Cathy for an illustration). Because these approaches are not based on a scientific theory, they are difficult to evaluate. Note, however, that an important strength is that they accord with everyday notions of personality.

The Behavioral Approach

The behavioral approach includes three major assumptions: *environmentalism,* the belief that all organisms are shaped by their environment; *experimentalism,* the sense that behavior has observable causes and can be studied experimentally; and *optimism,* the belief that behaviors can be changed. Abnormal behavior, according to the behavioral approach, consists of acquired habits that are maladaptive and can be changed by altering the environment to produce new, adaptive habits. This is accomplished using classical and operant conditioning. Keep in mind that the behavioral approach does not adhere to the medical model. Rather, in this approach, the symptoms of the disorder are the disorder. Once symptoms are relieved, the patient no longer has a mental illness. Know the basics of classical conditioning (see pp. 102–7, and Figure 3-1) and the therapies that are

based on them: *exposure,* which is used to extinguish maladaptive behaviors by exposing patients to feared objects; and *systematic desensitization,* in which the patient imagines the feared object while in a state of relaxation.

Know the basics of operant conditioning (pp. 107–10) and be clear on how this differs from classical conditioning. *Classical conditioning* explains how we learn "what goes with what" whereas *operant conditioning* explains how we learn "what to do to get what we want." Know the techniques that are used in operant therapies: *selective positive reinforcement,* in which a behavior is encouraged through systematic reinforcement; *selective punishment,* in which a behavior is discouraged by pairing an aversive event with the undesirable behavior; and *extinction,* the process by which a learned behavior ceases to be performed as the contingent reinforcer is withdrawn. See Table 3-3 for more information on the distinction between classical and operant therapies. Classical and operant conditioning are combined in *avoidance learning,* which involves learning what predicts an aversive event and learning how to escape from this event.

The Cognitive Approach

Psychologists who use this approach believe that what you think, believe, and expect influences how you behave. As with the behavioral approach, the symptoms are considered to be the disorder, and symptom relief is the main goal of therapy. Symptom relief is achieved by changing the thoughts that cause maladaptive behaviors. Therapists identify negative or distorted thoughts, challenge them using evidence from the client's life, and assist in changing those thoughts. Four specific techniques are described: altering *efficacy expectations* so that the patient believes that they can achieve a desired outcome; modifying *negative appraisals,* the negative automatic thoughts that evaluate what happens to us and what we do; changing *attributions,* the explanation for why an event has happened; and revising *long-term beliefs,* the unconscious dispositions that govern conscious mental events. Cognitive therapy is often combined with behavioral therapy in an attempt to change distorted cognitions and maladaptive behaviors. See Table 3-5 for an example of the various techniques used in cognitive-behavioral therapy (CBT). Note also that CBT has been combined with psychodynamic therapy in a technique called the *core conflictual relationship theme* (CCRT), which uses what a patient consciously thinks about to reveal underlying themes that affect their relationships (see p. 117 for more details).

Behavioral and cognitive therapy also have strengths and shortcomings (see pp. 117–18). In brief, the strengths include the following: their effectiveness in treating a number of disorders; the treatments are brief and inexpensive; the treatments are based on science and can be evaluated using scientific methodology. The main shortcoming is that they do not address the whole person or the deeper, underlying etiologies that produce symptoms.

TESTING YOUR UNDERSTANDING

Test your understanding of what you have read by working through the following tasks with a classmate.

1. Your roommate rarely studies, choosing instead to party, party, party. She is very sloppy, not very friendly, and sometimes yells at you for no apparent reason. Use Freud's structure of the mind to account for this behavior. What defense mechanisms might be operating here?

2. Explain your roommate's behavior from an existentialist perspective. What might an existentialist emphasize in treating your roommate?

3. Discuss ways in which you could use classical and operant conditioning to change your roommate's sloppy housekeeping behavior.

4. Your roommate's behavior is really bugging you, but you are stuck together until the end of the school year. What cognitive techniques might you use to restructure your thinking in order to make the rest of the year bearable?

5. When combining treatments, therapists often combine behavioral and cognitive interventions. Explain why these to approaches are so compatible with one another. What do they have in common?

6. Think about some aspect of yourself that you would like to change. Come up with strategies using each of the four different approaches that might help you make the change.

Multiple-Choice Questions

1. Jeanie fears dogs. In fact, this fear has progressed to the point that she is afraid to walk outside at all. When she sees a dog, she becomes extremely anxious and cannot escape fast enough. After a thorough assessment and several therapy sessions, Jeanie's therapist hypothesizes that Jeanie's parents were overresponsive to her fear and that this attention encouraged her fear. Jeanie's therapist is most likely using which approach?
   a. psychodynamic
   b. existential/humanistic
   c. behavioral
   d. cognitive

2. Jeanie fears dogs. Her therapist hypothesizes that Jeanie's parents unwittingly rewarded this behavior by being overresponsive to her fear. However, Jeanie disagrees; she thinks she is really afraid of something else, and that this fear may be related to her inability to maintain a relationship beyond the first few dates. Perhaps, she thinks, I am really afraid of men, but I am acting my fear out with dogs instead. Even thinking this makes her heart race. Jeanie's conceptualization is most consistent with which approach?
   a. psychodynamic
   b. existential/humanistic
   c. behavioral
   d. cognitive

3. Jeanie's therapist proposes that whenever she sees a dog or becomes anxious that she might encounter one, she should say to herself several times "I am safe" and "the dog cannot hurt me." This type of intervention is consistent with which approach?
   a. psychodynamic
   b. existential/humanistic
   c. behavioral
   d. cognitive

4. A therapist treats Jeanie's fear of dogs by seating her in a comfortable chair and instructing her to do some relaxation exercises. Then she has Jeanie imagine a friendly dog who is tied up, then an unfriendly dog who is tied up, and finally, an unfriendly dog who is not tied up. At each stage, the therapist makes sure that Jeanie stays in a relaxed state. Which type of behavior conditioning is the therapist using?
   a. classical conditioning
   b. operant conditioning
   c. cognitive-behavioral conditioning
   d. all of the above

5. John believes it is very important to do the right thing, and he strives to be the best person he can be. He strictly avoids anything he knows to be wrong, such as driving over the speed limit. He will often give up things he enjoys, such as certain foods, certain TV shows, etc., to build his character and he avoids temptations at all costs. According to Freudian theory, John has an overdeveloped:
   a. id.
   b. ego.
   c. superego.
   d. unconscious.

6. Which of the following processes takes place primarily in the conscious mind?
   a. id
   b. ego
   c. superego
   d. none of the above

7. Amy doesn't like to be angry; deep down, she feels it is unfeminine. When she occasionally loses her temper, she feels extremely ashamed. She attended her niece's birthday party and witnessed her sister getting a bit frustrated when the clown was late. After the party, she discussed her sister's "temper" at great length with her husband, declaring that it is hard for

her to like her sister because she is such an angry woman. Which of the following defense mechanisms is Amy employing?
a. repression
b. displacement
c. projection
d. sublimation

8. Which of the following neo-Freudians came up with the theory of "archetypes," described as universal ideas with which we are born?
a. Jung
b. Adler
c. Sullivan
d. Erikson

9. Neo-Freudians placed much more emphasis on _____, whereas modern psychodynamic theorists have focused more on _____.
a. social development; the self
b. the self; social development
c. sexual development; experience
d. experience; sexual development

10. All of the following are accurate descriptions of the differences between psychodynamic and cognitive-behavioral therapists EXCEPT:
a. Cognitive-behavioral therapists try to change thoughts and behaviors; psychodynamic therapists do not.
b. Psychodynamic therapists are nonreactive, whereas cognitive-behavioral therapists are more directive.
c. Psychodynamic therapists do not believe that treating the symptoms is enough; cognitive-behavioral therapists do.
d. Psychodynamic therapists adhere to the medical model of abnormality; cognitive-behavioral therapists do not.

11. Jen has been in therapy with a psychodynamic therapist for three months. After a difficult session, in which Jen discussed the harsh physical punishment she received from her father while growing up, Jen began to be afraid of the therapist. During the session, her heart started racing and she began to have thoughts that the therapist might hurt her. This phenomenon is best described as:
a. resistance.
b. projection.
c. transference.
d. sublimation.

12. Unlike some other approaches, psychodynamic theory:
a. focuses on the situation as well as the person.
b. can easily be evaluated using scientific methodology.
c. is a comprehensive theory of human personality.
d. has been supported by the majority of the studies.

13. All of the following are important aspects of the existential and humanistic approaches EXCEPT:
a. early attachment with caretakers.
b. freedom and choice.
c. responsibility and willingness.
d. fear of dying.

14. Bobby is a "people pleaser." He will often deny his own wants, needs, and desires in an attempt to make sure the people around him are happy. According to the existentialist and humanistic approaches, Bobby is:
a. exercising his freedom to make authentic choices.
b. taking personal responsibility for the way he reacts to the world.
c. using the notion of specialness to cope with his fear of dying.
d. using the notion of fusion to cope with his fear of dying.

15. Disorders of will, according to the existentialist and humanistic approaches, occur because people do not know what they want to do. According to these approaches, people may fail to know what they want for all of the following reasons EXCEPT:
a. what they want is repressed and they cannot access it.
b. they fear wanting.
c. they fear rejection.
d. they want others to magically discover their wants and fulfill them.

16. Which of the following approaches would be least likely to endorse the idea of "temporary insanity" as a defense in court?
a. psychodynamic
b. existentialist
c. behavioral
d. cognitive

17. Avoidance learning is an example of:
a. classical conditioning.
b. operant conditioning.
c. both a and b
d. neither a nor b

18. In Pavlov's famous experiment, he rang a bell just before his dog was fed. The dog began to salivate at the sound of the bell. The bell is the:
a. unconditioned stimulus.
b. conditioned stimulus.
c. unconditioned response.
d. conditioned response.

19. After the bell is sounded several times without food following, Pavlov's dog stops salivating at the sound of the bell. This phenomenon is known as:
a. unlearning.
b. extinction.
c. acquisition.
d. relearning.

20. Jose, who suffers from obsessive-compulsive disorder, always washes his hands fifty times after touching a doorknob, for fear he has picked up some germs. His therapist has him place his hands in a garbage can and makes him sit, without washing them, for half an hour. This is an example of what type of therapy?
    a. systematic desensitization
    b. selective positive reinforcement
    c. exposure
    d. selective negative reinforcement

21. When Anna does not do the dishes after dinner on Friday night, her parents tell her she cannot go out with her friends. This is an example of:
    a. punishment.
    b. negative reinforcement.
    c. positive reinforcement.
    d. none of the above

22. A parent of an autistic child splashes her with cold water whenever she begins to engage in self-mutilating behavior. The parent is using the therapeutic technique of:
    a. extinction.
    b. selective punishment.
    c. selective positive reinforcement.
    d. none of the above

23. A therapist using the cognitive approach would look for the cause of a mental disorder in:
    a. brain dysfunction.
    b. maladaptive behaviors.
    c. irrational thoughts.
    d. genetic inheritance.

24. Jody just failed her abnormal psychology test. She thinks that she failed because the test was unfair. What type of mental event is this?
    a. an expectation
    b. an appraisal
    c. an attribution
    d. a belief

25. Mitch just received an F on a test. He thinks he failed the test because his instructor's grading criteria were not sufficiently objective. Which of the following best characterizes Mitch's explanation?
    a. external
    b. stable
    c. global
    d. rationalization

26. Multimodal therapy, such as BASIC ID, involves the combined use of which approaches?
    a. psychodynamic and cognitive
    b. existential and behavioral
    c. behavioral and cognitive
    d. psychodynamic, behavioral, and cognitive

27. CCRT, the core conflictual relationship theme, is a technique that combines psychodynamic therapy with:
    a. existential/humanistic therapy.
    b. behavioral therapy.
    c. cognitive therapy.
    d. cognitive-behavioral therapy.

28. Behavioral and cognitive therapies have been shown to be effective in treating a number of disorders, are generally brief and inexpensive, and are easily tested using scientific methodology. However, these approaches have been criticized. Psychodynamic therapists have suggested that they _____, and existential therapists have suggested they _____
    a. do not recognize that people are free to choose; are too superficial.
    b. are too superficial; do not recognize that people are free to choose.
    c. do not hold people responsible for their actions; focus too exclusively on behavior.
    d. do not pay enough attention to unconscious processes; will simply lead to symptom substitution.

29. The failure of behavior treatment to produce long-term weight loss in obese people suggests that:
    a. obesity is probably biological in nature.
    b. sometimes symptom removal alone is not enough.
    c. both a and b
    d. neither a nor b

30. What is generally true regarding the effectiveness of the four different approaches?
    a. CBT is much more effective than psychodynamic or existential.
    b. They all work fairly well in the short term, but the psychodynamic approach works best for long-term change.
    c. They all appear to be effective for most of the disorders.
    d. Only a combination of approaches seems to be effective.

Fill in the Blank

1. Freud not only constructed a comprehensive theory of human personality and psychopathology, he also constructed a method of studying and changing personality. This method is known as _____.

   psychoanalysis

2. In Freudian theory, the _____ represents raw and urgent biological drives and is guided by the _____ principle.

   id

   pleasure

3. The _____ seeks to gratify desires in accordance with the requirements of reality; it is guided by the _____ principle.

   ego

   reality

4. The _____ represents conscience and idealistic striving.

   superego

5. _____ is a psychic pain caused by conflicts between the id, ego, and superego. It is relieved through the use of defense mechanisms.

   Anxiety

6. _____ is a defense by which the individual consciously forces unwanted thoughts of prohibited desires out of mind.

   Repression

7. _____ is a defense that consists of attributing to others those feelings and experiences that we deny having and usually repress.

   Projection

8. _____ is a defense in which the individual replaces the true target of his or her emotions with another, safer, target.

   Displacement

9. _____ is a defense that is similar to repression, but rather than doing away with inner facts, this does away with distressing external ones.

   Denial

10. _____ is the process of rechanneling psychic energies from socially undesirable goals to constructive and socially desirable ones.

    Sublimation

11. According to Jung, humans are born with memory traces of the experience of past generations; this is known as the _____ _____.

    collective unconscious

12. According to modern psychodynamic theory, three aspects of the self arise during development. The _____ self gives us our sense of separateness and identity; the _____ self gives us the sense that we can empathize with others; and the _____ self, which develops by using language, is our sense of self as a storehouse of knowledge and experience.

    core or body

    subjective

    verbal

13. According to Kohut and modern psychodynamic theory, the people who are important to us and who support our personality cohesiveness are called _____-_____.

    self-objects

14. The _____ model of abnormality recognizes that symptoms are not the illness, but merely reflect the underlying etiology.

    medical

15. For existential and humanist views, the will is very important. Two types of will are _____ will, which is willpower, and _____-_____ will, which is freely chosen and associated with future goals.

    exhortative; goal-directed

16. Two ways that people cope with their fear of dying are through a _____ _____ _____, in which a person believes the laws of nature do not apply to him or her, and _____, in which a person attaches him- or herself to others and refuses to stand apart.

notion of specialness

fusion

17. In behavior therapy, there are two basic learning processes. Through _____ conditioning, we learn what goes with what, and through _____ conditioning, we learn what to do to get what we want.

classical or Pavlovian

operant or instrumental

18. _____ is the learning of a response based on the contingency between a CS (conditioned stimulus) and a US (unconditioned stimulus).

Acquisition

19. _____ occurs when the CS loses its power to produce a formerly acquired response.

Extinction

20. An _____ is a response whose probability can either be increased by positive reinforcement or by the removal of negative reinforcement.

operant

21. A _____ _____ is a signal that means that reinforcement is available if the operant is made.

discriminative stimulus

22. _____ _____ are unconscious appraisals of what happens to us or what we do; they precede and cause emotion.

Automatic thoughts

23. A(n) _____ is an individual's explanation of why an event has befallen him or her.

attribution

Matching

Match the following definitions with the correct term and indicate in which approach each technique is used: psychodynamic (P), existential/humanist (E), behavioral (B), or cognitive (C). Put the letter of the matching technique in the blank at the beginning of each definition. Mark the corresponding approach (P, E, B, C) in the blank following the definition.

Definition

1. _____ Immersion in a feared situation (real or imagined) _____

2. _____ Processing momentary blocks in dealing with an issue _____

3. _____ Systematic delivery of positive reinforcement contingent on the occurrence of a behavior, in order to increase the behavior _____

4. _____ Shifting from negative explanations to more positive explanations of events _____

5. _____ Interpreting the emotions and expectations the patient has toward the therapist _____

6. _____ Imagining gradual more frightening scenes while in a state of relaxation _____

Technique

a. changing attributions

b. extinction

c. systematic desensitization

d. avoidance learning

e. changing long-term beliefs

f. catharsis

Definition   *Technique*

7. _____ Verbally and behaviorally countering superstitions   g. exposure
   and self-defeating propaganda _____

8. _____ Application of an aversive event following a behavior   h. CCRT
   to reduce the probability of its occurrence _____

9. _____ Patients learn what predicts an aversive event and how   i. interpreting transference
   to get away before the aversive event occurs _____

10. _____ Increasing a patient's belief that he or she can   j. selective positive reinforcement
    achieve a desired outcome _____

11. _____ Elimination of a highly desired event whenever a   k. free association
    behavior occurs in order to reduce the behavior _____

12. _____ The uncovering and reliving of early traumas _____   l. processing resistance

13. _____ Conscious thoughts are used to reveal underlying,   m. changing efficacy expectations uncon-
    scious themes about current
    and past relationships _____

14. _____ Saying whatever comes to mind without censoring _____   n. selective punishment

LEVELS OF ANALYSIS: EXAMINING THE CHAPTER'S THEMES

In a sense, the entire chapter embodies the levels of analysis theme, focusing, of course, on various psychological levels of analysis. The treatment of choice theme arises because the therapist must determine at what level to intervene. The science and practice theme is also prominent, inasmuch as each of the therapies is derived from a theory of human functioning.

Biological and Psychological Levels of Analysis

The four psychological approaches addressed in this chapter may be seen as levels of (psychological) analysis. They may be conceptualized as levels of "depth." At the surface level is the behavioral approach and its doctrine that the symptoms are the disorder; cognitive approaches achieve a little more depth by addressing the underlying conscious thoughts; existentialist and humanistic approaches go deeper in addressing will and responsibility; and the psychodynamic approach addresses the deepest level of all—abiding character traits.

Treatment of Choice

Because therapies are based on different theories of human functioning and vary as to level of depth, techniques can be chosen that are tailored to the level at which the therapist would like to intervene psychologically. The therapist must determine if the client wants to change a specific behavior or address more global personality issues. Outcome studies have shown little difference in the effectiveness rates among the different psychological interventions. However, some treatments have been shown to be particularly effective for certain disorders. This will continue to be addressed throughout the text.

Science and Practice

The therapeutic techniques described in the chapter are based on theories of human functioning. In psychodynamic psychotherapy, techniques such as free association, dream recall, interpreting resistance, and transference are based on the theory that humans repress unwanted feelings and early conflicts and that the only way to make them conscious is to tap into the unconscious mind. When these unconscious conflicts are brought to the surface, they are then more controllable by ego processes. Therapies based on existentialist and humanistic approaches focus on developing independence, goal-directed willing, and personal responsibility, based on the assumption that individuals are free and must use their freedom to make authentic choices based on their own desires and goals. Techniques used by behaviorists include classical conditioning techniques such as exposure and systematic desensitization. These techniques put into practice the scientific findings that people can learn to pair and unpair stimuli and responses. Operant conditioning techniques such as selective positive reinforcement, extinction, and selective punishment reflect the scientific findings that reinforced behaviors are more likely to reoccur, and behaviors that are punished are likely to diminish. Cognitive therapists try to change their patients' expectations, appraisals, attributions, and beliefs, based on the theory that mental events cause behavior and therefore changing mental events can lead to behavior changes.

In this chapter, there is also an interesting discussion of biological and psychological levels of analysis that addresses the effectiveness of psychological interventions for biologically based disorders. Because a person's genes and environment interact in the expression of many genetically based disorders, psychotherapy may be an ideal intervention to break the gene-environment covariance. See Box 3-1 for a detailed discussion. Also see Box 3-2 for a discussion of combining neuroscience with cognitive-behavioral therapy.

ANSWER KEY

Multiple-Choice Questions

1. c. The therapist's hypothesis is that Jeanie has been positively reinforced by her parents for displaying fear of dogs, thereby increasing the likelihood that she will display fear in the future. This is consistent with the behavioral notion that reinforced target behaviors are more likely to occur in the future.

2. a. Jeanie's hypothesis that her fear of dogs is based on a (mostly unconscious) fear of men is consistent with displacement, a defense mechanism proposed by Freud in which the individual replaces the true target of his or her emotions with another, safer, target.

3. d. The therapist is teaching Jeanie to alter her thoughts in an attempt to change her emotional response. This is consistent with the cognitive approach.

4. a. This question describes systematic desensitization, in which a patient imagines a set of gradually more frightening scenes and at the same time makes a response that is incompatible with fear (relaxation). This is a type of classical (or

Pavlovian) therapy, where the stimulus is paired with a new response.

5. c. According to Freudian theory, a person who is overly dominated by his or her superego seems wooden and moralistic, unable to be comfortable with pleasure and overly sensitive to "thou shalt not."

6. b. Id and superego processes are primarily (or entirely) subconscious, whereas ego processes are often conscious.

7. c. Projection consists of attributing to others those feelings and experiences that we personally deny having and that we usually repress. Although projection does involve some repression, repression alone is an incomplete answer.

8. a. Jung coined the term "archetypes," which are a part of the collective unconscious.

9. a. Neo-Freudians like Horney, Sullivan, Erikson, and Fromm departed from Freud by de-emphasizing sexual development and putting more emphasis on social development. Modern theorists, such as Kohut, focus on the self. For example, Kohut proposed three aspects of the self: the core self, the subjective self, and the verbal self.

10. a. Both types of therapists seek to change thoughts and behaviors, they just use different techniques to accomplish this goal.

11. c. Although Jen is projecting, transference is a better answer, because transference is the term specifically used to describe the transfer of emotions and conflicts from other sources onto a therapist by a client.

12. c. One of the strengths of this model is that it is a comprehensive theory of human personality. The shortcomings of the theory are that it is too difficult to test experimentally, that studies have failed to support it, and that the situational context has been neglected in the exclusive focus on the individual.

13. a. Freedom and choice, responsibility and willingness, and fear of dying are three important aspects of human experience, according to these models. Early attachment is a modern psychodynamic construct.

14. d. For existentialist and humanists, authenticity is very important. Authentic choices are those that are made based on one's own desires, not the desires of others. Denying your own desires in an attempt to fuse with others is a way of coping with the fear of dying and can be maladaptive.

15. a. Repression is a psychodynamic concept. All other answers are accurate descriptions based on the existentialist and humanistic approaches.

16. b. A core notion for existentialist approaches is the belief that people act freely, for better or for

worse, and that they should be held accountable for their actions.

17. c. Avoidance learning is an example of both types of conditioning; classical conditioning is used in learning what precedes an aversive event and operant conditioning is used in learning what to do to avoid that event.

18. b. By being paired with the unconditioned stimulus (food) the bell becomes the conditioned stimulus.

19. b. The term Pavlov coined to describe the loss of the conditioned stimulus's (bell's) power to produce a formally acquired response is extinction.

20. c. Exposure is a type of Pavlovian (or classical) therapy in which the patient is immersed in the situation that he or she fears.

21. b. A negative reinforcer is an event whose removal increases the probability of recurrence of a response that precedes it. Punishments are events in which the onset will decrease the probability of recurrence of a response that precedes it. In this case, Anna's parents are trying to increase a behavior (doing the dishes after dinner), therefore they are using negative reinforcement.

22. b. In selective punishment, an aversive event is applied whenever a maladaptive target behavior occurs, to reduce the probability of its occurrence. In extinction, a behavior is eliminated by omitting some highly desired event whenever the target behavior occurs.

23. c. Cognitive therapists believe that mental events can cause behavior and therefore behavior can be changed by changing mental events. They believe that disordered mental events or irrational thoughts are causal in the development of mental disorders.

24. c. An attribution is an individual's explanation of why an event has befallen him or her.

25. a. The three dimensions of attributions are: external or internal, stable or unstable, and global or specific. Mitch's attribution that he failed because the test is unfair is external, unstable, and specific.

26. c. BASIC ID is an approach that combines behavioral and cognitive treatments.

27. c. In CCRT, conscious thoughts about relationships are used as clues for underlying, often unconscious, relationship themes. This combines psychodynamic therapy with cognitive therapy.

28. b. Only answer b accurately portrays each of the model's criticisms.

29. a. Obesity does seem to be biological in nature, which indicates that the failure of behavioral approaches is due to their failure to address underlying causes (in this case, biological causes).

30. c. The most common finding is that each of the psychological approaches is effective with most of the disorders.

MATCHING

1. g, B
2. 1, P
3. j, B
4. a, C
5. i, P
6. c, B
7. e, C
8. n, B
9. d, B
10. m, C
11. b, B
12. f, P
13. h, C, B, & P
14. k, P

CHAPTER 4

The Biological Approach and Neuroscience

A GUIDE TO THE READING

This chapter provides an overview of the biological approach to abnormal behavior. The biological approach involves several levels of analysis: genetics, neurons, brain structure, neurodevelopment, and environmental input. It is helpful to focus on one level at a time, but keep in mind that the levels are very much interrelated in serving as the biological basis for abnormal behavior (see Figure 4-1 for an illustration). In addition, for many disorders, biological vulnerabilities must interact with environmental stress for abnormality to be expressed. The *diathesis-stress model* states that abnormal behavior is caused by a vulnerability to a disorder that is triggered (or buffered) by the environment. People may have high or low vulnerabilities and thus require different levels of stress to trigger a disorder. This model is fundamental to our understanding of many disorders and should be understood thoroughly (see p. 27 for further review). Keep in mind that vulnerabilities are typically biological but can also be acquired.

Genetics

Genes are the basic units of heredity that contain the code for our inherited traits. They are made up of DNA and are located on the chromosomes contained in the nucleus of every cell in our bodies. Figure 4-2 illustrates the structure and function of genes. Keep in mind that most behavioral phenomena are *polygenic* (influenced by a large number of genes), though some disorders are caused by a single gene (for example, Huntington's chorea). Be clear on the distinction between *genotype* (the specific genes we inherit) and

phenotype (the physical and behavioral characteristics associated with a particular genotype). Phenotypes are influenced by the environment within the cells themselves and within the uterus following conception. Be familiar with how genes are expressed (pp. 131–33; see Figure 4-4 for an illustration of the process). Also, keep in mind that just as the environment affects genetic expression, genes affect environment by influencing both our behavior (and in turn what kind of experiences we will have) and our perceptions of our life experiences. Be familiar with the research methods used in behavioral genetics (pp. 133–36), especially twin and adoption studies, which allow researchers to examine the relative contributions of genes and environment (be sure to review Figure 4-3 for an illustration of the formation of different types of twins and Box 4-1 for a summary of human gene therapy).

Neurons

Neurons, or nerve cells, are the cells that make up the human nervous system. They have been implicated in many psychological disorders and you should understand their structure and functioning well. This is summarized nicely in Figure 4-5. Our nerve cells use a combination of electrical impulses (within the cell) and chemicals ("neurotransmitters," between cells) to communicate in order to produce all of our mental and physical activities. Drugs used to treat psychological disorders work by altering the level of neurotransmitters in the synaptic gap (the area between neurons), by blocking postsynaptic receptors, or by increasing the synthesis of the neurotransmitter or blocking reuptake. Become familiar with the names of the neurotransmitters that have been implicated in psychological disorders: the catecholamines (dopamine, epinephrine, norepinephrine), serotonin, the amino acids (glutamate, GABA), and acetylcholine (review the discussion on pp. 137–39 of which neurotransmitters are implicated in which disorders; see Figure 4-6 for an illustration of the pathways of several important neurotransmitters). Hormones, another type of chemical messenger, are secreted by the endocrine glands (see Figure 4-7 for an overview). Note especially the importance on neural activity of sex hormones (which affect the development of brain structure and neural functioning) and stress hormones (which cause decreases in the performance of mental tasks and which hamper the healing process).

Brain Structures

It is important to have a basic understanding of the structure and function of the central nervous system (CNS) and the peripheral nervous system (PNS). The CNS is made up of the brain and spinal cord. There are two diagrams of the brain which should help in learning the basic structure, these are found in Figures 4-8 and 4-10. Know the parts of the brain and what they do (pp. 144–50). It may help to conceptualize the parts of the brain in terms of their evolutionary development: the oldest part of the brain is the brain stem, which controls automatic functions and contains the hindbrain and diencephalon. The hindbrain (including the medulla and the cerebellum) helps us process what we sense, keep our balance, and maintain automatic functions, such as heart rate. The diencephalon connects our two hemispheres and contains the thalamus and hypothalamus, which also help with processing sensory and motor information and controlling hormone secretions. The forebrain is the newest part of the brain and is unique to our species. It is important for conscious thought, reasoning, and memory. Be especially familiar with the structure and function of the forebrain. There are also some subcortical areas that have been implicated in psychopathology: the basal ganglia (involved in motor behavior), and the hippocampus and amygdala (parts of the limbic system involved in emotion and learning from rewards and punishments; see Figures 4-12A and B to review their structure). Remember, the structures of the brain work together to produce our complex behavior; be sure to know the basic systems and circuits discussed in the text, including the limbic system (Figure 4-13), the behavioral inhibition system and behavioral activating system (BIS and BAS, p. 148), and the HPA axis (p. 149). Be familiar with the basic structure and function of the PNS, which is divided into the somatic system (controls muscles and carries sensory input to the CNS) and the autonomic system (governs involuntary actions; be sure to review Figure 4-14 to understand this system).

Neurodevelopment

The development of the nervous system begins in the embryonic stage and continues through old age. Prenatal and postnatal periods have been shown to be particularly important in the development of future psychopathology. The prenatal period is important because chemicals inside and outside cells turn on or off the expression of genes, large amounts of neurons are lost, and nervous system structures go through critical periods of development (for a graph of critical periods, see Figure 4-15). Poor nutrition, exposure to drugs or alcohol, oxygen deprivation, and maternal stress can all negatively impact neurodevelopment. Growth of the nervous system continues postnatally, including cortical growth (cortical volume in infants is one-third of what it will be in adulthood), myelination (which speeds communication between neurons), and synaptic pruning (elimination of faulty or irrelevant connections). These changes are consistent with changes in metabolic activity in the brain, with the motor cortex, brain stem, etc., showing the greatest activity in newborns; the parietal and temporal regions in the first year; and the frontal cortex last. Beginning in middle age, our brains lose volume and show less metabolic activity; these age-related changes appear to be associated with the risk for certain psychological symptoms.

Environmental Input

The extent to which our environment affects our biological functioning varies over our lifespan. In certain critical periods, environment can have a large impact on biological and psychological functioning, particularly on learning and memory. Memories are formed through long-term potentiation (LTP), in which a permanent change is made in the firing patterns of an ensemble of neurons, with different regions of the brain being changed by different types of memories. This is evidenced by the fact that damage to different brain structures affects different types of memory. For example, damage to the hippocampus affects explicit memory (stored knowledge about objects, people, and events), whereas damage to the amygdala affects implicit memory (knowledge about skills and procedures).

The nervous system requires stimulation for development, as evidenced by studies that show that environmental enrichment can change the structure of the brain (see pp. 157–58 for a description of some of these studies). Studies have also clearly documented a relationship between exposure to stress and psychological problems; stress can trigger an underlying vulnerability to developing a disorder (recall the diathesis-stress model), and can worsen symptoms. Chronic or severe stress can have lasting effects on brain function (abnormality in the HPA axis, shrinkage of the hippocampus, etc.).

TESTING YOUR UNDERSTANDING

Test your understanding of what you have read by working through the following tasks with a classmate.

1. If you've ever known identical twins, you know that they are remarkable similar, yet also different from one another. In fact, identical twins are often different in many small ways at birth. Explain how environment interacts with genes to produce identical twins that are different. Consider both prenatal and postnatal factors.

2. What methods do researchers use to understand the effects of genes on behavior?

3. Explain why, in half the cases, a person who has an identical twin with schizophrenia does not become schizophrenic.

4. Draw a picture of two neurons and explain to a friend how they communicate with one another and why this is important in understanding abnormality.

5. Explain the nervous system, particularly the parts that are especially relevant to psychopathology.

6. Think of a newborn that you know or have known. Imagine how you would explain to the newborn's parents what changes have already taken place in the brain development of the child, what the child's brain is like now, and what will happen to the child's brain as he or she continues to grow.

Multiple-Choice Questions

1. A biological vulnerability to mental illness:
   a. is inherited genetically.
   b. is acquired through exposure to certain environmental factors.
   c. either a or b
   d. must always involve both a and b.

2. The biological approach has generated many different treatment methods over time. Which of the following is a treatment method whose use is now severely restricted?
   a. electroconvulsive therapy (ECT)
   b. psychosurgery
   c. medication
   d. both a and b

3. Why might Elaine, a college student, develop schizophrenia while her roommate, Danielle, does not?
   a. Elaine has inherited a vulnerability to schizophrenia; Danielle has not.
   b. Elaine is experiencing much more stress than Danielle.
   c. Elaine and Danielle are experiencing equal

amounts of stress, and both have inherited a vulnerability to schizophrenia, but Elaine's vulnerability to schizophrenia is more easily triggered than Danielle's.
   d. All of the above are reasons why Elaine might develop schizophrenia, while Danielle does not.

4. _____ consists of two strands of phosphate, sugar, and four nucleotide bases that are wrapped around each other like a double helix.
   a. DNA
   b. A gene
   c. A chromosome
   d. The nucleus of each human cell

5. Jen has blond hair, like her mother, and her sister has brown hair, like her father. Her father's mother has brown hair, though her father's father has blond hair. Jen marries a man with brown hair, whose parents both had brown hair, and all Jen's children have brown hair. In this case, blond hair appears to be:
   a. dominant.
   b. recessive.
   c. impossible to tell based on the information given.
   d. a genetic mutation.

6. Which of the following is true of monozygotic twins?
   a. They are always identical.
   b. They may not be identical because genetic mutations can occur during or after the separation of the two zygotes.
   c. They may not be identical because environmental influences begin at conception.
   d. both b and c

7. A gene has been expressed when _____, while the step that has the potential for influencing behavior is _____.
   a. the messenger RNA attaches to a ribosome and tells it to add amino acids to the protein it is synthesizing; the synthesis of proteins.
   b. the proteins are synthesized; when the messenger RNA attaches to a ribosome and tells it to add amino acids to the protein it is synthesizing.
   c. the proteins are synthesized; when the gene's coded information is transcribed from the template DNA into the messenger RNA.
   d. the gene's coded information is transcribed from the template DNA into the messenger RNA; the synthesis of proteins.

8. Some genes are virtually always expressed, while others are only expressed in certain circumstances. Which of the following is NOT a circumstance that could affect the expression of a gene?
   a. not inheriting the gene from the parents
   b. a lack of a certain biochemical in the biochemical environment surrounding the cell
   c. environmental factors in utero
   d. environmental factors after birth

9. Monozygotic twins (MZ) report more similar past experiences than dizygotic twins (DZ), even when the twins are raised apart. Which of the following is a reasonable hypothesis to explain this finding?
   a. Genes influence the likelihood that the twins will actually experience certain events.
   b. Genes influence the probability that the twins will remember certain past events.
   c. both a and b
   d. neither a nor b

10. Scientists employ many different types of research designs to explore the role of genes in behavior. _____ is used to document the occurrence of characteristics or disorders in individuals who vary in their genetic relatedness.
    a. The family study method
    b. The twin method
    c. The adoption method
    d. Genetic linkage analysis

11. Dr. M designs a study to determine whether the development of schizophrenia has a genetic basis. She locates families who have adopted a child whose biological mother had schizophrenia and compares them to adopted children whose biological mother did not have schizophrenia. She includes in her analysis only adoptive families with no history of schizophrenia and only adopted children who are now over 30 (since schizophrenia usually doesn't develop until early adulthood). She finds that the rate of schizophrenia among the adopted children is much higher for children whose biological mothers had schizophrenia. This provides evidence for:
    a. a genetic basis for schizophrenia.
    b. an environmental basis for schizophrenia.
    c. the hypothesis that environment has no impact on the development of schizophrenia.
    d. the hypothesis that genetics has no impact on the development of schizophrenia.

12. Researchers use a number of procedures with animals to aid in our understanding of how genes effect behavior. In one technique, researchers produce transgenic animals, animals whose genes have been artificially combined with other DNA. This is accomplished by:
    a. systematic breeding.
    b. quantitative genetic methods.
    c. injecting DNA into the nucleus of the single-celled zygotes.
    d. "knockout" procedures.

13. Most of our genes are devoted to the development and functioning of which system?
    a. the nervous system
    b. the endocrine system
    c. the autonomic nervous system
    d. the central nervous system

14. The nucleus of the neuron is located in the:
    a. dendrites.

b. soma.
c. axon.
d. myelin sheaths.

15. Neurons communicate electrochemically. Electrical signals are used to communicate within neurons, while chemicals, known as _____, are used to communicate among neurons.
    a. mitochondria
    b. action potentials
    c. receptors
    d. neurotransmitters

16. There are a number of ways that neurotransmitters are removed from the synaptic gap after information is transferred from one neuron to the next. Which of the following is not a way in which neurotransmitters are removed from the synaptic gap?
    a. diffusion
    b. degradation
    c. reuptake
    d. the use of agonists

17. Many neurotransmitters are thought to be involved in psychopathology. _____ influences attention, mood, and motivation and is involved in schizophrenia and Parkinson's disease, whereas _____ affects the way we process information and is implicated in depression and anxiety.
    a. GABA; norepinephrine
    b. Acetylcholine; glutamate
    c. Dopamine; serotonin
    d. Glutamate; GABA

18. Hormones also serve as chemical messengers, however, they are not released by neurons, but by _____.
    a. the endocrine glands
    b. the gonads
    c. the cerebrum
    d. the reticular activating system

19. Abnormal behavior can result from:
    a. too much neurotransmitter in the brain.
    b. too little neurotransmitter in the brain.
    c. abnormal hormonal levels.
    d. all of the above

20. The peripheral nervous system is made up of:
    a. the brain and the spinal cord.
    b. the sympathetic and parasympathetic nervous systems.
    c. the autonomic and somatic nervous systems.
    d. all of the above

21. The _____ is the oldest part of the brain, from the standpoint of evolution.
    a. brain stem
    b. hindbrain
    c. midbrain
    d. forebrain

22. The cerebral cortex, basal ganglia, amygdala, and hippocampus are major structures in the:
    a. midbrain.
    b. diencephalon.
    c. medulla.
    d. forebrain.

23. Trinh suffered a head injury in a car accident. Since the accident, she has had trouble with motor skills that involve spatial perception and has also had difficulty recognizing complex configurations. She most likely suffered damage in her _____ hemisphere.
    a. right
    b. left
    c. These symptoms are not consistent with either right- or left-brain injury.
    d. These symptoms indicate diffuse brain damage.

24. Which of the following association areas or axes is associated with integrating past memories, emotional/motivational impulses, and motor plans?
    a. the profrontal association area
    b. the limbic association area
    c. the HPA axis
    d. none of the above

25. Perseveration, a difficulty in making transitions between one action and the next, is often seen in patients with _____ damage.
    a. midbrain
    b. limbic system
    c. frontal lobe
    d. neuronal

26. Which of the following is NOT one of the subcortical regions that appear to be especially relevant to psychopathology?
    a. basal ganglia
    b. hypothalamus
    c. hippocampus
    d. amygdala

27. Which of the following systems is sensitive to pleasure and reward?
    a. behavioral activation system
    b. behavioral inhibition system
    c. fight/flight system
    d. all of the above

28. Which of the following periods are critical for the development of nervous system structures?
    a. the first trimester
    b. the second trimester
    c. the entire pregnancy
    d. the first and second trimesters

29. Memories are represented in the nervous system by:
    a. the creation of new neural connections.
    b. relatively permanent changes in the firing pattern of an ensemble of neurons.
    c. changes in the brain structure.
    d. increases in neurotransmitters.

30. Chronic or severe stress can cause changes both in the brain's function, as evidenced by _____, and in the brain's structure, such as shrinkage of the _____.
    a. chronic decrease in glucocorticoid release; hippocampus
    b. chronic decrease in glucocorticoid release; thalamus
    c. chronic increase in glucocorticoid release; hippocampus
    d. chronic increase in glucocorticoid release; thalamus

Fill in the Blank

1. The _____ model applied the same terms to psychological and behavioral abnormalities that were used to describe physical illnesses.

   biomedical

2. The _____-_____ model emphasizes the interplay between biology and experience in the development of psychopathology.

   diathesis-stress

3. _____ are the basic units of heredity that contain the code for our inherited traits.

   Genes

4. _____ refers to the development of the nervous system.

   Neurodevelopment

5. The _____ molecule is formed like a double helix and stores the template for the production of proteins from amino acids.

   DNA

6. A _____ gene can produce a trait on its own, whereas a _____ gene requires another like it to produce a trait.

    dominant; recessive

7. The specific genes inherited by an individual are called the _____, whereas the specific physical or behavioral characteristics that are expressed are known as the _____.

    genotype

    phenotype

8. Characteristics that are influenced by multiple genes are called _____.

    polygenic

9. _____ twins originate from two fertilized eggs and _____ twins develop from a single fertilized egg.

    Dizygotic or fraternal; monozygotic or identical

10. The term _____ is used by scientists to refer to the likelihood that a particular gene will be expressed.

    penetrance

11. _____ is the process by which DNA synthesizes RNA.

    Transcription

12. In behavioral genetics, the _____ _____ method simply documents the occurrence of disorders in individuals who vary in their genetic relatedness; _____ _____ _____ involves looking for a "marker" gene in a family in which several members suffer from the same disorder.

    family study

    genetic linkage analysis

13. _____, or nerve cells, are the building blocks of the nervous system.

    Neurons

14. _____ are the nerve cell's primary chemical messengers.

    Neurotransmitters

15. There are several ways to remove neurotransmitters from the synapse: _____ occurs when the neurotransmitters mix with other substances and their concentration is reduced; _____ involves the decomposition of neurotransmitters by enzymes; and _____ occurs when the excess neurotransmitters are taken back by the presynaptic neuron.

    diffusion

    degradation

    reuptake

16. Drugs that increase activity in particular neurotransmitter systems are called _____.

    agonists

17. The brain and the spinal cord make up the _____ _____ system; the _____ _____ system includes the autonomic and somatic nervous systems.

    central nervous

    peripheral nervous

18. The _____ system activates our "fight or flight" response; the _____ system calms us down.

    sympathetic; parasympathetic

19. _____ _____ is the process in which connections among neurons are eliminated during development.

    Synaptic pruning

20. _____ memory refers to stored knowledge about objects, people, and events and _____ memory refers to stored knowledge about perceptual and motor skills and various procedures and principles.

    Explicit

    implicit

Matching

Can you match the parts of the brain with their functions?

1. _____ Brain stem

    a. processes sensory and motor information and directs it to the cortex

2. _____ Cerebellum

    b. integrates past memories, emotion/motivation, and motor plans

3. _____ Medulla

    c. a system of cavities containing cerebral spinal fluid

4. _____ Thalamus

    d. triggers emotional responses and our ability to learn from rewards and punishments

5. _____ Hypothalamus

    e. controls posture, balance, and movements

6. _____ Corpus callosum

    f. essential to motor behavior; involved in the behavioral activating system

7. _____ Limbic system

    g. regulates breathing, heart rate, and blood pressure

8. _____ Ventricles

    h. governs executive functions such as formulating and executing plans

9. _____ Cerebral cortex

    i. controls automatic functions such as coughing or swallowing

10. _____ Basal ganglia

    j. connects right and left hemispheres, enabling communication

11. _____ Amygdala

    k. controls hormone secretion from pituitary gland; regulates appetite and sexual interest

LEVELS OF ANALYSIS: EXAMINING THE CHAPTER'S THEMES

Like Chapter 3, this entire chapter embodies the levels of analysis theme, with a primary focus on the biological approach. The reciprocal relationship between biology and environment is emphasized throughout. The development theme appears in the context of neurodevelopment, and the chapter also addresses some science and practice issues.

Biological and Psychological Levels of Analysis

Although the focus of this chapter is on the biological approach, the chapter stresses that biological processes are influenced by environment and experience at the cellular level, during prenatal growth, and throughout human development. One example of the impact of environment on biological processes is that monozygotic twins are not always born identical. Changes at the cellular level during the zygote phase as well as other conditions in the prenatal environment can result in clear biological differences, such as monozygotic twins of different genders. The prenatal and postnatal cellular environment also plays an important role in whether or not the genes we inherit are expressed. During brain development, which lasts through early adulthood, the environment shapes our brains and neural connections by changing the activities of our genes. Evidence also suggests

that exposure to certain types of environments (stressful, enriched, etc.) can alter brain structure and function. So the relationship between biology and environment begins with conception and continues throughout adulthood. Genes also influence our environment, since they influence our behavior, which in turn influences the kinds of experiences we will have. The relationship between genes and environment is clarified by the diathesis-stress model, which suggests that disorders result from a vulnerability (often an inherited vulnerability) which is triggered or suppressed by the environment.

Development

Neurodevelopment (the development of the nervous system) occurs throughout a person's life; however, evidence suggests there is a critical period during which the system is particularly vulnerable. It appears that the critical period for neurodevelopment is during the first two trimesters of pregnancy (see Figure 4-15 for an illustration of other critical periods). Maternal exposure to toxins, stress, nutritional deficits, and oxygen deprivation can disrupt neurodevelopment in offspring. This is one of the reasons good prenatal health has been stressed in our country. After birth, the brain continues to develop, and changes in activity levels indicate which parts of the brain are developing during which periods. In newborns, the greatest activity occurs in the motor cortex, the thalamus, the brain stem, and the cerebrum, whereas frontal cortex activity is the greatest starting at about age six.

Science and Practice

Animal models are often used to investigate the biological processes and the relative contribution of biology and environment to disease. Some have raised questions about the validity of applying information based on animal research to humans. There is a great deal of similarity between the biological processes of humans and animals. However, especially in psychological research, the complexity of the human brain clearly limits the extent to which animal research can be applied. See Box 4-2 for a discussion of this controversy.

ANSWER KEY

MULTIPLE-CHOICE QUESTIONS

1. c. Biological vulnerability may be inherited or acquired through exposure to environmental factors, or may result in an interaction between the two.

2. b. Psychosurgery is now rarely used. ECT, while less commonly used compared to medications, is still used as an effective treatment for depression and mania.

3. d. According to the diathesis-stress model, a mental disorder develops (1) if the person has a vulnerability to the particular disorder and (2) if they encounter sufficient stress in their environment. Vulnerability levels vary, such that the amount of stress needed to trigger the onset of a disorder varies, depending on how vulnerable a person is.

4. a. DNA consists of two strands wrapped around each other like a double helix. Genes are specific sequences of DNA and are located on the chromosomes which are contained in the nucleus of each human cell.

5. b. Recessive genes can only be expressed if both gene pairs have the trait. In Jen's case, she has blond hair because she inherited a blond recessive gene from each of her parents. Her father carried a recessive blond gene from his father, but has brown hair himself because of the dominant brown gene he inherited from his mother.

6. d. Monozygotic twins are not always identical. Reasons for differences include genetic mutations and differences in prenatal environment.

7. d. The transcription of DNA into RNA is the process by which a gene is expressed while the actual synthesis of proteins, the final step in the process, is the one that has the potential for influencing behavior.

8. a. Gene expression has been found to be very influenced by environmental factors at the cellular level, in utero, and even after birth. Remember that expression has to do with whether the genes you inherit (genotype) are expressed as specific physical or behavioral characteristics.

9. c. There is evidence that genes influence both our behavior (which in turn influences the kinds of experiences we have) and the way we view our life experiences.

10. a. This is a description of the family study method. Genetic linkage analysis involves finding genetic markers for particular disorders.

11. a. The adoption method helps to determine whether a disorder has a biological or environmental basis (or both). In this case, schizophrenia clearly has a genetic basis. However, environment cannot be ruled out entirely, because the prenatal environment was experienced with the biological mother.

12. c. Transgenic animals are produced by injecting DNA into the single-celled zygotes. Quantitative genetic methods involve gathering data on large samples of people to estimate how much a person's genotype (versus the environment) contributes to a particular trait or disorder. "Knockout" procedures involve the elimination of genes in embryos.

13. a. Most of our genes are devoted to the nervous system. The autonomic nervous system and the central nervous system are parts of the nervous system.

14. b. The nucleus of the neuron, which is the command center of the cell, is located in the cell body, or soma.

15. d. As their name implies, neurotransmitters are the chemicals used to transmit information among neurons. For a complete map of the parts and functioning of a neuron, review Figure 4-5.

16. d. Diffusion of the chemicals, degradation (elimination through the action of enzymes), and reuptake (excess neurotransmitter taken back by the presynaptic neuron) are all ways of removing neurotransmitters from the synaptic gap. Agonists are drugs that increase the activity of a particular neurotransmitter (for instance, by blocking the reuptake). Antagonists, in contrast, reduce the activity of a neurotransmitter.

17. c. Dopamine is involved in schizophrenia and Parkinson's disease; serotonin is implicated in depression and anxiety (remember Prozac is a "SSRI," or selective serotonin reuptake inhibitor).

18. a. Hormones are released by the endocrine glands. See Figure 4-7 for a detailed map of the endocrine

system and the hormones released by each part.

19. d. Abnormal levels of hormones or neurotransmitters can lead to abnormal behavior.

20. c. The peripheral nervous system is made up of the autonomic and somatic systems. The sympathetic and parasympathetic systems make up the autonomic system. The brain and spinal cord make up the central nervous system.

21. a. The brain stem is the oldest part of the brain and is divided into the hindbrain, the midbrain, and the diencephalon. It controls automatic functions such as breathing and swallowing.

22. d. All of these structures are located in the forebrain, the newest part of the brain, which is most highly developed in human beings.

23. a. The right hemisphere is specialized for spatial/holistic functions whereas the left hemisphere is specialized for linguistic/analytic functions.

24. b. The limbic association area is associated with memory, emotion, and motor plans.

25. c. Damage to the frontal lobes can result in changes to the entire personality, violent behavior, and perseveration.

26. b. The basal ganglia, hippocampus, and amygdala are subcortical regions that seem to be especially relevant to psychopathology, especially to the experience of emotions and stress. They are involved in the behavioral inhibition system and the behavioral activation system.

27. a. The BAS is sensitive to pleasure and reward. The BIS plays a role in the experience of anxiety, and the FFS overrides both and is associated with intense arousal and attempts to flee or resist a threat.

28. d. The first two trimesters are critical periods for the development of nervous system structures in human beings.

29. b. The brain processes sensory information using the simultaneous activity of "ensembles," or groups of neurons. Memories are represented by relatively permanent changes in the firing pattern of these ensembles.

30. c. Chronic or severe stress can cause chronic increases in the release of glucocorticoid, a stress hormone, resulting in greater biological and behavioral responses to later stressors. Women with histories of abuse and men who were exposed to intense combat showed shrinkage in the hippocampus.

MATCHING

1. i
2. e
3. g
4. a
5. k
6. j
7. b
8. c
9. h
10. f
11. d

CHAPTER 5 | Anxiety Disorders

A GUIDE TO THE READING

At the beginning of the chapter, fear and anxiety are defined and then six anxiety disorders are presented: phobias, post-traumatic stress disorder (PTSD), panic disorder, agoraphobia, generalized anxiety disorder (GAD), and obsessive-compulsive disorder (OCD). *Fear* is characterized by distress about specific, dangerous objects (as in phobias and PTSD), whereas *anxiety* is a general feeling of unease about an unspecified danger (as in panic and GAD). Review carefully the four elements of fear, as they will reappear throughout the chapter: *cognitive* (discernment of threat), *somatic* (the body's reaction), *emotional* (feelings of dread or terror), and *behavioral* (fleeing, freezing, or fighting). Keep in mind that abnormal fear is the same as normal fear; it is just out of proportion to the danger. Anxiety has the same components as fear, but the cognitive element is the expectation of a more diffuse and uncertain danger. You'll need to be familiar with DSM-IV criteria, the etiology, and the effective treatments for each of the anxiety disorders discussed in the chapter.

Phobias

Criteria. The DSM-IV criteria for specific phobias appear on p. 170. Review these carefully. Note that phobic fear is excessive or unreasonable, cued by a specific object or situation, avoided or endured with intense anxiety, and interferes significantly with a person's normal routine (for example, a person afraid of bridges stops going to work because he must cross a bridge on the way). The objects of fear vary quite a bit, see Table 5-1 for a list of common phobias. The criteria for social phobias appear on p. 171. Note that social phobias are very similar to specific phobias, but the focus of the fear is embarrassment or humiliation in social situations.

Etiology. Specific and social phobias are best explained in evolutionary terms as prepared classical conditioning. People develop phobias of objects or situations that were evolutionarily dangerous to humans (dangerous animals, insects, etc.) through either classical conditioning (the feared object was paired with a frightening experience) or vicarious conditioning (for example, a child observes her father's fear of dogs). There is also evidence that some people are more likely to develop phobias due to genetic vulnerabilities and/or neurophysiological factors (such as abnormal levels of serotonin, dopamine, and GABA).

Treatment. Three behavior therapies have proven to be 80 to 90 percent effective in treating phobias: systematic desensitization, exposure, and modeling. The goal of all these therapies is to extinguish fear conditioning. *Systematic desensitization* is a process whereby the patient gradually faces the feared object while in a state of relaxation. In *exposure therapy,* the patient is exposed to the feared object or situation without the feared consequence (for example, plane travel for a patient who fears flying). In *modeling,* the patient observes another person perform the behavior they fear (for example, watching someone else handle snakes). Drug treatments have not been useful for long-term treatment of phobias. See Table 5-2 for a summary of the treatments for phobias.

Post-traumatic stress disorder (PTSD)

Criteria. Post-traumatic stress disorder is the re-experiencing, through dreams, flashbacks, etc., of a traumatic event in which a person experienced or witnessed an event that threatened bodily integrity. People with PTSD avoid stimuli associated with the trauma and experience increased arousal. See p. 182 for DSM-IV criteria for diagnosis. The text provides good descriptions of the experiences of the most common traumatic events: rape (pp. 186–87) and combat (pp. 187–89).

Etiology. Not everyone develops PTSD in response to a traumatic event. Predictors of PTSD include the degree of threat experienced in the trauma, pretrauma psychological health, pretrauma preparation, and levels of income and education. There is also evidence for genetic predispositions to developing the disorder (for instance, abnormalities in the HPA axis and amygdala) and cognitive vulnerabilities (for example, the tendency to make catastrophic interpretations of bad events).

Treatment. Drug treatment can be helpful in reducing some but not all of the symptoms. Psychotherapy is more promising, particularly exposure and disclosure therapy. *Exposure* involves reliving the trauma in one's imagination. *Disclosure* involves talking about the traumatic event. See Table 5-4 for a comparison of treatments and Box 5-1 for a description of the controversial EMDR treatment.

Panic Disorder

Criteria. Panic attacks are sudden attacks of extreme anxiety involving all four elements of fear. People with panic disorder experience panic attacks that are unexpected and that cause significant concern about the possibility and implications of having additional attacks (see pp. 193–94 for an illustration of an attack and p. 194 for DSM-IV criteria).

Etiology. There are biological and cognitive explanations for the cause of panic attacks. See Table 5-5 for a comparison of these explanations. For panic, the cognitive explanation subsumes the biological; that is, there are certainly biological correlates, but the development of the disorder is probably best explained from a cognitive perspective. People with panic disorder catastrophically misinterpret bodily sensations (for instance, someone who just finished exercising interprets her increased heart rate as "I'm having a heart attack"). These interpretations cause anxiety and more physical symptoms, which confirm the catastrophic interpretation; this feedback loop leads to a full-blown panic attack.

Treatment. Various drugs can relieve panic during an attack, but they have side effects and a relapse may occur once they are taken away. Psychological treatments for panic are equally effective, and work better in the long term. Cognitive therapy is used to help patients reinterpret their bodily sensations in less catastrophic ways, thus short-circuiting the feedback loop that leads to panic (see pp. 198–99 for an example of cognitive therapy). See Table 5-6 for a comparison of cognitive therapy and medication.

Agoraphobia

Criteria. Agoraphobia, the fear of open or public places, usually occurs in the context of panic. People with agora-

phobia are highly anxious about having a panic attack and being unable to get help; thus, they avoid situations where this might happen (sometimes becoming housebound) or endure these situations with great distress (see p. 200 for DSM-IV criteria).

Etiology. Agoraphobia is a conditioned response based on an initial experience of panic in a place where the person cannot get help (in a mall, driving a car, etc.). The conditioned stimulus is the place where the panic occurred, the unconditioned stimulus is the first panic attack, the unconditioned response is the panic response, and the conditioned response is fear and avoidance of the situation in which panic might occur and help not come.

Treatment. Imipramine (an antidepressant) relieves panic. When combined with exposure to the feared situation, the patient does not experience a panic attack and the fear is extinguished. Review Table 5-7 for a comparison of drug treatment, exposure therapy, and the combination of the two.

Generalized Anxiety Disorder (GAD)

Criteria. GAD is experienced as chronic anxiety about a number of things, making it therefore difficult to control. It includes symptoms of anxiety almost every day for at least six months (review p. 203 for DSM-IV criteria). The four elements of anxiety are present (see p. 202 for an illustration).

Etiology. People with GAD experience chronic activation of the behavioral inhibition system (BIS; the system that triggers fears during threat). This may occur due to "kindling," in which groups of repeatedly activated neurons develop lower thresholds for subsequent activation. GABA deficiencies are associated with the disorder. Maladaptive thoughts and feelings of having no control may also contribute to GAD.

Treatment. Benzodiazepines (antianxiety medications) enhance the release of GABA and reduce anxiety for as long as they are taken. They are addictive, however, and have a high relapse rate. Nonaddictive alternatives include Buspar and the SSRIs. Cognitive-behavioral therapy is also effective in relieving GAD, is not addictive, and has more lasting effects (see Table 5-8 for a comparison).

Obsessive-Compulsive Disorder (OCD)

Criteria. OCD involves *obsessions,* repetitive thoughts that are distressing and difficult to control, and *compulsions,* rigid rituals that are aimed at reducing the anxiety caused by the obsessions. These obsessions and compulsions are recognized by the person as excessive or unreasonable and they interfere with the person's functioning (see p. 206 for DSM-IV criteria).

Etiology. OCD may be partially hereditary, with relatives

of patients with OCD suffering from a range of anxiety disorders. According to psychodynamic theory, obsessions are a defense against unwelcome, unconscious thoughts and the content of the obsessions symbolizes the underlying conflict. Cognitive-behavioral theory suggests that people with OCD are unable to dismiss or distract themselves from the normal obsessional thoughts that all people experience. Compulsive rituals are maintained because they are reinforced by anxiety reduction. Neuroscience researchers point to brain dysfunction and neurological signs, such as the tendency to develop OCD after right brain trauma and the high concordance of OCD with epilepsy and Tourette's syndrome. See Table 5-9 for a summary of views of OCD from these three perspectives.

Treatment. Behavior therapy and drug therapy are effective in treating OCD (see Table 5-10 for a comparison). In behavior therapy, response prevention, exposure, and modeling are used as treatments (see p. 214 for an example). Clomipramine, an antidepressant drug, reduces obsessions and helps patients to resist compulsions, but, again, tends to lead to relapse when the drug is removed.

Everyday Anxiety

There is a useful instrument for assessing whether the common, everyday anxiety that people experience is too high in Box 5-4. Techniques that have been useful in dealing with everyday anxiety include progressive relaxation and meditation (described on p. 217).

TESTING YOUR UNDERSTANDING

Test your understanding of what you have read by working through the following tasks with a classmate.

1. What is the difference between fear and anxiety? What are the four elements that they share?

2. Think of someone you know who experiences a phobia. Why does this person fears what he or she fears? How could you help him or her deal with the phobia?

3. Why do some people develop PTSD after a trauma and some do not? Would you be likely to? If you did, what would you do to cope with it?

4. Your uncle calls to tell you that your cousin has recently been diagnosed with panic disorder. He explains that your cousin's therapist is using a cognitive approach to treat your cousin, but your uncle is concerned because he's heard that panic is a biological problem. Explain to your uncle why the cognitive approach makes sense, even in light of the evidence that there are biological correlates to panic disorder.

5. Explain how agoraphobia is different from the other phobias.

6. Think of someone you know who is chronically anxious. Explain what might be causing this chronic anxiety, biologically and psychologically.

7. Why does a person with OCD engage in compulsions? How are these obsessions and compulsions related to depression?

Multiple-Choice Questions

1. Which of the following best describes fear and anxiety?
   a. Disorders involving fear and anxiety are simply the extreme end of the continuum of normal fear and anxiety, and the difference between fear and anxiety is primarily in the emotional content.
   b. Disorders involving fear and anxiety are simply the extreme end of the continuum of normal fear and anxiety, and the difference between fear and anxiety is primarily in the cognitive content.
   c. Disorders involving fear and anxiety are fundamentally different from normal fear and anxiety, and the difference between fear and anxiety is primarily in the emotional content.
   d. Disorders involving fear and anxiety are fundamentally different from normal fear and anxiety, and the difference between fear and anxiety is primarily in the cognitive content

2. In which of the following disorders does a person experience fear (as opposed to anxiety)?
   a. panic disorder
   b. generalized anxiety disorder (GAD)
   c. post-traumatic stress disorder (PTSD)
   d. agoraphobia

3. Social phobias usually begin:
   a. in childhood.
   b. in adolescence.
   c. after age twenty-five.
   d. after age thirty-five.

4. According to your text, which of the following is probably the most useful way to understand phobias?
   a. They represent a deeper, underlying, unconscious conflict.
   b. They are a result of maladaptive cognitions.
   c. They are a result of operant conditioning.
   d. They are a result of prepared classical conditioning.

5. Phobic fears are quite resistant to extinction. Which of the following explains this resistance to change?
   a. People with phobias rarely test the reality of their fears.

b. Brain circuits in the amygdala are difficult or impossible to delete.

c. There may be a genetic predisposition to phobias.

d. all of the above

6. Systematic desensitization, exposure, and modeling are highly effective treatments for phobias. What do each of these treatments have in common?

a. They all employ relaxation techniques.

b. They all extinguish fear conditioning.

c. They all involve vicarious learning.

d. all of the above

7. Which of the following is true regarding the relative effectiveness of drug therapy versus extinction therapies in treating phobias?

a. Improvement is shown in 60 to 80 percent of patients being treated with drug therapy; extinction therapies are probably better than a placebo.

b. The cost for both is about the same.

c. Both involve moderate side effects.

d. Drugs involve high relapse rates, whereas extinction therapies result in low relapse rates.

8. Which of the following is true regarding the course of post-traumatic stress disorder (PTSD)?

a. It usually remits on its own, based on a natural healing process.

b. It often does not remit unless the person is treated.

c. It can only be diagnosed based on a natural disaster.

d. It can only be diagnosed based on a manmade disaster.

9. Following rape, a woman typically goes through a "disorganization" phase which can involve all of the following EXCEPT:

a. expressive emotions such as crying, anxiety, anger, etc.

b. controlled emotions such as showing a calm exterior.

c. difficulty resuming normal sexual activity.

d. taking action to ensure safety.

10. Which person is LEAST likely to develop PTSD in response to a trauma?

a. Jim, who had prior experience with trauma

b. Mavis, whose parents were Holocaust survivors

c. Stan, who has always been highly neurotic and has a history of mental disorders

d. Jennifer, who has a history of high anxiety

11. Malcolm, who is suffering from PTSD, is encouraged by his therapist to relive the trauma in his imagination, while overcoming the tendency to dissociate from the experience. His therapist is using:

a. disclosure therapy.

b. systematic desensitization.

c. exposure therapy.

d. modeling.

12. Which of the following is true regarding the use of drugs to treat PTSD?

a. They are probably better than a placebo.

b. They are very useful in treating PTSD.

c. They are very expensive.

d. They have no side effects.

13. Agoraphobia usually occurs with which other anxiety disorder?

a. obsessive-compulsive disorder (OCD)

b. post-traumatic stress disorder (PTSD)

c. generalized anxiety disorder (GAD)

d. panic disorder

14. Though there is evidence that panic can be explained by at least two different levels of analysis, the _____ level subsumes, or totally explains, all the evidence from the _____ level.

a. biological; behavioral

b. biological; cognitive

c. behavioral; biological

d. cognitive; biological

15. Which of the following is NOT true regarding the evidence for a biological basis of panic disorder?

a. Panic can be induced chemically.

b. If one of two identical twins has panic disorder, there is a 65 to 75 percent chance the other will have it.

c. Medication is quite effective in controlling panic attacks.

d. People with panic disorder have poorly regulated fight/flight systems.

16. What is the core cognitive component of panic disorder?

a. low self-efficacy regarding ability to deal with attacks

b. catastrophic misinterpretation of bodily sensations

c. maladaptive attributions for why a panic attack happened

d. all of the above

17. What percent of patients with panic disorder are panic free following cognitive therapy?

a. more than 30 percent

b. more than 50 percent

c. more than 75 percent

d. more than 95 percent

18. Which of the following best represents the official treatment guidelines recommended by the American Psychiatric Association for panic disorder?

a. Drug therapy and cognitive therapy are equally effective in the short term; cognitive therapy has greater durability than drug therapy.

b. Drug therapy and cognitive therapy are equally effective in the short term; drug therapy has greater durability than cognitive therapy.

c. Cognitive therapy is more effective in the short term and has greater durability than drug therapy.

d. Drug therapy is more effective in the short term; cognitive therapy has greater durability than drug therapy.

19. All of the following frequently occur along with agoraphobia EXCEPT:
    a. depression
    b. substance abuse
    c. avoidant personality disorder
    d. obsessive-compulsive disorder

20. Which of the following models provides the best explanation for the etiology of agoraphobia?
    a. psychodynamic
    b. behavioral
    c. biological
    d. cognitive

21. The treatments of choice for agoraphobia include:
    a. in vivo (real life) exposure and cognitive therapy.
    b. in vivo exposure and modeling.
    c. imaginal exposure and cognitive therapy.
    d. imaginal exposure and modeling.

22. Of the following, which provides the best explanation for generalized anxiety disorder (GAD)?
    a. the behavioral model
    b. the humanistic model
    c. the biological model
    d. the psychodynamic model

23. The effectiveness of benzodiazepines in treating GAD is probably due that fact that the benzodiazepines:
    a. enhance the release of serotonin.
    b. enhance the release of GABA.
    c. enhance the release of dopamine.
    d. enhance the release of norepinephrine.

24. People with obsessive-compulsive disorder (OCD) often also suffer from _____, during which the incidence of obsession triples.
    a. substance abuse
    b. schizophrenia
    c. depression
    d. panic

25. Men and women with OCD differ in the things they obsess about. Women are more likely to be _____, while men are more likely to be _____.
    a. "cleaners"; "checkers"
    b. "checkers"; "cleaners"
    c. "hoarders"; "checkers"
    d. "checkers"; "hoarders"

26. Which of the following models best explains OCD?
    a. psychodynamic
    b. cognitive-behavioral
    c. neuroscience
    d. all of the above

27. The fact that the content of obsessions and of compulsive rituals is narrow and selective (that is, people typically obsess about only a few things: germs, violence, etc.) provides support for which level of analysis?
    a. psychodynamic
    b. cognitive-behavioral
    c. neuroscience
    d. all of the above

28. The treatments that are most effective for OCD are:
    a. behavioral therapy and drug therapy.
    b. cognitive therapy and drug therapy.
    c. short-term psychodynamic therapy and drug therapy.
    d. cognitive therapy and behavior therapy.

29. Three techniques are mentioned in the text for coping with everyday anxiety: meditation, relaxation, and tranquilizers. Which is the least effective of these three techniques?
    a. meditation
    b. relaxation
    c. tranquilizers
    d. all are about equally effective

30. Progressive relaxation blocks the _____ components of anxiety, whereas meditation blocks the _____ components of anxiety.
    a. thought; motor
    b. motor; thought
    c. emotional; thought
    d. thought; emotional

Fill in the Blank

1. The _____ _____ _____ response involves the activation of the autonomic nervous system, causing our heart rate to increase, our spleen to contract, our respiration to accelerate, etc.

   flight or fight

2. When a threat is encountered, there are two types of flight responses: In _____ responding, the harmful event occurs and then the person leaves the scene. In _____ responding, the person leaves before the harmful event occurs.

   escape

   avoidance

3. Anxiety and depression are highly comorbid (that is, people with anxiety are also highly likely to have depression). One explanation for this is that both anxiety and depression are part of a more basic general level of distress termed _____ _____.

negative affect

4. People acquire phobias by _____ conditioning when they observe others display the phobia.

vicarious

5. People tend to develop phobias only for objects that are evolutionarily dangerous. This is known as _____ classical conditioning.

prepared

6. _____ _____ is a treatment that involves training in relaxation, hierarchy construction, and counter conditioning.

Systematic desensitization

7. _____ therapy involves a person forcing themselves to be in the presence of a feared stimulus.

Exposure

8. _____ therapy involves the patient opening up and talking about a traumatic event.

Disclosure

9. _____ therapy involves moving your eyes back and forth while concentrating on a disturbing image.

EMDR or Eye Movement Desensitization and Reprocessing

10. _____ is a fear of going out to places of assembly, open spaces, and crowds, or being in any situation in which a person might get sick, not be able to escape, and not get help.

Agoraphobia

11. _____ is a neurophysiological phenomenon in which groups of neurons that are activated repeatedly develop lower thresholds for subsequent activation.

Kindling

12. _____ are repetitive thoughts, images, or impulses that invade consciousness, are often abhorrent, and are very difficult to dismiss or control.

Obsessions

13. _____ consist of rigid rituals or mental acts that the person feels driven to perform in response to an obsession.

Compulsions

14. _____ _____ is a technique in which you tighten and then release each of the major muscle groups of your body until your muscles are wholly flaccid.

Progressive relaxation

15. _____ involves closing your eyes and repeating a mantra to yourself.

Meditation or Transcendental meditation

16. _____ is the neurotransmitter implicated in GAD, whereas _____ and _____ are implicated in panic disorder.

GABA; norepinephrine serotonin

17. _____ _____, _____, and the _____ _____ are the brain structures that malfunction in panic disorder, whereas OCD is related to a malfunction in the _____ _____.

Brain stem, amygdala, frontal cortex

basal ganglia

18. Obsessive compulsive disorder responds especially well to _____ and _____.

antidepressants (the SSRIs)

exposure

19. Specific phobias are very effectively treated by _____ and _____ _____.

exposure; systematic desensitization

20. GAD is best treated using _____-_____ _____ and
_____ _____.

anxiety-reducing medications

relaxation training

21. People who suffer from PTSD often improve with _____ and _____
_____.

exposure; group

treatment

Additional Exercise: Epidemiology

Can you remember the epidemiological characteristic of each disorder? Write the prevalence rate (percent of people who have this disorder) for the major anxiety disorders and the gender in which each disorder and each type of phobia occurs more frequently.

Disorder	*Prevalence Rate (%)*	*Gender*
1. Specific phobia	_____	_____
2. Animal phobia	N/A	_____
3. Natural environment phobias	N/A	_____
4. Situational phobias	N/A	_____
5. Blood injection injury phobias	N/A	_____
6. Social phobia	_____	_____
7. Post-traumatic stress disorder (PTSD)	_____	_____
8. Panic disorder	_____	_____
9. Agoraphobia	_____	_____
10. Generalized anxiety disorder (GAD)	_____	_____
11. Obsessive-compulsive disorder (OCD)	_____	_____

LEVELS OF ANALYSIS: EXAMINING THE CHAPTER'S THEMES

Two themes are highlighted throughout this chapter: levels of analysis and treatment of choice.

Biological and Psychological Levels of Analysis

The biological and psychological levels of analysis are used to explain each of the anxiety disorders. Phobias develop as a result of classical conditioning, but only for select objects and situations (those that were dangerous to pretechnological humans). The vulnerability to develop phobias may be genetic and/or based on neurophysiology (for example, low levels of GABA). In PTSD, the experience of trauma is a necessary, but not sufficient, cause for the disorder. Those who develop PTSD in response to trauma may have psychological (previous mental problems, high anxiety), biological (genetic predisposition, abnormal neural circuitry), and/or social (lower income and education) factors that make them vulnerable. In panic disorder, the cognitive level of analysis completely subsumes the biological level. While there are clearly biological correlates to panic, it appears that it is the catastrophic misinterpretation of bodily sensations that best explains the development of the disorder. Agoraphobia, which may accompany panic, is best explained by classical conditioning. In GAD, biological explanations include chronic activation of the behavioral inhibition system and GABA deficiencies. Psychological explanations include feelings of uncontrollability and maladaptive thoughts. OCD is best explained using three models: psychodynamic (having specific unconscious conflicts), cognitive-behavioral (inability to distract oneself from troubling thoughts, depression), and neuroscience (overactive cortical-striatal-thalamic circuit).

Treatment of Choice

The treatments of choice provided for each disorder are based on treatment outcome research and our current understanding of etiology. Drug therapy and psychotherapy have proven effective for treating anxiety, but some antianxiety drugs are addictive and most result in relapse when the drug is no longer taken. Therefore, for long-term treatment, psychotherapy or a combination of therapy and medication is recommended. The treatment of choice for phobias is behavioral therapy, specifically systematic desensitization, exposure, and modeling. The treatment of choice for PTSD is exposure therapy, and there is evidence that disclosure therapy and EMDR are very effective. The effectiveness of drug treatment on PTSD is marginal. For panic disorder, drug treatment and cognitive therapy are the treatments of choice, with cognitive therapy having a lower relapse rate. In treating agoraphobia, exposure, cognitive therapy, and the combination of these psychological treatments with medication are most effective. For GAD, drugs provide relief, but only for as long as they are taken; cognitive-behavioral treatment provides more lasting relief. Behavioral therapy and drug therapy (clomipramine) are the treatments of choice for OCD.

ANSWER KEY

MULTIPLE-CHOICE QUESTIONS

1. b. The fear and anxiety experienced in mental disorders is similar to normal fear and anxiety; it is just excessive compared to the threat. The difference between fear and anxiety is in the cognitive content. With fear, the person thinks there is a clear and specific danger; with anxiety, there is an expectation of a more diffuse and uncertain danger.

2. c. Fear is experienced in phobia and PTSD; anxiety is experienced in panic, agoraphobia, GAD, and agoraphobia.

3. b. Social phobias usually begin in adolescence, occasionally in childhood, and only rarely after age twenty-five.

4. d. Phobias develop as a result of classical conditioning; however, only objects and situations that were dangerous to pretechnological humans appear to act as phobic objects.

5. d. All of the explanations given are valid explanations of why it is difficult to extinguish a phobic fear.

6. b. Systematic desensitization and exposure employ relaxation techniques, whereas modeling employs vicarious learning. All three are designed to extinguish fear conditioning.

7. d. As with most anxiety disorders, drugs help with anxiety only until patients stop taking them. For a complete review of the relative effectiveness of the two approaches, see Table 5-2.

8. b. People who suffer from PTSD have been shown to be just as bad off seven years later as they were four years later, indicating that a natural healing process doesn't seem to be going on. PTSD can be diagnosed following any trauma that involves a threat to one's bodily integrity.

9. d. During the disorganization phase, a woman may display expressive or controlled emotions and has difficulty resuming normal activities. Taking action to ensure safety occurs during the "reorganization" phase.

10. a. People who have prior experience with trauma, have training in mental and physical stoicism, or who expected the trauma are less likely to develop PTSD. Children of Holocaust survivors and people with a history of mental disorders are more likely to develop PTSD in response to a trauma.

11. c. Exposure therapy involves reliving the trauma in the imagination while overcoming the tendency to dissociate from it.

12. a. Drugs are better than placebos in treating PTSD, but are only moderately useful and have moderate side effects. They are not very expensive (Table 5-4).

13. d. Agoraphobia, the fear of going out to places of assembly, open spaces, and crowds, usually occurs in the context of panic disorder. The person fears that another panic attack will occur if he or she goes out into a public place.

14. d. The cognitive explanation can completely account for all the biological correlates of panic disorder. For a summary, see Table 5-6.

15. b. The concordance rate for panic disorder for identical twins is 25–30 percent. Even for the most biologically based disorders, concordance rates for identical twins rarely exceed 50 percent.

16. b. According to the cognitive level of analysis, the basic cause of panic disorder is catastrophic misinterpretation of bodily sensations.

17. c. Studies indicate that more than 75 percent of patients are panic free and remain panic free up to two years following cognitive therapy.

18. a. The statements in option a are most representative of the practice guidelines recommended by the APA.

19. c. Agoraphobia is often comorbid with depression, substance abuse, and OCD.

20. b. Agoraphobia is best explained by classical conditioning (the behavioral model), in which the first panic attack is paired with being in a public place.

21. a. Several studies indicate that in vivo exposure and cognitive therapy are the psychological treatments of choice for agoraphobia.

22. c. Researchers have proposed biological and psychological explanations for GAD. The psychological explanation focuses on the cognitive model; therefore, the biological model is the best choice among the options given.

23. b. Benzodiazepines enhance the release of GABA (a neurotransmitter that inhibits anxiety), which helps GAD patients who probably have too few GABA receptors or otherwise process GABA inadequately.

24. c. As many as 67 percent of people with OCD also experience depression, which exacerbates the occurrence of obsessions.

25. a. Women with OCD are more likely to be "cleaners," whereas men are more likely to be "checkers."

26. d. Psychodynamic, cognitive-behavioral, and neuroscience models of OCD together yield an integrated picture of how OCD is caused.

27. c. The selective and primitive content of obsessions and compulsions is consistent with the evolutionary and neuroscience view of OCD.

28. a. Response prevention, exposure, and modeling are all behavioral therapies that provide relief for patients with OCD. Clomipramine, an antidepressant drug, also reduces obsessive and compulsive behavior.

29. c. Overall, meditation and relaxation are useful techniques.

30. b. Progressive relaxation blocks the motor components of anxiety, whereas meditation blocks the thoughts that produce anxiety.

ADDITIONAL EXERCISE

1. 11 percent; women
2. N/A; women
3. N/A; none
4. N/A; women
5. N/A; women
6. 13 percent; women
7. 8 percent; women
8. 2 percent; women
9. 3 percent; women
10. 5 percent; women
11. 2–3 percent; women

CHAPTER 6 | Somatoform and Dissociative Disorders

A GUIDE TO THE READING

This chapter presents two categories of disorders that may be less familiar to you than the anxiety disorders discussed in the previous chapter: the somatoform disorders and the dissociative disorders. Anxiety is thought to play a key role in the development of these disorders, but it is not usually felt by those who suffer from the disorders. The somatoform disorders are characterized by a loss of physical functioning, apparently resulting from psychological conflict. The dissociative disorders involve identity fragmentation.

Somatoform Disorders

Criteria. Be familiar with the five factors that are used to diagnose a patient with a somatoform disorder (p. 222): (1) loss of physical functioning; (2) no known physical cause; (3) psychological factors related to symptom(s); (4) indifference to physical loss; and (5) symptoms not under voluntary control. *Conversion* occurs when psychological stress is converted into a physical symptom (for example, hysterical blindness following a trauma). *Somatization* involves many physical complaints that cannot be explained by known physical causes. *Pain disorder* is characterized by pain that causes marked distress or impairment, with the onset or the severity due to psychological factors (see p. 224 for DSM-IV criteria). *Hypochondriasis* is the conviction that one has a serious medical disease, in spite of evidence to the contrary (see p. 225 for DSM-IV criteria). Finally, *body dysmorphic disorder* involves the exaggeration of a slight bodily defect, the concern over which comes to dominate the person's life (see p. 226 for DSM-IV criteria).

It is sometimes difficult to distinguish the somatoform disorders from malingering, psychosomatic disorders, factitious disorders, or undiagnosed physical illness. In malingering, the person is deliberately faking a disorder in order to gain something. The symptoms are under the patient's voluntary control, whereas in somatoform disorders, they are not. In psychosomatic disorders, there is a physical basis to the symptoms (ulcers, hypertension), though the symptoms are exaggerated by psychological factors. In factitious disorder, a patient deliberately causes illness or injury to him- or herself in order to gain medical attention. Finally, it is certainly possible that what appears to be a somatoform disorder is actually an undiagnosed physical illness.

Etiology. There is only marginal evidence that the somatoform disorders run in families, except for somatization (female relatives of those with the disorder are ten times more likely to develop it). The most viable explanation for the etiology of the somatoform disorders appears to be psychodynamic. According to this model, the physical symptoms are a defense against an unacceptable idea and the nature of the symptoms symbolizes the underlying conflict (see the explanation of Bear's paralysis on p. 230). Because the anxiety is "converted" into the physical symptom(s), people with somatoform disorders do not experience anxiety and seem strangely indifferent to their physical symptoms. Other models used to explain these disorders include the communication model (those who have difficulty verbally communicating their distress unconsciously use physical symptoms as a way of communicating their distress; see pp. 230–231) and the percept blocking view (perceptions are still used as input, but are blocked from conscious awareness; see pp. 231-32).

Treatment. Confrontation may result in a temporary relief of symptoms, but the relapse rate is high and such a confrontation may produce conflict and loss of self-esteem. Treatment involving strong suggestions that the symptoms will improve over time has been shown to be effective for up to 75 percent of patients for four to six years following the intervention. Treatments providing insight into the underlying conflict have been shown to be effective by a number of case studies but remain to be studied under controlled conditions. Antidepressants, sensible advice about pain control, and family therapy all appear to be helpful and deserve further study.

Dissociative Disorders

Criteria. Dissociative disorders occur as a result of strong psychological trauma and involve a profound and lasting disturbance of memory. The word *dissociative* refers to the phenomenon of two or more mental processes co-existing or alternating without influencing each other (review the description of the experience of dissociation on p. 233). In *dissociative amnesia,* a substantial block of time in one's life is forgotten (see p. 234 for DSM-IV criteria). Be familiar with the different types of amnesia: generalized (involving all details of one's personal life; see case of Timmy pp. 233–34), retrograde (the events preceding a trauma are forgotten), post-traumatic (the loss of memory of events after a trauma), anterograde (difficulty remembering new material), and selective (memory loss of events related to a particular theme). Be clear on the difference between organic and dissociative amnesia. Organic amnesia is physically based and affects a person's memory of personal knowledge, general knowledge, and recent events. The anterograde amnesia is severe, and memory recovery is difficult and gradual. Dissociative amnesia is psychologically based and involves recent memory, past memory, and loss of personal (but not general) knowledge. It involves no anterograde loss and can reverse abruptly. *Depersonalization disorder* involves feeling detached from one's body or mind (see p. 236 for DSM-IV criteria). *Dissociative identity disorder (DID)* is defined as the occurrence of two or more distinct identities in the same individual. Each identity has a stable life and the identities alternate in controlling the body. Alternate personalities differ in their memories, gender, age, and physiological indices (for instance, EEG). People with DID often do not remember what occurred when an alternate personality was in control, though some alternates are aware of the others' identities (see p. 237 for DSM-IV criteria). Be aware of the reasons for the recent increase in diagnosed cases of DID (p. 237). There is some debate about whether DID actually exists; review the arguments on both sides (pp. 243–46).

Etiology. The cause of the dissociative disorders remains a mystery. One speculation for the cause of amnesia is that it is a global defense against anxiety produced by very traumatic circumstances. DID is theorized to be caused by a trauma occurring between the ages of four and six (as many as 97 percent of those with DID report that they experienced child abuse). Children who are highly susceptible to self-hypnosis then create alternate identities in order to relieve themselves of the emotional burden of the abuse (see Figure 6-2 for a graph of the development of DID).

Treatment. Long-term psychotherapy is the most common treatment for DID. Cognitive therapists treat patients with DID using tactical integration, in which the therapist teaches the patient skills of disputing and challenging irrational thoughts and tries to find the basis for why these irrational thoughts were credible to the patient in the first place. Psychodynamic therapists treat DID by making the patient aware that he or she has the disorder, using hypnosis to talk with other identities, and working to reintegrate them. There is evidence that 94 percent of patients treated by experienced psychodynamic therapist show strong improvement. Antidepressants and antianxiety drugs provide moderate relief for the patients.

TESTING YOUR UNDERSTANDING

Test your understanding of what you have read by working through the following tasks with a classmate.

1. Many people have never heard of the somatoform disorders. See if you can explain the five general symptoms of somatoform disorders to a friend who doesn't know what they are.

2. Imagine you experience a painful physical symptom but are told by your doctors that they can find nothing physically wrong with you. How might you go about deciding whether your symptom is psychologically or physically based?

3. Though many of the somatoform disorders do not appear to run in families, there is evidence for a genetic etiology of somatization disorder. Can you verbalize the evidence that supports this?

4. Imagine you are a psychologist, who, after extensive testing, determines that your patient is indeed suffering from a somatoform disorder. How might you explain this to the patient? What treatment would you use for your patient?

5. There are many ways a person can dissociate from a painful experience. Can you list and explain each of these methods of dissociation?

6. One of the clues that psychologists look for when diagnosing a patient with dissociative identity disorder (DID) is gaps in memory. Explain why gaps in memory may suggest DID.

7. See if you can present the arguments both for and against the existence of DID.

Multiple-Choice Questions

1. Julie had been under a lot of stress at school over the past month. One morning she awoke with terrible pain in her stomach. She went to the emergency room, but the doctor could not find anything physically wrong with her. Julie would most likely be diagnosed with:
   a. body dysmorphic disorder.
   b. conversion disorder.
   c. pain disorder.
   d. hypochondriasis.

2. Eddie always seems to have problems with his health and visits doctors often. He often feels pain in various parts of his body, gets nauseous easily, has difficulty tolerating certain foods, and gets dizzy frequently. He is frustrated because the doctors don't really seem to be able to help him. They never seem to be able to pinpoint the cause of his various problems. Eddie most likely suffers from:
   a. somatization disorder.
   b. hypochondriasis.
   c. conversion disorder.
   d. body dysmorphic disorder.

3. Cerise arrived at the emergency room complaining of blurred vision. She was unable to read the eye chart, but more detailed neurological testing showed no physical problems with her eyes. Cerise is most likely suffering from:
   a. body dysmorphic disorder.
   b. conversion disorder.
   c. somatization disorder.
   d. hypochondriasis.

4. Anxiety disorders and somatoform disorders have several things in common. Which of the following is NOT something that they have in common?
   a. physical symptoms
   b. feelings of anxiety
   c. impairment in functioning
   d. none of the above

5. A patient who is diagnosed with somatoform disorder would have all of the following EXCEPT:
   a. symptoms that cannot be explained by a known physical or neurological condition.
   b. psychological factors related to the symptom.
   c. lost or altered physical functioning.
   d. symptoms that are under voluntary control.

6. Which is the somatoform disorder that is commonly linked to unnecessary surgery, addiction to prescription drugs, and attempted suicide?
   a. body dysmorphic disorder
   b. conversion disorder
   c. somatization disorder
   d. hypochondriasis

7. What part of the brain appears to be involved in somatization disorder?
   a. basal ganglia
   b. amygdala
   c. right hemisphere
   d. left hemisphere

8. Which is the most frequent of the somatoform disorders?
   a. pain disorder
   b. conversion disorder
   c. somatization disorder
   d. hypochondriasis

9. *Koro,* panic among Chinese males about the possibility that one's penis will retract into the abdomen and *dhat,* a preoccupation among men in India about losing semen, are both culturally influenced forms of:
   a. body dysmorphic disorder.
   b. conversion disorder.
   c. somatization disorder.
   d. hypochondriasis.

10. Which is the somatoform disorder that is commonly linked to depression, suicide, and repeated plastic surgery?
    a. body dysmorphic disorder
    b. conversion disorder
    c. somatization disorder
    d. hypochondriasis

11. Faking symptoms in order to gain some benefit is called:
    a. malingering.
    b. secondary gain.
    c. factitious disorder.
    d. Munchausen's syndrome.

12. Evidence suggests that which of the following runs in families?
    a. body dysmorphic disorder
    b. conversion disorder
    c. somatization disorder
    d. hypochondriasis

13. Which of the following disorders may share the same genetic diathesis as somatization disorder?
    a. eating disorders and schizophrenia
    b. depression and anxiety
    c. alcoholism and antisocial personality disorder
    d. learning disabilities and attention deficit disorder

14. Which approach is probably the most viable for understanding somatoform disorders?
    a. cognitive
    b. psychodynamic
    c. humanistic
    d. behavioral

15. The idea that people with somatoform disorders have difficulty expressing their feelings is most consistent with the _____ view.
    a. psychodynamic
    b. percept blocking
    c. communicative
    d. cognitive

16. Which of the following therapies for somatoform disorders is probably the least effective over time?
    a. confrontation
    b. suggestion
    c. insight
    d. family therapy

17. Will, a sixteen-year-old boy, is brought into the emergency room by the police, who found him wandering around the streets in apparent confusion. He cannot remember where he lives, who his family is, or where he goes to school. He is, however, able to remember the date and who the president of the United States is. Will is treated for dehydration and allowed to sleep for six hours. Upon awakening, he is suddenly able to recall everything. What is the best diagnosis for Will?
    a. dissociative amnesia
    b. organic amnesia
    c. dissociative identity disorder
    d. depersonalization disorder

18. With no warning, Maria's boyfriend of three years called her and told her it was over. He wouldn't explain why and hung up the phone. Maria was shocked, and she began to feel as though she was in a dream or a movie. She continued to feel detached from herself, as if she was outside looking in, and she found it very difficult to go to class or do any homework. What is the best diagnosis for Maria?
    a. dissociative amnesia
    b. organic amnesia
    c. dissociative identity disorder
    d. depersonalization disorder

19. Dr. Montoia is having his first session with a new patient. The patient comes in complaining of depression, but as the interview proceeds, Dr. Montoia learns that she also cannot remember several significant periods of time over the past year. She denies substance abuse. What is the most likely diagnosis for this patient?
    a. dissociative amnesia
    b. organic amnesia
    c. dissociative identity disorder
    d. depersonalization disorder

20. When people experience trauma they can react in a number of different ways. People who develop dissociative disorders react to trauma by:
    a. having flashbacks and dreams about the trauma.
    b. experiencing a great deal of anxiety about the trauma.

    c. experiencing physical problems related to their psychological problems.
    d. experiencing a profound and lasting disturbance of memory.

21. Which of the following is NOT a form of dissociation?
    a. derealization
    b. identity confusion
    c. identity derealization
    d. identity alteration

22. Following a car accident, Stephanie is unable to recall the events that occurred immediately after the crash. Stephanie has _____ amnesia.
    a. retrograde
    b. post-traumatic
    c. anterograde
    d. selective

23. Severe anterograde amnesia is the primary symptom of:
    a. trauma.
    b. dissociative amnesia.
    c. organic amnesia.
    d. none of the above

24. Which of the following dissociative disorders has not been universally accepted as actually existing?
    a. dissociative amnesia
    b. dissociative identity disorder
    c. both of the above
    d. neither of the above

25. Which of the following dissociative disorders is comorbid with depression, hypochondriases, and substance abuse?
    a. dissociative amnesia
    b. depersonalization disorder
    c. dissociative identity disorder
    d. none of the above

26. The frequency of cases of dissociative identity disorder (DID) has increased dramatically in the last twenty-five years. Which of the following is NOT one of the reasons cited in the text?
    a. The stress of modern culture causes more cases of DID.
    b. Recently, psychologists have done a better job probing for the disorder.
    c. Psychodynamic therapists are eager to diagnose it.
    d. The new and highly visible awareness of child abuse.

27. Which statement best describes the awareness of the various identities, or alters, about one another?
    a. All alters know about each other.
    b. Some alters know about the others and some don't.
    c. All alters are unaware of the others.
    d. Only the core alter knows about the others.

28. There is evidence that alternative identities are generally created first between ages:
    a. two and four.
    b. four and six.
    c. six and eight.
    d. eight and ten.

29. Which of the following factors best explains why some children create alternate identities in response to trauma and others do not?
    a. the level of trauma
    b. genetic vulnerability

    c. hypnotizability
    d. the frequency of trauma

30. Which of the following is a doubt that affects the argument about the existence of dissociative identity disorder?
    a. doubt about the memories of childhood sexual abuse
    b. doubt about the existence of the unconscious
    c. doubt based on the use of the diagnosis by criminals as a defense in court
    d. none of the above

Fill in the Blank

1. _____ is a disorder that typically involves one neurological symptom but has no physical basis.

   Conversion

2. _____ involves many physical complaints that cannot be explained fully by physical causes and that are not under voluntary control.

   Somatization or Briquet's syndrome

3. _____ _____ involves pain in one or more parts of the body, causing marked distress or impairment.

   Pain disorder or Psychalgia

4. _____ is the conviction that one has a serious medical disease in spite of extensive evidence and reassurance to the contrary.

   Hypochondriasis

5. _____, which is reported primarily in India, involves a preoccupation about losing semen. It causes dizziness and fatigue.

   Dhat

6. _____ _____ _____ involves the exaggeration of a slight bodily defect into the perception of wholesale ugliness.

   Body dysmorphic disorder

7. _____ means faking symptoms.

   Malingering

8. _____ _____ consists of deriving benefits from one's environment as a consequence of having abnormal symptoms.

   Secondary gain

9. _____ _____ involve symptoms that may be initiated or exaggerated by psychological factors but that have a physical basis.

   Psychosomatic disorders

10. _____ _____ is a conversion symptom in which nothing can be felt in the hand or fingers, but in which sensation is intact from the wrist up.

    Glove anathesia

11. _____ _____ involves deliberately hurting oneself in order to get medical attention.

    Factitious disorder or Munchhausen syndrome

12. _____ refers to people who cannot easily express their feelings; it literally means no words for feelings.

    Alexithymia

13. _____ involves feeling detached from one's body or mind.

    Depersonalization

14. _____ occurs when the world, not the self, seems unreal.

    Derealization

15. _____ _____ involves confusion or uncertainty about who one is.   Identity confusion

16. _____ _____ involves the display of some surprising skill that one did not know one had.   Identity alteration

17. A _____ _____ involves loss of memory of one's identity and sudden travel away from one's home.   fugue state

18. _____ amnesia involves loss of all details of one's personal life.   Global or generalized

19. _____ amnesia involves the loss of memory of all events that occurred immediately before a trauma.   Retrograde

20. _____-_____ amnesia involves the loss of memory of all events that occurred after a trauma.   Post-traumatic

21. _____ amnesia involves difficulties remembering new material.   Anterograde

22. _____ amnesia involves the loss of memory for select events that are related to a specific theme.   Selective or categorical

Additional Exercise: Epidemiology

Can you remember the epidemiological characteristics of each disorder? Write the prevalence rate (percent of people who have this disorder), the age at which it is most likely to occur developmentally, and which gender is more likely to be diagnosed with the disorder.

Disorder	Prevalence rate (%)	Age at which it is most likely to occur	Gender difference
1. Conversion	_____	_____	_____
2. Somatization	_____	_____	_____
3. Pain disorder	_____	_____	_____
4. Hypochondriases	_____	_____	_____
5. Body dysmorphic disorder	_____	_____	_____
6. Dissociative amnesia	_____	_____	_____
7. Depersonalization	_____	_____	_____
8. Dissociative identity disorder	_____	_____	_____

LEVELS OF ANALYSIS: EXAMINING THE CHAPTER'S THEMES

Three themes emerge in this chapter: biological and psychological levels of analysis, development, and treatment of choice.

Biological and Psychological Levels of Analysis

The somatoform disorders and the dissociative disorders appear to be almost exclusively psychological in nature. In the case of amnesia, amnesia resulting from psychological causes (dissociative amnesia) is clearly distinguishable from amnesia based on biological causes (organic amnesia). These disorders are therefore fairly unique, as most disorders appear to require both the biological and psychological levels of analysis to explain them completely. One exception among the somatoform disorders is somatization disorder, which does appear to run in families (among female relatives) and to appear in conjunction with alcoholism and antisocial personality disorder (in male relatives). Clearly, culture and environment can also play a role in the incidence of the disorders; more dissociative disorders occur during war, and somatoform disorders may appear more frequently as a result of political oppression (for instance, conversion disorders appeared under the regime of Cambodian leader Pol Pot; see p. 229).

Development

Dissociative identity disorder is associated with developmental processes. The disorder appears to originate in childhood due to severe abuse. Most patients with DID create their first alternate personality between ages four and six.

Treatment of Choice

Treatment for the somatoform and dissociative disorders has been spearheaded by psychodynamic psychotherapists. Psychodynamic therapy still appears to be the treatment of choice, especially for dissociative disorders, though psychodynamic approaches still need empirical validation. Cognitive approaches also seem to be successful in treating these disorders. Antidepressants have some positive effects for both somatoform and dissociative disorders.

ANSWER KEY

MULTIPLE-CHOICE QUESTIONS

1. c. Severe pain at one or more anatomical sites is the predominant complaint of patients with pain disorders.

2. a. People with somatization disorder experience many physical complaints across many major systems of the body. People with hypochondriasis are preoccupied with fears that they have a serious disease, despite evidence to the contrary.

3. b. Conversion disorder typically centers around one symptom that affects motor or sensory function and that suggests a neurological condition.

4. b. Though anxiety is theorized to be at the root of the somatoform disorders, people who suffer from them are surprisingly indifferent to their symptoms. This is sometimes referred to as "la belle indifference."

5. d. The symptoms that patients with somatoform disorder experience are not under voluntary control.

6. c. According to the text, unnecessary surgery, addiction to prescription drugs, and attempted suicide are commonly linked to somatization disorder.

7. d. The presenting symptoms of somatization disorder occur more often on the right side of the body, suggesting left hemisphere involvement.

8. a. Statistically, pain disorder (psychalgia) may be the most frequent of the somatoform disorders.

9. d. *Koro* and *dhat* are both forms of hypochondriasis, in which the particular physical problem is greatly influenced by culture.

10. a. Body dysmorphic disorder, which involves a fixation on a slight bodily defect, is linked to depression, suicide, and repeated plastic surgery.

11. a. Malingering involves faking symptoms in order to gain some benefit. Secondary gain (deriving benefits as a consequence of having abnormal symptoms) can occur in malingering and in the somatoform disorders, in which the symptoms are not faked. Factitious disorder and Munchausen's syndrome are the same thing, and they involve deliberately making oneself ill in order to get medical attention.

12. c. The female relatives of people with somatization disorder are ten times more likely to develop it than women in the general population.

13. c. Daughters of alcoholics show unexpectedly high rates of somatization disorder when raised in adoptive families. Compared to other adopted children, sons of alcoholics are more likely to be alcoholic or have antisocial personality disorders.

14. b. The psychodynamic view remains quite viable in explaining the somatoform disorders. It is the only model that can account for the indifference the patients with somatoform disorders feel about their symptoms.

15. c. The communicative view suggests that people with somatoform disorders develop physical symptoms as a way of communicating their distress because they are unable to verbally communicate their psychological distress to others.

16. a. Although many of the therapies mentioned in your text require further study, confrontation appears to be only temporarily effective.

17. a. Patients with dissociative amnesia lose their memory of the recent and remote past, but retain their store of general knowledge (for example, who the president is). Dissociative amnesia also reverses abruptly. Patients with organic amnesia can remember the remote past, cannot remember general knowledge, and only experience gradual improvement in memory.

18. d. Depersonalization disorder involves persistent experiences of feeling detached from one's mental processes or body, causing impairment in functioning.

19. c. In DID, patients cannot remember periods when the alternate identities are in control of the body. This is one of the central features and also one of the best clues to the disorder.

20. d. Dissociative disorders result in a profound lack of memory following a severe trauma. Flashbacks are consistent with PTSD; felt anxiety is consistent with the anxiety disorders, and physical problems are consistent with the somatoform disorders.

21. c. The experience of dissociation consists of either: (1) amnesia, (2) depersonalization, (3) derealization, (4) identity confusion, or (5) identity alteration.

22. b. Retrograde amnesia involves events immediately preceding a trauma; post-traumatic amnesia involves events immediately following the trauma; anterograde amnesia involves difficulty remembering new material; and selective amnesia involves difficulty remembering events related to a particular theme.

23. c. Patients with organic amnesia have severe anterograde amnesia, and this is their primary symptom.

24. c. Neither dissociative amnesia nor DID has been universally accepted as actually existing.

25. b. Patients with depersonalization disorder are highly hypnotizable, experience distortions in the shapes and sizes of objects, and are susceptible to depression, hypochondriases, and substance abuse.

26. a. DID is not associated with stress, nor does it seem likely that there are more cases now than before. Psychologists now probe for amnesia, which has helped to identify DID. Psychodynamic therapists are eager to diagnose it because it fits their model so well. Finally, up to 97 percent of people diagnosed with DID report child abuse.

27. b. It is common for one of the identities to be aware of the experiences of the other identities and for one of the identities to be unaware of the others. The core personality is typically unaware of the others.

28. b. Bliss's study indicated that alternative identities are first created between the ages four and six.

29. c. According to Bliss's model, children who are skilled at self-hypnosis use it to develop a second personality, while children who are less easily hypnotized use other coping strategies.

30. a. The most salient grounds for doubting the existence of DID concerns the memories of childhood sexual abuse. Almost all reports are uncorroborated and there is evidence that false memories can occur or even be implanted.

ADDITIONAL EXERCISE

1. >1%; late adolescence to early adulthood; women
2. 2–10%; adulthood; women
3. Most frequent of the somatoform disorders; not reported in text; none
4. 4%; adolescence, middle age, 60+; none
5. Uncommon; adolescence onward; men
6. Rare, but more common during war and disasters; more common in younger people; men
7. 50% report brief episodes, disorder itself is rare; not reported in text; not reported in text
8. 5% of psychiatric admissions in some clinics; begins in childhood; women

CHAPTER 7

Mood Disorders

A GUIDE TO THE READING

A great deal of research has been done on the course and treatment of depression, and there are well-developed theories of what causes this disorder. You'll need to be familiar with the detailed information provided in the text about this research. You will also need to be familiar with the symptoms, causes, and treatments of bipolar disorder and seasonal affective disorder (SAD), an interesting form of mood disorder based on the seasons. Suicide is linked to mood disorders and you should know who is at risk and what can prevent it.

Depression

Criteria and vulnerability. Major depressive disorder is similar to normal depression, but the symptoms are more severe, more frequent, and last much longer. It is typically episodic but can be chronic, as in *dysthymic disorder,* a low level of depression that lasts at least two years. Depression usually dissipates over time, but it tends to recur. It may occur with *melancholia,* which involves a lack of pleasure in all activities, severe symptoms, and somatic complaints. The criteria for a depressive disorder include four types of symptoms: mood symptoms, such as sadness and guilt; cognitive symptoms, such as belief that one is a failure; motivational symptoms, such as difficulty getting up for work; and physical symptoms, such as the loss of appetite; see p. 252 for the DSM-IV criteria. You can assess your own periods of depression and become familiar with the four types of symptoms by completing the assessment in Box 7-1.

Everyone is vulnerable to depression and there is a one in seven chance that you will experience a major depressive episode in your lifetime. Young people are at particularly high risk, as demonstrated by four lines of evidence: the ECA study, a national epidemiological study, found much lower rates of depression for those born earlier in the twentieth century; an international epidemiological study showed dramatic increases in risk throughout the twentieth century; family studies show that younger relatives of people with depression are much more susceptible than older relatives; studies of the Amish show that they have about one-fifth to one-tenth the risk for depression compared to Americans from modern culture (see pp. 256–57 for more details on these studies; see Box 7-2 for a discussion of why young Americans are suffering an epidemic of depression). Women are also at increased risk; they are diagnosed with depression about twice as much as men. This may be due to their willingness to admit to depression, hormonal vulnerability, genetics, social learning, or because women tend to ruminate more about bad events. There are also ethnic differences, with the rate of mood disorders significantly lower among blacks. Bad life events can lead to depression, but life events are not a strong predictor of depression. Previous depression and a genetic predisposition both overshadow life events as predictors of depression.

Causes. The two major theories of depression—one based on biological evidence and one based on cognition—can explain a great deal about the disorder. Depression has many biological aspects, including genetic predispositions (relatives of patients are two to five times more at risk), alterations in neurotransmitter and hormone systems (inadequate levels of serotonin, testosterone, and estrogen), and changes in specific areas of the brain (brain damage to left hemisphere, smaller prefrontal cortex). Be familiar with how biological irregularities are related to depression, see pp. 264–69; Figures 7-2 and 7-3 are especially useful for explaining the neurochemical processes involved.

In addition to these biological aspects, there are clearly

cognitive components to depression as well. Two major theories that have been well-supported by research include Beck's cognitive theory of depression and Seligman's learned helplessness model. According to Beck, two mechanisms cause depression: the *cognitive triad,* which consists of negative thoughts about the self, the world, and the future; and *errors in logic,* which are logical errors that can lead to or maintain depression, such as magnifying small bad events and minimizing large good events; see p. 270 for a list of common logical errors made by people with depression. Seligman has found that animals and people who experience negative, inescapable events develop *learned helplessness,* which involves expectations that bad events will occur and that there is nothing that can be done to stop them. How helpless people feel is based on their attribution of a bad event as: *internal-external* (due to them or outside circumstances), *stable-unstable,* (permanent or temporary), *global-specific* (affecting many areas of life or only a few specific areas; see Figure 7-5 for an example). People who attribute bad events as stable and global may experience hopelessness, a subtype of depression that is characterized by the expectation of no control and the certainty that something bad will happen.

Treatment. There are three classes of drugs used to treat depression. *Tricyclic antidepressants* block the reuptake of norepinephrine and help 60 to 75 percent of patients who take them. *Monamine oxidase inhibitors (MAOIs)* prevent the breakdown of norepinephrine by inhibiting the enzyme MAO. They also work well, but are prescribed less often due to potential lethal side effects when combined with certain foods. *Selective serotonin reuptake inhibitors (SSRIs)* selectively inhibit the reuptake of serotonin. They help 60 to 70 percent of patients and have a lower risk of overdose and fewer side effects compared to the tricyclics. New *atypical antidepressants,* such as Wellbutrin, are now being prescribed. They affect the availability of dopamine and are free of the sexual side effects that can occur with the other drugs. Keep in mind that around 30 to 40 percent of the effect of antidepressant drugs is due to a placebo effect. In addition, drugs have high relapse rates once stopped, and psychotherapy has been shown to be as effective as drugs (thought drugs start to work more quickly). Another biological treatment is electroconvulsive shock treatment (ECT). It is highly effective and has few side effects, though depression does tend to recur the next year following treatment.

Beck's cognitive therapy employs techniques for detecting automatic negative thoughts and replacing them with realistic and less depressing thoughts (see pp. 279–80 for a transcript of a cognitive therapist using these techniques with a client). Techniques based on Seligman's approach include teaching social and assertiveness skills, criticizing automatic thoughts, and changing from pessimistic to optimistic attributions. Interpersonal therapy, a brief form of psychodynamic therapy, focuses on current interpersonal problems (see pp. 280–82 for more details about these approaches). These therapies work about as well as medication, and result in lower rates of relapse. See Table 7-3 for a summary of the effectiveness of these approaches and Box 7-4 for a discussion about deciding the treatment of choice.

Bipolar Disorder

People with bipolar disorder experience fluctuating depressive and manic episodes. Manic episodes involve euphoric or irritable mood, grandiose and/or racing thoughts, hyperactive and reckless behavior, and a greatly lessened need for sleep (see pp. 284–85 for an case example). Bipolar disorder affects 0.6 to 1.1 percent of the U.S. population in their lifetimes and affects men and women equally. It typically occurs suddenly between the ages of twenty and thirty. The disorder can be very debilitating, leading to divorce, chronic social or occupational impairment, and suicide. The cause of the disorder is unknown, though it clearly involves disruptions in neurochemistry and in various systems in the brain (for instance, the reward system, the movement processing system, and the disinhibition-inhibition process). There is clearly a strong genetic component, with identical twins having five times the concordance rate compared to fraternal twins. The treatment of choice for bipolar disorder is *lithium carbonate*, a naturally occurring salt. About 80 percent of patients experience full or partial relief from lithium. It is quite toxic in overdose, so new drugs have been developed, such as Depakote.

Seasonal Affective Disorder (SAD)

Seasonal Affective Disorder is a specifier in the DSM-IV that can be used with any of the mood disorders (see p. 290 for DSM-IV criteria). It is characterized by depression that begins with the onset of winter and fully remits as the days lengthen. People with SAD experience fatigue, oversleeping, and cravings for carbohydrates. Women are diagnosed more than men and the rates vary a great deal, depending on the number of short days that occur in the geographical area. The use of artificial light during short days provides relief of symptoms.

Suicide

Depressed individuals are the single group most at risk for suicide, with a suicide rate twenty-five times that of the general population. Suicide is also linked to alcohol abuse, schizophrenia, and homicidal people. There has been a recent rise in suicide among young people, making it the third leading cause of death among high school and college students. Women make roughly three times as many suicide attempts as men (probably because the rate of depression is higher in women), but men succeed four times more often than women (probably because of the methods they use). Rates of suicide vary: suicide is more common in industrialized countries and in regions with strong political antagonism and forced social changes (see Table 7-6 for rates of suicides by country). Men over age eighty-five have the highest rate of all age groups. The strongest predictor of suicide is a previous attempt at suicide. Review pages 296–97 for a discussion of the various motivations for suicide. Suicide centers and psychosocial interventions appear to help to prevent suicide.

TESTING YOUR UNDERSTANDING

Test your understanding of what you have read by working through the following tasks with a classmate.

1. Your mother is worried that one of her friends is depressed. Tell her the symptoms that would indicate that her friend is suffering from depressive disorder.

2. Explain why young people and women are particularly at risk for depression.

3. Your mother decides that her friend is indeed clinically depressed. She wants to know why her friend developed depression. Explain both the biological and psychological reasons for depression to your mother.

4. Your mother tells you her friend is taking Prozac. She's worried that this might not be the right treatment for her friend. Explain to your mother how drugs for depression work and the reasons for considering psychotherapy instead of drugs.

5. Christie McNicole, a famous actress, was diagnosed with bipolar disorder. Explain how this disorder differs from depression and describe the symptoms, causes, and treatments for bipolar disorder.

6. Why are people in Alaska more likely to experience depression during the winter months? What treatment is used to help alleviate that depression?

7. Psychologists often deal with people who are considering suicide. Which patients are at the greatest risk for suicide and how might suicide be prevented?

Multiple-Choice Questions

1. Carlotta is feeling blue. When she thinks about it, she realizes she has been feeling blue for a long time, probably more than three years. Without knowing any more, what is the most likely diagnosis for Carlotta?
   a. bipolar disorder
   b. major depressive disorder
   c. dysthymic disorder
   d. depression with melancholia

2. Jody experiences terrible depression about once every six months. She also experiences times when she's very irritable, quite talkative, and has difficulty sleeping more than two hours a night. Jody would best be diagnosed as having:
   a. bipolar disorder.
   b. major depressive disorder.
   c. dysthymic disorder.
   d. depression with melancholia.

3. Joshua is feeling quite blue. His friends notice that he moves very slowly, and appears to have lost interest in almost everything. He wakes very early in the morning and feels better as the day progresses. He is lethargic and has lost weight. Joshua is best diagnosed as having:
   a. bipolar disorder.
   b. major depressive disorder.
   c. dysthymic disorder.
   d. depression with melancholia.

4. Which of the following is true regarding changes in the rates of depression over the last two generations?
   a. Fewer people are depressed, but depression is more widespread among teenagers.
   b. Fewer people are depressed, and the rates of depression among teenagers are lower.
   c. Depression has become the most widespread psychological disorder, though rates of depression among teenagers are lower.
   d. Depression has become the most widespread psychological disorder, and depression is more widespread among teenagers.

5. Ambivalence, the feeling that every decision is momentous, and the fear of a wrong decision are all typical of which type of depressive symptoms?
   a. mood symptoms
   b. cognitive symptoms
   c. motivational symptoms
   d. physical symptoms

6. Who is the least likely to experience a depressive episode?
   a. Mike, a fifty-year-old African-American businessman
   b. Sheila, a thirty-five-year-old Caucasian teacher
   c. Benjamin, a sixteen-year-old Latino high school student
   d. Mike, Sheila, and Benjamin are equally at risk for depression.

7. Why are women more likely than men to be diagnosed with depression?
   a. They aren't actually more depressed; they are just more willing to admit it.
   b. hormonal changes

c. genetic proneness
d. all of the above

8. Who is least likely to experience a depressive episode?
   a. Kelly, who has several relatives with depression
   b. Jill, who just separated from her spouse
   c. Jennifer, who has experienced past depressive episodes
   d. Genetics, bad life events, and past depressive episodes all predict depression equally well.

9. Most depressions improve over time, even without treatment. However, the rate of relapse or recurrence is pretty high. Which of the following is NOT a predictor of relapse or recurrence?
   a. being married
   b. the presence of a personality disorder
   c. the presence of pessimism
   d. being a woman

10. Which of the following is a neurotransmitter that has been implicated in depression?
    a. serotonin
    b. norepinephrine
    c. dopamine
    d. all of the above

11. There is quite a bit of evidence that depression is related to the biological effects of stress. Which of the following is NOT evidence for this?
    a. Depressed patients show greatly increased levels of cortisol in their blood.
    b. Depressed patients in one study each had a smaller hippocampus than nondepressed patients.
    c. Individuals with underactive thyroid glands (hypothyroidism) show many of the features of depression.
    d. The infusion of CRF (corticotropin releasing factor) in the brains of animals produces many of the signs of depression.

12. Carlos received one of the highest grades in the class on a recent examination. He has been feeling depressed lately and when the professor tells the class that she is disappointed with their scores, Carlos feels guilty and feels that he should have studied more. Carlos is making which error in logic common in depression?
    a. arbitrary inference
    b. overgeneralization
    c. minimization
    d. personalization

13. The Santana family tragically lost their farm (which was their livelihood) when a tornado hit without warning two years ago. They now live in a small apartment in town. Mr. Santana spends most of his day watching TV, not bothering to look for a job. He and his wife both feel that it's not worth it to try to rebuild their lives because it could all just disappear again.

Which theory of depression best describes their situation?
   a. Beck's cognitive theory of depression
   b. the learned helplessness model
   c. the psychodynamic model
   d. the behavioral model

14. Imagine that you miss 80 percent of the questions on this practice quiz. If you say to yourself that it is because you have a cold and cannot think clearly, you are making a(n) _____ attribution.
    a. internal, stable, and global
    b. external, stable, and specific
    c. internal, unstable, and global
    d. external, unstable, and specific

15. The _____ class of antidepressant medications is prescribed most frequently because of their relatively benign side effects and the low risk of overdose.
    a. tricylic
    b. MAO inhibitor
    c. SSRI
    d. atypical antidepressant

16. _____ are prescribed less frequently because of the potential fatal side effects when combined with foods such as wine or aged cheese.
    a. Tricyclic antidepressants
    b. MAO inhibitors
    c. SSRIs
    d. Atypical antidepressants

17. In which of the following instances would drug therapy clearly be superior to psychotherapy for depression?
    a. in all instances
    b. in cases of severe depression
    c. in cases of psychotic depression
    d. in cases when you want to prevent relapse once the intervention is stopped

18. Which of the following is true about electroconvulsive shock treatment (ECT)?
    a. It is not used anymore.
    b. It is used, but it doesn't really work very well.
    c. It is used, but only in the worst situations, because it has profound side effects.
    d. It works very well, but it is associated with a high rate of recurrence.

19. Detecting automatic thoughts, reality testing automatic thoughts, training in changing attributions, and changing depressogenic assumptions are the four specific techniques used in:
    a. Beck's cognitive therapy.
    b. therapy for learned helplessness.
    c. interpersonal therapy.
    d. rational-emotive therapy.

20. Soo is seeing a therapist for depression. Her therapist encourages her to discuss her recent break-up with her boyfriend and has her role-play ways to meet new people and ways to be more assertive. What type of therapy is Soo probably in?
    a. Beck's cognitive therapy
    b. therapy for learned helplessness
    c. interpersonal therapy
    d. rational-emotive therapy

21. Which of the following is NOT true of bipolar disorder compared to major depressive disorder?
    a. Bipolar disorder is more severe.
    b. Bipolar depression is associated more with overeating and sleeping too much, whereas unipolar depression tends to be associated with reduced appetite and insomnia.
    c. Prozac can sometimes make things worse by bringing on a manic episode.
    d. Women are more likely than men to be diagnosed with bipolar disorder.

22. A case described in the text includes the following: "I know I suffered terribly. . . . I tried to remember what had been beautiful in my life. I did not think about love or how I had wandered all over the world. . . . I remembered most the river I had loved most in my life. Before I could fish in it again I would take its water in the shell of my hands and kiss it as I would kiss a woman. Sometimes, when I sat at the barred window and fished in memory, the pain was almost unbearable. I had to block it out, the beauty, and I had to remind myself that dirt, foulness, and muddy waters also ran the world. . . ." What symptom common in mania does this description illustrate?
    a. flight of ideas
    b. frenetic activity
    c. grandiosity
    d. euphoric mood

23. The cause of bipolar disorder is unknown, but evidence suggests that the _____ approach is the most useful in understanding the disorder.
    a. cognitive
    b. biological
    c. behavioral
    d. psychodynamic

24. The clear treatment of choice for bipolar disorder is:
    a. lithium carbonate.
    b. cognitive therapy.
    c. intensive psychodynamic therapy.
    d. behavioral therapy.

25. Fatigue, oversleeping, and carbohydrate craving are symptoms that are typical of:
    a. depression with melancholia.
    b. bipolar disorder.
    c. seasonal affective disorder.
    d. dysthymia.

26. Suicide is the _____ most frequent cause of death among high school and college students.
    a. first
    b. second
    c. third
    d. fourth

27. Mood disorders are precursors to the majority of suicides. In fact, people with mood disorders have _____ times the rate of people in the general population.
    a. five
    b. ten
    c. twenty
    d. twenty-five

28. What is the biggest risk factor for suicide?
    a. depression
    b. age
    c. a previous attempt at suicide
    d. a family history of suicide

29. Which of the following is NOT associated with a high suicide rate?
    a. generalized anxiety disorder
    b. alcohol abuse
    c. schizophrenia
    d. homicidal people

30. Which of the following has the highest suicide rate?
    a. United States
    b. Mexico
    c. Hungary
    d. Egypt

Fill in the Blank

1. In _____ _____, an individual suffers only from depressive symptoms without ever experiencing mania.

   major depression or unipolar depression

2. In _____, the individual experiences symptoms of excessive elation, expansiveness, irritability, talkativeness, inflated self-esteem, and flight of ideas.

   mania

3. In _____ _____, the individual experiences both depression and mania.

    bipolar disorder or manic depression

4. _____ disorder is chronic depression in which the individual has been depressed for at least two years without more than a two-month return to normal functioning.

    Dysthymic

5. In _____ _____, people have both chronic depression and episodic depression at the same time.

    double depression

6. Biologically based depression is sometimes called _____, meaning coming from within the body.

    endogenous

7. Psychologically based depression is sometimes called _____, meaning coming from outside the body.

    reactive or exogenous

8. _____ features in a diagnosis of depression refer to a loss of pleasure in all activities, a general lack of reaction to pleasurable activities (worst in the morning), early morning awakening, lethargy, weight loss, and guilt.

    Melancholic

9. _____ refers to the return of depressive symptoms following at least six months without significant symptoms.

    Recurrence

10. _____ refers to a return of depressive symptoms in less than six months.

    Relapse

11. _____ theory suggests that the numbers of postsynaptic monoamine receptors are inadequate in people with depression.

    Downregulation

12. _____ is a process by which certain neurons, by firing repeatedly, make themselves more sensitive to subsequent stimulation.

    Kindling

13. The _____ triad consists of negative thoughts about the self, ongoing experience, and the future.

    cognitive

14. _____ _____ refers to drawing a conclusion when there is little or no evidence to support it.

    Arbitrary inference

15. _____ _____ consists of focusing on one insignificant detail while ignoring the more important features of the situation.

    Selective abstraction

16. _____ refers to drawing global conclusions about worth, ability, or performance on the basis of a single fact.

    Overgeneralization

17. _____ and _____ are gross errors of evaluation, in which small bad events are magnified and large good events are minimized.

    Magnification; minimization

18. _____ refers to incorrectly taking responsibility for bad events in the world.

    Personalization

19. The _____ _____ model holds that the basic cause of depression is an expectation. The individual expects that bad events will happen and that nothing can be done to prevent their occurrence.

    learned helplessness

20. When making _____-_____ attributions, a person considers whether a bad event- is due to herself or circumstances outside herself.

    internal-external

21. When making _____-_____ attributions, a person asks herself, "Is the cause of my failure something permanent or something temporary?"

    stable-unstable

22. When making _____-_____ attributions, an individual asks herself whether the cause of her failure will produce failure in a wide variety of circumstances or only in similar circumstances.

    global-specific

23. The _____ theory of depression emphasizes the stable and global dimensions for negative events.

    hopelessness

24. Antidepressant medications are _____ rather than curative. That is, they suppress the symptoms of depression, but the symptoms have the same risk of returning once medication is discontinued.

    palliative

25. _____ _____ _____ is a symptom of mania in which a person's thoughts or ideas race to his mind faster than he can write them down or say them.

    Flight of ideas

26. _____ _____ _____ is characterized by depressions that begin each year in October or November and fully remit, sometimes switching to mania, as the days lengthen.

    Seasonal affective disorder

27. _____ suicide occurs when the individual has too few ties to his or her fellow humans. Societal demands, principal among them the demand to live, are not registered.

    Egoistic

28. _____ suicide is for the sake of society; the individual takes his or her own life in order to benefit to the community.

    Altruistic

LEVELS OF ANALYSIS: EXAMINING THE CHAPTER'S THEMES

Interestingly, depression is clearly a disorder that requires both a complex biological and psychological analysis, whereas bipolar disorder appears primarily biological. This has implications for how the disorders are understood and treated. The emergence of new medications for treating the mood disorders has led to some controversy between science and practice.

Biological and Psychological Levels of Analysis

Depression is a disorder that clearly can only be understood by using both psychological and biological levels of analysis. In contrast, bipolar disorder appears to be best explained using a biological model. For unipolar depression, there are clear links to biological functioning (for instance, genetic predisposition, alterations in neurotransmitters and hormones, and brain structure) as well as to negative cognitions (automatic and negative attributions, for example). Changes in neurochemistry and changes in cognitions can lead to the relief of symptoms. Further, cognitions and biology interact: helplessness and hopelessness can reduce serotonin levels, and lowered serotonin levels can increase helplessness and hopelessness. Likewise, when treating depression, positive changes in behavior can induce changes in neurotransmitter levels, and changes in neurotransmitter levels induced by medication can effect positive changes in behavior.

Treatment of Choice

About 60–70 percent of patients with depression experience relief from antidepressant medications. The medications act quickly and the newest antidepressants have few side effects. There are, however, higher recurrence and relapse rates when the drugs are discontinued. In profound psychotic depression, medication or ECT are necessary to treat the patient. ECT is also effective; about 80 percent of depressed patients respond well to ECT and modern techniques have greatly reduced the side effects. Psychotherapy, particularly cognitive therapy and interpersonal therapy (IPT), has been shown to be as effective as medication, with no side effects, and a lower rate of relapse and recurrence.

So which is the treatment of choice? Patient factors must be considered. Patients who have difficulty talking about their problems, or who are severely depressed and require immediate relief may be better candidates for drug therapy. Patients who cannot take drugs or who are unwilling to use them may be best treated with psychotherapy. To decide the treatment of choice, one must ask, "For which patient, and for which kind of depression?" See Box 7-4 for a detailed discussion of treatment of choice.

Science and Practice

Box 7-3 discusses the controversy over the claim that Prozac can cause suicide. Though there is little scientific support for this claim, at least one lawsuit has been brought against the company that manufactures Prozac on behalf of a depressed patient. Box 7-3 describes the case of Bill Forsythe, who killed his wife and himself after taking the drug. An expert witness for the plaintiffs testified that some patients have an abnormal reaction to Prozac called "akathisia," in which they experience intense thoughts of harming themselves or someone else. The challenge in weighing this claim is to separate whether the symptoms were caused by the drug or by the underlying depression. The jury decided in favor of Eli Lilly, the manufacturer of Prozac. However, some experts believe it is important for Eli Lilly to include a warning on the drug advising doctors to closely monitor first-time users of the drug. They claim that Eli Lilly is unwilling to do so because it will damage their sales.

ANSWER KEY

MULTIPLE-CHOICE QUESTIONS

1. c. Dysthymic disorder is chronic depression in which the individual has been depressed for at least two years without more than a two-month return to normal functioning.

2. a. People with bipolar disorder experience periods of depression and periods of mania, during which the individual experiences symptoms such as elation, expansiveness, irritability, and talkativeness.

3. d. Depression with melancholia includes a loss of pleasure in all activities, numbing, early morning awakening, lethargy, weight loss, and guilt.

4. d. Depression is the most widespread psychological disorder. If you were born after 1975, you are ten times more likely to become depressed than were your grandparents. In 1960, the average age for the first depressive episode was thirty, now it is less than fifteen.

5. c. Motivational symptoms include difficulty getting up, difficulty planning, ambivalence, fear of making a wrong decision, and "paralysis of the will," when patients cannot bring themselves to do even those things that are necessary to life.

6. a. Young people, females, and Latinos are all more likely to experience depression than older people, males, Caucasians, and African Americans.

7. d. Several hypotheses have been advanced to account for why women have higher rates of depression: women are more willing to admit they are depressed; they experience hormonal changes such as premenstrual depression or postnatal depression; the depressive gene is expressed as depression in females, but as alcoholism in males; women have a tendency to ruminate about bad life events; and women can fall into a cycle of failure and helplessness through the pursuit of thinness.

8. b. Prior depression and genetic predisposition both overshadow life events in predicting depression. In fact, about 90 percent of people who experience bad life events do not become depressed.

9. a. The predictors of relapse and recurrence include having a personality disorder, being pessimistic, being a woman, never marrying, and having suffered more depressive episodes in a shorter period of time.

10. d. Serotonin, norepinephrine, and dopamine have all been implicated in depression.

11. c. Hypothyroidism is related to depression, but is not a stress-related condition. All the other choices provide evidence that stress-related changes are linked to depression.

12. a. Arbitrary inference refers to drawing conclusions when there is little or no evidence to support them. Overgeneralization refers to drawing global conclusions about worth, ability, or performance on the basis of a single fact. Minimization occurs when large good events are minimized. Personalization refers to incorrectly taking responsibility for bad events in the world.

13. b. The learned helplessness model says that people and animals given inescapable events (for instance, a tornado) will become profoundly passive later on when they are given escapable events (such as lack of money due to unemployment).

14. c. Internal, unstable, and global attributions are internal to the person, will change over time, and affect everything the person does. See Figure 7-5 for a chart of the different types of attributions.

15. c. The SSRIs are prescribed often because they have fewer side effects than the other types and because of the low risk of overdose.

16. b. MAO inhibitors can have fatal side effects when combined with certain foods or medications.

17. c. In cases of profound psychotic depression, only drugs or ECT will work. Psychotherapy has been demonstrated to work as well as drug treatment for severe and moderate depression, and medications are linked to higher rates of relapse once the drug is removed.

18. d. ECT is used and is very effective. The side effects have been greatly reduced by modern techniques and up to 80 percent of patients respond to it. It is associated with a high rate of recurrence, with almost 60 percent of those treated becoming depressed again the next year.

19. a. This is a description of the techniques used in Beck's cognitive therapy.

20. c. IPT deals with current relationship problems and teaches social, communication, and assertiveness skills.

21. d. Men and women are equally likely to be diagnosed with bipolar disorder. The other choices are all true.

22. a. This description illustrates flight of ideas, or racing thoughts.

23. b. Much of the evidence is consistent with the biological model. For example, disturbances in biochemistry, disturbances in various systems of the brain, and evidence for genetic transmission have all been noted in conjunction with bipolar disorder.

24. a. Drug therapy, classically lithium carbonate, is clearly the treatment of choice for bipolar disorder. Other drugs being prescribed for the disorder are anticonvulsant drugs such as Tegretol and Depakote.

25. c. Fatigue, oversleeping, and carbohydrate craving are symptoms that are typical of seasonal affective disorder.

26. c. Suicide is the third most frequent cause of death among high school and college students. This age group now accounts for more than 15 percent of all suicides.

27. d. People with mood disorders have twenty-five times the rate of suicide compared to people in the general population.

28. c. In the year following an attempted suicide, the individual carries a risk for a completed suicide one hundred times greater than average.

29. a. Alcohol abusers make up 20 percent of suicides, 5 to 10 percent are people with schizophrenia, and white murderers have a rate that is seven hundred times the national average.

30. c. Hungary, Sri Lanka, and Russia have the highest suicide rates; Mexico and Egypt have very low suicide rates. The U.S. has an average suicide rate.

CHAPTER 8 | Early-Onset Disorders

A GUIDE TO THE READING

Perhaps the most challenging aspect of this chapter is its breadth; eighteen childhood disorders are presented, some in more depth than others. The disorders are divided into four types: emotional, developmental, eating and habit, and disruptive behavior. You will probably have an easier time remembering the various disorders if you learn them by category. Be sure to start by reading pages 305–6 carefully for a general overview of childhood disorders. Table 8-1 is particularly helpful; it presents all the disorders, their typical age of onset, and their prevalence.

Emotional Disorders

The emotional disorders include reactive attachment disorder, separation anxiety disorder, phobias, and childhood depression. The chief symptom of reactive attachment disorder is a marked disturbance in the child's ability to relate to other people, beginning before age five (see p. 307 for DSM-IV criteria). These children may either fail to respond to people at all (the *inhibited* subtype), or they may respond to people indiscriminately (the *disinhibited* subtype). It is assumed that inadequate care causes the syndrome. Relatively little research has been done on its prevalence, specific causes, or treatments.

Separation anxiety disorder, in contrast, involves an excessive need for contact with the caregiver and resistance to separation (see p. 310 for DSM-IV criteria). Genetic influences and modeling of parental fears contribute to the development of the disorder. Successful treatments have included cognitive-behavioral treatment and antidepressant medication.

Common phobias for children appear in Table 8-2. They are associated with a traumatic event, general anxiety, and the influence of phobic parents. The most common phobia is school phobia. Behavioral treatments can be quite effective, including systematic desensitization and working with parents.

As noted in Chapter 7, the age of onset of depression is going down. Symptoms of depression in children are similar to those in adults, as are the risk factors (family history of depression, stress, low self-esteem, pessimism). Antidepressant medications can be helpful, but there are concerns about the side effects. Therefore, psychotherapy is the treatment of choice.

Developmental Disorders

The essential feature of developmental disorders is a disturbance in the acquisition of cognitive, language, motor, or social skills. Developmental disorders include autism, Rett's disorder, childhood disintegrative disorder, Asperger's disorder, mental retardation, and learning disorders.

Children with autism do not respond to others normally, have great difficulty developing language, insist on sameness, and have impaired intellectual development (see p. 316 for DSM-IV criteria; review pp. 318–21 for more details on specific symptoms). There is strong evidence that autism is a biologically based disorder (for example, the presence of larger brain volumes but smaller cerebellums, high rates of epileptic seizures, abnormalities in dopamine and serotonin levels, and obstetrical complications). Medications are used to treat specific symptoms, but intensive behavioral therapy is the main treatment (see p. 324 for a description of an effective treatment spearheaded by Lovaas).

Rett's disorder involves normal development in the first year, then a slowing down of head growth, a decline in motor and communication skills, social withdrawal, rigidity, stereotypic movements, and mental retardation (see p. 326 for DSM-IV criteria). It is caused by a genetic mutation on the X chromosome, probably due to a prenatal event.

In childhood disintegrative disorder, autistic-like symptoms occur, but not until after age two (see p. 327 for DSM-IV criteria). The cause is unknown, but it is perhaps due to some abnormality in early development of nervous system. The treatments are the same as those used for autism.

Asperger's disorder involves less severe deficits, primarily impairment in social interaction, and is not detected until preschool age (see p. 328 for DSM-IV criteria).

Mental retardation involves subaverage intellectual functioning and limitations in two or more adaptive skill areas (communication, self-care, etc.; see p. 330 for DSM-IV criteria). Measures of intelligence and adaptive behavior scales are used to make a diagnosis. Be familiar with the levels of retardation presented on pages 331–32 and the multitude of causes for the disorder, as described on pages 332–35 (Table 8-4 provides a nice summary). Although there is no treatment that can reverse mental retardation, most individuals with the disorder are provided with special education opportunities that prepare them to live in the community as adults.

Learning disabilities are more specific than the other developmental disorders and typically involve either reading, math, or writing. Theories of causes include a delay in the development of the brain, an abnormality in the structure of the brain, and some abnormality in the "wiring" of the left hemisphere. Treatment involves special training in the deficient skills as well as behavior therapy designed to maintain the child's interest.

Finally, pervasive developmental disorder not otherwise specified (PDD-NOS) is used to diagnose children with autistic-like abnormalities but who do not meet criteria for any of the other pervasive developmental disorders.

Eating and Habit Disorders

The eating disorders include anorexia, which involves an intense fear of gaining weight (despite being extremely underweight) and a distorted body image, and bulimia, which involves out-of-control binge eating and the use of compensatory mechanisms, such as purging (see pp. 339 and 340 for DSM-IV criteria). A good summary of the explanatory models of the disorders appears in Table 8-5. There are biological correlates to the eating disorders (for example, a malfunction of the hypothalamus) as well as psychosocial theories (cultural norms, maladaptive family patterns, etc.; review pp. 340–42 for detailed description of causes). Recent approaches to treatment include behavioral and cognitive techniques for the patients and their families. Antidepressants are sometimes prescribed, but only as an adjunct (see the treatment tables, Table 8-6 and 8-7, for a summary).

Disorders of habit include *enuresis* (bed-wetting), *speech disorders* (stuttering), and *Tourette's disorder,* which involves multiple motor and verbal tics. Enuresis is a common childhood problem, so in order to be diagnosed it must be severe (see p. 344 for DSM-IV criteria). A predisposition to enuresis can be inherited; physical illness, stress, and less sensitivity to the cues from the bladder can also contribute to the problem. Behavioral methods, such as the "bell and pad" method (see p. 345), and medication are both effective, though the effects of behavioral treatments may be more lasting compared to medications (see Table 8-8).

Stuttering involves a dysrhythmia in speech that is pronounced and prolonged (see p. 346 for DSM-IV criteria). The causes are unclear, though abnormalities in the left hemisphere and genetic factors appear to play a role. Psychotherapy and reeducational techniques are effective in treating stuttering; review pages 345–46 for a description of specific techniques.

Tourette's disorder involves multiple tics that last for at least one year (see p. 347 for DSM-IV criteria) and can also involve *coprolalia,* the repetition of socially unacceptable words. It appears to be biologically based; the basal ganglia, the thalamus, and genetic factors all seem to play a role. Drugs that block dopamine receptors are the most effective treatment; behavioral management and stress reduction are also used as an adjunct.

Disruptive Behavior Disorders

The disruptive behavior disorders include conduct disorder, oppositional defiant disorder, and attention deficit/hyperactivity disorder. Conduct disorder involves the repeated violation of very basic norms for interpersonal behavior. Some behaviors connected with the disorder include physical aggression, lying, and cheating (see p. 350 for DSM-IV criteria). Be familiar with the detailed description of the disorder provided on pages 349–55. Factors that probably play a role in the causing the disorder include the increased availability of guns, the influence of the media, maladaptive families, poverty, genetic predisposition, pregnancy complications, low levels of serotonin, abnormalities in the frontal lobe of the brain, reduced physical arousal, and reduced empathy. Treatments that use multiple strategies, such as behavioral reinforcement, family therapy, and parent training, are the most effective in treating conduct disorder (see Table 8-9 for a summary of treatment approaches for conduct disorder).

Oppositional defiant disorder (ODD) is less severe than conduct disorder, and involves defiance, hostility, and negativity (see p. 361 for DSM-IV criteria). The causes and treatment of ODD are similar to those of conduct disorder.

Attention deficit/hyperactivity disorder (ADHD) is the most frequent of the disruptive behavior disorders and can involve attentional difficulties, hyperactive behavior, or both (see p. 363 for DSM-IV criteria). There are several possible causes of ADHD, including genetic factors, abnormality in the dopamine receptors, prenatal complications, environmental toxins, high blood levels of lead (from eating lead paint chips), underarousal of the limbic system, and disruptive families. The two main treatment approaches to ADHD are medication (Ritalin) and behavioral therapy (see Table 8-10 for a summary of the effectiveness of these treatment approaches). Medication appears to be more effective than behavioral therapy, though a combination of drug therapy and behavioral therapy is the most effective treatment for some of the conduct problems associated with ADHD. Be sure to review Box 8-3 to understand the controversy about prescribing Ritalin.

TESTING YOUR UNDERSTANDING

Test your understanding of what you have read by working through the following tasks with a classmate.

1. Think of a child who you suspect might have a childhood disorder. Diagnose the child and provide a rationale for your diagnosis. How might this child best be treated?

2. Boys and girls suffer from depression at about the same rates, but women are diagnosed twice as often as men. Why does the female-to-male ratio change with age?

3. Imagine you hear about a child who has developed almost no social or language skills and who rigidly adheres to routines. What questions would you ask to determine whether this child is suffering from autism, Rett's disorder, childhood disintegrative disorder, or Asperger's disorder?

4. Explain the criteria for a diagnosis of mental retardation and list as many causes as you can.

5. Explain why the United States, which has an abundance of food, has such high rates of eating disorders compared to countries where food is quite scarce.

6. All children misbehave, but some children persistently violate even the most basic rules of conduct. Describe how a child's behavior becomes problematic enough to be diagnosed with conduct disorder, and how such a child (and his or her family) might change this behavior.

7. Explain to a friend why some believe that ADHD is overdiagnosed and Ritalin overprescribed in the United States.

Multiple-Choice Questions

1. At any point in time, between _____ and _____ of children suffer from moderate to severe psychological problems.
   a. 1 percent; 5 percent
   b. 5 percent; 14 percent
   c. 14 percent; 20 percent
   d. 20 percent; 25 percent

2. Autistic disorder falls into which diagnostic class?
   a. emotional disorders
   b. developmental disorders
   c. eating and habit disorders
   d. disruptive behavior disorders

3. Separation anxiety disorder falls into which diagnostic class?
   a. emotional disorders
   b. developmental disorders
   c. eating and habit disorders
   d. disruptive behavior disorders

4. Which of the following is NOT true regarding the differences between the disorders that first occur in childhood and the disorders that first occur in adulthood?
   a. In children, psychologists must differentiate normal variability in rates of development from psychological problems that indicate a need for treatment.
   b. Childhood psychological problems are more predictable than adult disorders.
   c. A child's distress is more likely to be manifest indirectly through disruptive behaviors.
   d. Children's problems are quite specific to particular situations or contexts.

5. Reactive attachment disorder is unique among the DSM-IV disorders because there are specific assumptions about the etiology of the disorder. The diagnostic criteria for reactive attachment disorder assume that it is caused by:
   a. neurological problems.
   b. poverty.
   c. prenatal factors.
   d. inadequate care.

6. Demetria worries that bad things will happen to her parents when they go out. She cries a lot when they leave and experiences terrible headaches while they are away. Demetria would be best diagnosed with which emotional disorder?
   a. reactive attachment disorder
   b. separation anxiety disorder
   c. phobias
   d. childhood depression

7. Which of the following is the most common and problematic childhood phobia?
   a. separation
   b. animals
   c. school
   d. the dark

8. The essential feature of autism is:
   a. delayed language development.
   b. stereotypical patterns of behavior.
   c. inability to relate to others in a normal way.
   d. rigid adherence to schedules.

9. Which of the following is mentioned as one of the best predictors of later progress for children with autism?
   a. the severity of the language delay
   b. the severity of the impairment in social interactions
   c. measured IQ
   d. both a and c

10. The childhood disorder that is most clearly based solely on biological, rather than psychological or social factors, is:
    a. childhood depression.
    b. autism.
    c. bulimia nervosa.
    d. conduct disorder.

11. Intensive behavioral treatment programs have proven to be effective for at least some children with autistic disorder. Children who participate in these programs for several years have shown increases in IQ of up to _____ points.
    a. five
    b. twelve
    c. nineteen
    d. twenty-eight

12. Marisa developed normally during her first year, and then suddenly began to withdraw from social interactions and adhere rigidly to routines and rituals. She experienced a decline in motor and communication skills and a slowing down in head growth. She is best diagnosed as having:
    a. autistic disorder.
    b. Rett's disorder.
    c. childhood disintegrative disorder.
    d. Asperger's disorder.

13. Which of the following developmental disorders is clearly due to a mutation in the X chromosome?
    a. autistic disorder
    b. Rett's disorder
    c. childhood disintegrative disorder
    d. Asperger's disorder

14. Chad was a friendly boy who seemed to develop normally. When he reached kindergarten, however, he began to engage in repetitive patterns of behavior and had difficulty relating to others. He stopped making eye contact, and his facial expressions always seemed to be the same. Chad is best diagnosed with:
    a. autistic disorder.
    b. Rett's disorder.
    c. childhood disintegrative disorder.
    d. Asperger's disorder.

15. People with _____ mental retardation can acquire skills through a sixth grade level and can function adequately in unskilled and semiskilled jobs. They are the largest group with mental retardation.
    a. mild
    b. moderate
    c. severe
    d. profound

16. People with _____ mental retardation show poor motor development and develop little or no communicative speech. They are unable to profit from vocational training, though they may be able to perform simple, unskilled job tasks under supervision.
    a. mild
    b. moderate
    c. severe
    d. profound

17. John is a very affectionate child who suffers from mental retardation. He has wide-set, slanted eyes and faces an increased risk of Alzheimer's disease. John's mental retardation is probably due to:
    a. Down syndrome.
    b. Fragile X syndrome.
    c. an inability to metabolize phenylalanine (PKU).
    d. his mother's drinking of alcohol during pregnancy.

18. Jill was born with a normal IQ, but now she cannot walk or talk and has an IQ under 20. What is her mental retardation probably due to?
    a. Down syndrome
    b. Fragile X syndrome
    c. an inability to metabolize phenylalanine (PKU)
    d. her mother's drinking of alcohol during pregnancy

19. When educating children with mental retardation, the best approach seems to be:
    a. special educational approaches.
    b. mainstream classrooms.
    c. a combination of special education and mainstream classroom experiences.
    d. both approaches seem to work equally well.

20. Carlito continues to wet his bed just about every night, even though he is six years old. This problem fits in which diagnostic class?
    a. emotional disorders
    b. developmental disorders
    c. eating and habit disorders
    d. disruptive behavior disorders

21. Lee is very underweight, though she sees herself as still needing to lose a few pounds. She is afraid of gaining weight, so much so that she often vomits after eating. Lee would best be diagnosed as having:
    a. bulimia nervosa.
    b. anorexia nervosa.
    c. both bulimia and anorexia.
    d. normal adolescent worries about weight.

22. Which of the following appears to be the best treatment for bulimia?
    a. interpersonal therapy
    b. behavior therapy
    c. cognitive-behavioral therapy
    d. antidepressant medication

23. Which of the following appears to be the best treatment for enuresis?
    a. drug therapy
    b. cognitive therapy
    c. parent training
    d. the "bell and pad" method

24. Todd often loses his temper, is defiant toward his teacher and parents, is hostile, defies rules and requests, deliberately does things to annoy other people, and is spiteful and vindictive. Todd would best be diagnosed as having:
    a. conduct disorder.
    b. oppositional defiant disorder (ODD).
    c. attention deficit/hyperactivity disorder (ADHD).
    d. no disorder; Todd's behavior is within the normal range.

25. Which is the most accurate statement regarding the cause of conduct disorder?
    a. It is primarily related to parenting techniques, such as the use of harsh and inconsistent punishment.
    b. It is primarily due to social factors, such as the increased availability of guns, violence in the media, and poverty.
    c. It is primarily caused by genetic inheritance.
    d. It is a disorder that can only be fully explained by taking into account genetics, psychological, and social factors.

26. There are several methods used to treat conduct disorder. Which method uses a family-based approach that involves intensive work with the child in his or her environment at home, school, and in peer groups?
    a. cognitive problem skills training (PSST)
    b. parent management training
    c. treatment homes, such as Achievement Place
    d. multisystemic therapy (MST)

27. Which neurotransmitter is implicated in oppositional defiant disorder?
    a. serotonin
    b. norepinephrine
    c. dopamine
    d. none of the above; children with ODD show no biological abnormalities.

28. Which of the following is the most frequently diagnosed childhood disruptive disorder?
    a. conduct disorder
    b. oppositional defiant disorder (ODD)
    c. attention deficit/hyperactivity disorder (ADHD)
    d. depression

29. Which neurotransmitter is implicated in attention deficit/hyperactivity disorder?
    a. serotonin
    b. norepinephrine
    c. dopamine
    d. none of the above; children with ADHD show no biological abnormalities.

30. Which of the following is true regarding the treatment of ADHD?
    a. Medication is more effective than behavioral therapy, and the combination of both does not increase effectivness.
    b. Behavioral therapy is more effective than medication, and the combination of both does not increase effectivness.
    c. Medication is more effective than behavioral therapy, and the combination of both is the most effective for reducing the conduct problems associated with ADHD.
    d. Behavioral therapy is more effective than medication, and the combination of both is the most effective for reducing the conduct problems associated with ADHD.

Fill in the Blank

1. The _____ disorders of childhood involve negative affective states, particularly insecurity, fear, anxiety, and sadness.   emotional

2. The _____ disorders of childhood are characterized by marked deficiencies in the child's acquisition of intellectual, communicative, and social skills.   developmental

3. The _____ disorders include a rather wide variety of symptoms that involve repetitive maladaptive or nonfunctional behaviors, for example, bed wetting and stuttering.

habit

4. _____ _____ disorders are characterized by deficits in self-control and involve behavior tendencies like hyperactivity, inattention, aggressiveness, destructiveness, and defiance of authority.

Disruptive behavior

5. _____ _____ disorder is a marked disturbance in the child's ability to relate to other people.

Reactive attachment

6. _____ developmental disorders involve noticeable abnormalities in the child's social adjustment and include autism, Rett's disorder, childhood disintegrative disorder, and Asperger's disorder.

Pervasive

7. _____ is the tendency to repeat or echo precisely what one has just heard.

Echolalia

8. _____ means to repeat the actions of others.

Echopraxia

9. _____ _____ is the tendency to use "I" where "you" is meant and vice versa.

Pronominal reversal

10. _____ involves the repetition of a sound, word, or phrase over an extended period of time.

Perseveration

11. A _____ is someone with an unusually high area of ability in one particular area and little or moderate ability in other areas.

savant

12. _____ disorder occurs only in females and involves a slowing in head growth and withdrawal from social interactions beginning after age one.

Rett's

13. _____ disorder is usually not detected until the preschool period or later; some believe that it is a mild form of autism.

Asperger's

14. A major cause of mental retardation is the chromosomal disorder known as _____ _____, which involves an extra chromosome 21.

Down syndrome

15. _____ _____ _____ is a condition involving physical defects, deformities, and mental retardation in fetuses exposed to alcohol through the mother's drinking during pregnancy.

Fetal alcohol syndrome

16. _____ is defined as involuntary urination at least twice a month for children between five and six, and once a month for those who are older.

Enuresis

17. In _____, a treatment for stuttering, a therapist reads from a book and the stutterer repeats the therapist's words shortly after the latter has spoken them.

shadowing

18. _____-_____ _____ requires stutterers to speak in time to a metronome or beeper that sounds in an earpiece.

Syllable-timed speech

19. A _____ is a repetitive, involuntary movement or vocalization that has a very sudden onset.

tic

20. _____ involves the repetition of socially unacceptable words.

Coprolalia

Additional Exercise: Early-Onset Disorders

Identify whether girls or boys are more likely to be diagnosed with the following childhood disorders.

Disorder	*Girls or Boys?*
1. Separation anxiety disorder	_____
2. Phobias	_____
3. Autistic disorder	_____
4. Rett's disorder	_____
5. Asperger's disorder	_____
6. Learning disorder	_____
7. Bulimia nervosa	_____
8. Anorexia nervosa	_____
9. Enuresis	_____
10. Speech disorders	_____
11. Tourette's disorder	_____
12. Conduct disorder	_____
13. Oppositional defiant disorder	_____
14. ADHD	_____

LEVELS OF ANALYSIS: EXAMINING THE CHAPTER'S THEMES

In this chapter, all four themes are discussed. Childhood disorders are best understood as being caused by multiple factors, requiring multiple levels of analysis. They are very much tied to the developmental process and treatment must take development into account. Finally, some types of treatment that have received little or no scientific research support are regularly used by clinicians in the hope of improving the fates of children with particularly devastating childhood disorders.

Biological and Psychological Levels of Analysis

The extent to which biological, psychological, and social factors play a role in the childhood disorders varies from disorder to disorder. Some, such as autism, are primarily biological in nature; others, such as anxiety disorder following exposure to trauma, are primary psychological. The most striking characteristic about the etiology of the childhood disorders, however, is that virtually all of them are the consequence of multiple causal factors. Mental retardation is a particularly interesting disorder in that a very similar cluster of symptoms (low IQ, impairment in functioning) can be caused by many different biological and environmental fac-

tors. Recent discoveries of the biological underpinnings of some forms of mental retardation, such as Fragile X syndrome (see Box 8-2) and the inability to metabolize phenylalanine, have led to regular testing in order to prevent or better treat mental retardation.

Development

The childhood disorders are very much related to development, due to the human brain's prolonged period of maturation. In fact, diagnosing a child with a mental disorder is particularly difficult because many problems experienced in childhood are simply outgrown. Therefore, psychologists are faced with the challenge of discerning which problems are temporary and which will persist and/or lead to more serious difficulties. In addition, the onset of different disorders occurs at different stages of development. For example, separation anxiety usually occurs during the preschool years, whereas eating disorders do not appear until adolescence. Clearly, the type of disorder that develops is related to the developmental processes the child is going through. The extent to which disorders affect males and females can also change with age; depression is experienced at about the same rates in boys and girls until adolescence, when girls start to experience it at much higher rates.

Treatment of Choice

There has been increasing evidence that medications can be very useful for treating a variety of childhood disorders. In the case of ADHD, medication has been demonstrated to be the most effective treatment. This has caused some controversy, however, because of the side effects of medication and the concern that certain medications may adversely impact development. As a result, most psychologists recommend psychological treatment, such as behavioral or cognitive therapy, for children with disorders. Because Ritalin is so effective in treating ADHD, however, it continues to be widely prescribed. Critics are concerned that we are using Ritalin to control normal childhood behaviors that adults don't like to deal with. See Box 8-3 for more information about this debate.

Science and Practice

Practitioners have implemented their own therapies for some childhood disorders that have been historically difficult to treat. Examples include "holding" or "rage reduction" therapy for reactive attachment disorder and facilitated communication for autistic disorder (see Box 8-1). These therapies have received little or no research support, and some clinicians have expressed concern that they are inappropriate and may even hurt the clients. The fact that they continue to be practiced is probably due to the frustration on the part of parents and clinicians that effective therapies have not yet been developed. These therapies may serve as a way for parents and clinicians to maintain hope that something can be done to help the child.

ANSWER KEY

MULTIPLE-CHOICE QUESTIONS

1. c. According to the text, at any given time, between 14 percent and 20 percent of children suffer from moderate to severe psychological problems.

2. b. Developmental disorders include autism, Rett's disorder, childhood disintegrative disorder, Asperger's disorder, mental retardation, and learning disorders.

3. a. The emotional disorders include reactive attachment disorder, separation anxiety disorder, phobias, and childhood depression.

4. b. Childhood psychological problems are less predictable than adult disorders, because children change so dramatically over time.

5. d. In order to receive the diagnosis, a child must have been exposed to serious neglect or outright abuse during some period before the symptoms began. It is assumed that inadequate care causes the syndrome.

6. b. Worries that bad things will happen to parents, resisting separation, and physical symptoms of anxiety, such as headaches, are all symptoms of separation anxiety disorder.

7. c. According to the text, school phobia is the most common and problematic childhood phobia, experienced by 1 percent of children in the general population.

8. c. All the responses are characteristic of children with autism, but the inability to relate to others is the essential feature of autism.

9. d. Both a and c are mentioned as one of the best predictors of later progress for children with autism.

10. b. There is little evidence that autism has psychogenic origins. There are also no differences in rates of autism across social classes and ethnicities.

11. d. IQ increases of seven to twenty-eight points have been demonstrated for children with autism who participate in behavioral programs.

12. b. All of the disorders mentioned have autistic-like symptoms. Rett's disorder is distinguished by no observable abnormalities during the first year.

After the first year, there is a slowing down of head growth. The disorder only occurs in females, as it is a genetically determined disorder that is lethal to the male fetus.

13. b. Rett's disorder is caused by a mutation in the X chromosome that occurs prenatally. This mutation causes Rett's disorder in the female fetus and is lethal to the male fetus.

14. d. All of the disorders mentioned have autistic-like symptoms. What distinguishes Asperger's syndrome is the late onset; it is usually not detected until the preschool period or later. It also involves less severe deficits than autism.

15. a. About 85 percent of children with mental retardation fall into this category.

16. c. This is a description of severe mental retardation. Those with profound mental retardation require custodial care and often have severe physical deformities, central nervous system difficulties, and retarded growth.

17. a. All of the above can cause mental retardation. Down syndrome is distinguished by a characteristic facial expression, increased risk for Alzheimer's disease, and an affectionate nature.

18. c. All of the above can cause mental retardation. What distinguishes PKU is that the child is normal at birth, but the central nervous system is poisoned by phenylalanine resulting in an inability to walk or talk and a very low IQ.

19. c. A combination of special education and mainstream classroom experiences appears to be the optimal approach to educating children with mental retardation.

20. c. The eating and habit disorders include bulimia, anorexia, elimination disorders (enuresis and encopresis), speech disorders, and Tourette's disorder.

21. b. Lee is best diagnosed as having anorexia nervosa, purging type, because she is underweight, afraid of gaining weight, and has a distorted body image. She does not binge (eat a lot of food at one sitting while feeling out of control about the eating), which is the hallmark symptom of bulimia.

22. c. While the other interventions do help about 50 percent of patients with bulimia, cognitive-behavioral therapy helps more than 50 percent (see Table 8-6). Cognitive-behavioral therapy combined with antidepressants is also an effective treatment, helping about 60 percent of patients.

23. d. While drug therapy can be useful, the "bell and pad" method, where a bell rings and wakens the child when he or she starts to urinate in bed, is just as effective and may have longer-lasting effects.

24. b. Todd's behavior is consistent with the criteria for ODD. Conduct disorder is more severe, involving

behaviors such as lying, stealing and running away. ADHD involves an inability to concentrate and/or hyperactive behavior.

25. d. All of the responses are explanations for the development of conduct disorder. They must all be taken into account in order to explain the disorder fully.

26. d. This is a description of MST. PSST focuses on developing interpersonal problem solving skills; PMT helps parents use new approaches to manage the child's behavior at home; and treatment homes take the child out of the home environment.

27. a. Children with ODD show a reduction in serotonin activity.

28. c. ADHD is the most frequently diagnosed disruptive disorder of childhood; in fact, some experts believe it is overdiagnosed in the United States.

29. c. Children with ADHD show some abnormality in the dopamine system.

30. c. Outcome studies have shown that medication is more effective than behavioral therapy, and the combination of both is the most effective for reducing the conduct problems associated with ADHD.

ADDITIONAL EXERCISE

1. girls
2. girls
3. boys
4. girls
5. boys
6. boys
7. girls
8. girls
9. boys
10. boys
11. boys
12. boys
13. boys
14. boys

| Personality Disorders

A GUIDE TO THE READING

As with Chapter 8, this chapter is challenging because of the number of disorders that it covers. The ten personality disorders are arranged in three clusters: odd-eccentric disorders, dramatic-erratic disorders, and anxious-fearful disorders. You will probably have an easier time remembering the various disorders if you learn them by cluster. Be sure to review the DSM-IV boxes that contain the criteria for each of the ten disorders. Personality disorders are enduring, maladaptive ways of perceiving, relating to, and thinking about the world and oneself. They can be difficult to diagnose; be sure to review the section "Diagnosing Personality Disorders" for a complete understanding of the many issues involved in diagnosing personality disorders.

Cluster A: Odd-Eccentric Disorders

The odd-eccentric disorders involve some form of discomfort with or suspicion about other people. It may be easier to remember them by noting that each shares some symptoms with the Axis I disorder schizophrenia. *Schizotypal personality disorder* involves oddities in thinking, perceiving, communicating, and behavior that are similar to, but less severe than, the positive symptoms of schizophrenia. *Schizoid personality disorder* involves the inability to form social relationships; it is similar to the negative symptoms of schizophrenia. *Paranoid personality disorder* involves a pervasive and long-standing distrust of others; it is similar to the paranoia observed in paranoid schizophrenia. The disorders all have a genetic component, appearing more frequently in families of patients with schizophrenia, and all are more common in men than in women. Researchers have also found similarities between schizotypal personality dis-

order and schizophrenia including similar physical and behavioral abnormalities, similar childhood adjustment problems, and parallel cognitive functions and brain structure. Cognitive-behavioral therapy is used for all the Cluster A disorders. Treatment for schizotypal personality disorder may also include social skills training and antipsychotic medications. Group therapy is useful for schizoid personality disorder; for paranoid personality disorder, it is essential to establish a collaborative relationship between the therapist and client.

Cluster B: Dramatic-Erratic Disorders

Cluster B disorders involve overt behavior that is inappropriate and/or extreme. Cluster B disorders include antisocial, histrionic, narcissistic, and borderline personality disorders. Quite a bit has been written about antisocial personality disorder and this is the disorder that is covered in the most depth in the chapter.

Antisocial personality disorder is diagnosed when a patient meets criteria that involve a pervasive pattern of disregard for and violation of the rights of others occurring since age fifteen. This is distinguished from *psychopathy*, which is based on personality traits. Although some people who have psychopathic traits do not meet the criteria for antisocial personality disorder, there is a great deal of overlap between psychopathy and antisocial personality disorder. The personality traits include inadequately motivated antisocial behavior, the absence of a conscience or sense of responsibility to others, and emotional poverty. The absence of shame or remorse is one of the most common characteristics of antisocial personality disorder. The disorder originates as a childhood conduct disorder and is much more common in males than in females. The disorder appears to have multiple, interactive causes. There is evidence for inherited vulnerabilities, such as higher concordance rates in MZ twins than in DZ twins. Adopted children with biological fathers possessing criminal records were more likely to develop the disorder, and adopted children with both a criminal biological father and an unstable adoptive family were even more likely to develop the disorder, illustrating the interaction of genes and environment. Birth and prenatal complications, including maternal drinking and smoking, increase risk of the disorder. Physiological differences have been found in people with antisocial personality disorder, who have generalized reductions in psychophysiological responses including low resting heart rate and decreased activity in the frontal lobes. Family and social factors also contribute to higher rates of antisocial personality disorder including: poverty, high levels of conflict, parental instability, early experiences of witnessing violence, and abuse or neglect. People with antisocial personality disorder also seem to learn differently compared to controls (see Table 9-4 for a summary of these findings and review "response modulation theory" on pp. 395–96). The interaction of all these factors leads to the development of the disorder; see Figure 9-1 for a helpful graph. Antisocial personality disorder is difficult to treat, because the problems are long standing and the client has limited capacity for trust and commitment. Treatment has focused on improving the client's ability to empathize and to process subtle cues that certain behaviors should be inhibited. Behavioral techniques are also used to correct negative patterns of behavior. No specific drug treatments have been found to be helpful. Prevention approaches have focused on changing the environments of at-risk youth.

People with *histrionic personality disorder* draw attention to themselves and react to insignificant events with dramatic emotional displays. Histrionic personality disorder occurs more frequently in women, perhaps because the same underlying causes (a lack of concern for others) are manifested as antisocial personality disorder in men and histrionic personality disorder in women. Theories about the causes of histrionic personality disorder suggest that the extreme dependency need stems from both a fixation at the oral stage of development and inconsistent patterns of reinforcement provided by parents. Little is known about treatment for this disorder, though therapists are encouraged to focus on the highly defensive style and interpersonal dependency needs of the client.

Narcissistic personality disorder is characterized by an inflated sense of self-importance and a lack of empathy. People may develop this disorder if they did not experience an empathic connection with a caregiver when they were very young.

Borderline personality disorder involves instability in four areas: interpersonal relationships, behavior, mood, and self-image. This is a serious disorder that can lead to suicide,

substance abuse, and many other types of self-destructive behavior. The disorder may result from early childhood abuse, a tendency to "split" the world into extremes of good and bad, or biological dysfunction (for example, low serotonin activity and brain trauma). It appears that the best explanation is a diathesis-stress model, wherein heritable traits are triggered by psychosocial experiences. Psychotherapy and certain medications appear to be useful in treating the disorder (see Table 9-5 for a summary, and be sure to review the description of dialectical behavioral therapy on page 405, as it is particularly useful for treating borderline personality disorder).

Cluster C: Anxious-Fearful Disorders

Anxious-fearful disorders are characterized by high levels of worry and anxiety and a tendency to hold feelings in. These disorders are similar to the anxiety disorders diagnosed in Axis I, but they involve pervasive personality traits rather than acute anxiety symptoms. *Avoidant personality disorder* is similar to social phobia and it involves a turning away from relationships due to a fear of appearing foolish. It is different from schizoid personality disorder because patients with avoidant personality disorder want to be close to others, but are unwilling to risk rejection. Biologically based differences in temperament are involved in avoidant personality disorder and treatment is similar to treatment for social phobia (graduated exposure to social settings, social skills training, etc.). *Dependent personality disorder* involves a pervasive and excessive need to be taken care of, which can lead to submissive behavior and fears of separation. Parental behavior that is overprotective and authoritarian probably leads to the development of this disorder. *Obsessive-compulsive personality disorder* involves a pervasive pattern of perfectionism, that can lead to procrastination, overinvolvement in details, and difficulty expressing emotion. It is more frequent among men and is rooted in punitive parental responses to everyday childhood mishaps. Cognitive approaches and supportive psychotherapy have been used to treat the disorder.

TESTING YOUR UNDERSTANDING

Test your understanding of what you have read by working through the following tasks with a classmate.

1. How might you distinguish between someone who is "really shy" and someone who suffers from a personality disorder such as avoidant personality disorder or schizoid personality disorder?

2. There is evidence supporting a genetic factor in some of the personality disorders. List the disorders for

which there is evidence for heritability and describe how the genetic vulnerability develops into a full-blown personality disorder.

3. How would you distinguish between someone with schizotypal disorder and someone with schizophrenia?

4. The shootings at Columbine High School raised a lot of questions about how two teenagers could perpetrate such terrible violence. Based on your knowledge of antisocial personality disorder, explain why this happened and how it might be prevented in the future.

5. Think of someone you know who has unstable relationships with others. Identify which personality disorder the person most resembles, and describe why his or her relationships are so unstable.

6. Borderline personality disorder is commonly diagnosed—perhaps too often. How can you be sure that someone truly has the disorder?

7. Describe how the anxious-fearful personality disorders differ from Axis I anxiety disorders.

Multiple-Choice Questions

1. Personality disorders are diagnosed on which axis?
   a. Axis I
   b. Axis II
   c. Axis III
   d. Axis IV

2. What percentage of the population would meet diagnostic criteria for a personality disorder?
   a. .1 percent
   b. 1 percent
   c. 10 percent
   d. 25 percent

3. One important question researchers have tried to address is the number of personality dimensions that exist. The most well-known theory proposes that there are _____ personality dimensions.
   a. five
   b. ten
   c. sixteen
   d. twenty-three

4. According to Cloninger, who has proposed a biological basis for personality dimensions, people with antisocial personality disorder would be:
   a. high in novelty seeking and harm avoidance, and low in reward dependence and self-directedness.
   b. high in novelty seeking and reward dependence, and low in harm avoidance, and self-directedness.
   c. high in novelty seeking and low in harm avoidance, reward dependence, and self-directedness.
   d. high in novelty seeking and self-directedness, and low in harm avoidance and reward dependence.

5. _____ disorders tend to be more common in men, whereas _____ disorders occur more often in women.
   a. Antisocial; histrionic
   b. Antisocial; borderline
   c. Paranoid; borderline
   d. Paranoid; schizoid

6. Which of the following disorders includes oddities in thinking, perceiving, communicating, and behavior that are serious, but not serious enough to warrant a diagnosis of schizophrenia?
   a. schizoid personality disorder
   b. schizotypal personality disorder
   c. paranoid personality disorder
   d. obsessive-compulsive personality disorder

7. For which Cluster A personality disorder is there the most evidence for the influence of genetic factors?
   a. schizoid personality disorder
   b. schizotypal personality disorder
   c. paranoid personality disorder
   d. There is no evidence for the influence of genetics on any of the Cluster A personality disorders.

8. Malcolm has no friends, seems indifferent to praise and criticism, and is clearly lacking in social skills. Upon questioning, it appears that Malcolm has no desire to form friendships. Malcolm would best be diagnosed with:
   a. schizoid personality disorder.
   b. schizotypal personality disorder.
   c. avoidant personality disorder.
   d. paranoid personality disorder.

9. Robert has always been hypersensitive and seems to always be checking people to make sure they are not trying to hurt him. He seems ready to attack for any little reason and finds special meanings in the innocent behavior of others. Robert would best be diagnosed as having:
   a. schizoid personality disorder.
   b. schizotypal personality disorder.
   c. avoidant personality disorder.
   d. paranoid personality disorder.

10. What type of therapy is used for all of the Cluster A disorders?
    a. group therapy
    b. social skills training
    c. cognitive-behavioral therapy
    d. therapy that emphasizes therapist/patient collaboration

11. Which of the following is true regarding the relationship between psychopathy and antisocial personality disorder?
    a. All patients who score high on measures of psychopathy are diagnosable as antisocial personality disorder.
    b. All patients diagnosed with antisocial personality disorder score high on measures of psychopathy.
    c. Antisocial personality disorder and psychopathy are different constructs and have little overlap.
    d. Antisocial personality disorder and psychopathy are different constructs and there is considerable overlap between them.

12. One of the difficulties in diagnosing antisocial personality disorder is the difference between how people describe themselves and the way others describe them. In diagnosing antisocial personality disorder, which is the best approach?
    a. use information provided by the patient
    b. use information provided by the patient's family
    c. use information provided by the patient's friends
    d. all of the above

13. Which of the following is NOT characteristic of people with antisocial personality disorder?
    a. Their crimes often seem random and impulsive.
    b. They lack conscience.
    c. They do not have the capacity to care deeply about other people.
    d. They experience deep and passionate emotions.

14. Which of the following is NOT true regarding the heritability of antisocial personality disorder?
    a. MZ twins show a higher concordance rate for criminal behavior than DZ twins.
    b. The concordance rates of antisocial personality disorder in MZ twins were higher for traits measured before age eighteen, but not as high for traits measured in adulthood.
    c. The heritability for adult antisocial traits suggests a moderate genetic effect.
    d. Adopted children with criminal biological fathers are more likely to develop antisocial personality disorder than adopted children with criminal adoptive fathers.

15. In a study of reaction times, male prison inmates who scored high on a measure of psychopathic tendencies had _____ than inmates who did not have psychopathic tendencies.
    a. faster reaction times
    b. slower reaction times
    c. faster reaction times for emotional words only
    d. slower reaction times for emotional words only

16. All of the following are true regarding the physiological differences in people with antisocial personality disorder EXCEPT:
    a. increases in frontal lobe activity.
    b. decreases in behavioral inhibition.
    c. low resting heart rate.
    d. reduced skin conductance responses.

17. Which of the following is NOT characteristic of the families of people with antisocial personality disorder?
    a. parental loss through divorce
    b. parental loss through death
    c. high levels of conflict
    d. abuse and/or neglect of children

18. In a famous experiment examining the effects of punishment on learning in a group of individuals with psychopathic tendencies, subjects were presented with a series of trials in which they were to select the "right" lever. If the wrong lever was selected, either a red light would flash or the subject would get an electric shock. David Lykken found that:
    a. those who scored high on measures of psychopathy learned more quickly compared to controls.
    b. those who scored high on measures of psychopathy learned more slowly compared to controls.
    c. those who scored high on measures of psychopathy made more errors resulting in a flashing red light.
    d. those who scored high on measures of psychopathy made more errors resulting in electric shocks.

19. The "response modulation theory" proposes that people who score high on measures of psychopathy have difficulty avoiding punishment. There are several factors, however, that result in those individuals having less difficulty avoiding punishment. Which of the following is NOT one of those factors?
    a. Avoidance is the only goal.
    b. The avoidance goal is made clear in the beginning.
    c. Social disapproval is given when punishment is avoided.
    d. There is an extended period of time between trials.

20. Psychologists have been pessimistic about treating people with antisocial personality disorder for all of the following reasons EXCEPT:
    a. There are no specific drug treatments for antisocial personality disorder.
    b. Cognitive interventions have proven ineffective.
    c. The symptoms are characterological in nature.
    d. The clients have limited capacity for trust and commitment.

21. Olds and his colleagues tested four intervention programs to see if changes in the environment could reduce the risk of developing antisocial personality disorder. Groups 1 and 2 were provided with prenatal and well-child care. Group 3 was provided with prenatal and well-child care and a nurse who visited the women at home during their pregnancy. Group 4 was provided with prenatal and well-child care and a

nurse who visited the women at home through the child's second birthday. Adolescents from which group demonstrated decreases in antisocial behaviors?
a. Groups 1 and 2
b. Group 3
c. Group 4
d. There were no group differences.

22. It has been proposed that the same underlying causes lead to antisocial personality disorder in men and _____ in women.
a. histrionic personality disorder
b. borderline personality disorder
c. narcissistic personality disorder
d. dependent personality disorder

23. Todd asked his roommate to try to keep their room neater, and his roommate refused to speak to him for days. The other day, his roommate flew into a rage because he received a C on a test, even though he had not studied for the test at all. His roommate is constantly talking about schemes for getting rich very quickly, but they all seem pretty farfetched. Todd's roommate would best be diagnosed as having:
a. histrionic personality disorder.
b. borderline personality disorder.
c. narcissistic personality disorder.
d. dependent personality disorder.

24. Sheila seems to be terrified of being abandoned. She has had many relationships, none of which has lasted more than a few months. She is never alone, instead she begins a new relationship as soon as the previous one ends. She is moody and impulsive. She has little control over her anger and experiences chronic feelings of emptiness. Sheila would best be diagnosed as having:
a. histrionic personality disorder.
b. borderline personality disorder.
c. narcissistic personality disorder.
d. dependent personality disorder.

25. According to the text, all of the following are involved in the development of borderline personality disorder EXCEPT:
a. early childhood abuse.
b. a history of head trauma.
c. a tendency to split the world into extremes of good and bad.
d. maladaptive cognitions.

26. Dialectical behavioral therapy appears to be an effective treatment for borderline personality disorder, at least in the short term. This model presumes that patients lack all of the following skills EXCEPT:
a. interpersonal skills.
b. cognitive skills.
c. self-regulation skills.
d. distress tolerance skills.

27. Jennifer is a loner. She avoids new experiences and meeting new people whenever possible. Though she would really like to have some friends, she is always afraid that she will seem stupid if she tries to form a friendship. Jennifer most likely suffers from:
a. schizoid personality disorder.
b. avoidant personality disorder.
c. obsessive-compulsive personality disorder.
d. paranoid personality disorder.

28. Jose, a college student, is sometimes annoying to his friends because he can never decide what classes to take. He asks them every quarter and always calls his parents to get their advice as well. He seems to need advice about everything—where to work, whom to date, and what to wear. Sometimes his friends wish he would just figure some things out for himself. Jose most likely suffers from:
a. avoidant personality disorder.
b. borderline personality disorder.
c. dependent personality disorder.
d. obsessive-compulsive personality disorder.

29. Maria is a procrastinator. She leaves the most important things until last, and gets caught up in less important details. She spends lots of time making long lists and detailed schedules. She is not very emotional and tends to be pretty moralistic. Maria would best be diagnosed with:
a. obsessive-compulsive personality disorder.
b. avoidant personality disorder.
c. histrionic personality disorder.
d. borderline personality disorder.

30. Which of the following is probably least useful in treating obsessive-compulsive personality disorder?
a. cognitive therapy
b. supportive therapy
c. medication
d. all of the above are about equally effective

Fill in the Blank

1. _____ refers to the relatively stable psychological and behavioral characteristics of an individual—the way a person views the world and relates to it.

Personality

2. Various aspects of personality such as optimism and extroversion are referred to as

    _____ _____.   personality traits

3. People with _____ _____ have enduring, inflexible, and maladaptive   personality disorders

    patterns or traits that can affect their thinking, emotional responses, interpersonal

    relations, and impulse control.

4. The tendency for people to meet criteria for more than one personality disorder is

    referred to as _____.   comorbidity

5. The _____ approach is used when a person either meets the behavioral   categorical

    criteria, and falls into a category, or fails to meet criteria and is deemed to not have that

    particular disorder.

6. A _____ approach is used by those who view the behaviors and traits that   dimensional

    define the personality disorders as falling on a continuum.

7. The five personality dimensions in the five-factor model are conscientiousness,

    agreeableness, emotional stability, _____, and _____.   extroversion; openness

8. Cluster A, or the _____-_____ personality disorders, involve   odd-eccentric

    some form of discomfort with or suspicion about other people.

9. _____ _____ _____ is the feeling that one is the object of   Idea of reference

    special attention from others and is one of the symptoms of schizotypal personality

    disorder.

10. _____ is a sense of estrangement from oneself and from one's environment   Depersonalization

    and is a symptom of schizotypal personality disorder.

11. Cluster B disorders, or _____-_____ disorders, involve overt behavior   dramatic-erratic

    that is inappropriate and/or extreme.

12. Antisocial personality disorder is based on behavioral diagnostic criteria, whereas

    _____ is based on personality traits that are assessed with a checklist or   psychopathy

    questionnaire.

13. In the nineteenth century, people who showed persistent antisocial tendencies were

    said to be afflicted by _____ _____, which was viewed as the   moral insanity

    disorder of the will.

14. _____ _____ theory was proposed to make sense of the research   Response modulation

    findings on passive avoidance in patients with antisocial personality disorder.

15. _____ practice is a behavioral technique in which the individual's negative   Positive

    patterns of behavior are corrected and appropriate behavior repeatedly presented. It is

    used to treat patients with antisocial personality disorder.

16. Cluster C disorders, or the _____-_____ disorders, are characterized   anxious-fearful

    by high levels of worry and anxiety, and the tendency to hold feelings in.

LEVELS OF ANALYSIS: EXAMINING THE CHAPTER'S THEMES

Two important themes in this chapter are biological and psychological levels of analysis and treatment of choice.

Biological and Psychological Levels of Analysis

Though it is clear that environmental factors are involved in the formation of a personality disorder, there is also evidence to suggest that at least some of the personality disorders have genetic and biological underpinnings. Some researchers have proposed that personality dimensions, both normal and abnormal, are heritable and involve specific neurotransmitter systems (review Cloninger's work on p. 374 as an example). It is well established that Cluster A disorders are influenced by genetic factors; the biological relatives of schizophrenics are more likely to develop schizotypal, schizoid, and paranoid personality disorders. There are other biological parallels between schizotypal personality disorder and schizophrenia including physical and behavioral abnormalities, cognitive functions, and brain structure. Inherited vulnerabilities clearly play a role in antisocial personality disorder as well; the concordance rate for MZ twins is 35 percent whereas the concordance rate for DZ twins is 13 percent. Birth and prenatal complications can also cause or increase vulnerability, and physiological responses differ in those with antisocial personality disorder compared to controls. These biological factors interact with environmental factors (for instance, parental divorce) to produce antisocial personality disorder. Borderline personality disorder also appears to have some biological correlates, including reduced serotonin and smaller frontal lobes. Like antisocial personality disorder, the diathesis-stress model best explains how borderline personality disorder develops. Biologically based differences in temperament probably lead to the development of avoidant personality disorder. The remaining disorders—narcissistic, histrionic, dependent, and obsessive-compulsive personality disorder—appear to be caused primarily by psychological factors.

Treatment of Choice

Generally, the treatment of choice for personality disorders is some form of psychotherapy. Medications are used for some disorders, but tend to be useful only for treating some of the symptoms. Recently, evidence has been building that the SSRIs are particularly useful for treating personality disorders. In a study comparing drug treatments to psychotherapy, however, researchers found that 82 percent of patients with personality disorders improved when treated with psychotherapy compared to 47 percent of those using medica-

tion (see Box 9-2 for a detailed description of the study).

ANSWER KEY

MULTIPLE-CHOICE QUESTIONS

1. b. Axis I disorders are behavioral syndromes, such as major depression or schizophrenia, that are typically associated with severe symptoms that other people can readily notice. In personality disorders, diagnosed on Axis II, the suffering is often muted.

2. c. The best estimates indicate that 10 to 13 percent of people would meet diagnostic criteria for a personality disorder.

3. a. The five-factor model proposes that there are five personality dimensions: extroversion, conscientiousness, agreeableness, emotional stability, and openness to experience.

4. c. Using Cloninger's model, someone with antisocial personality disorder would be characterized by high novelty seeking, but low harm avoidance, reward dependence, persistence, self-directedness, cooperativeness, and self-transcendence.

5. a. Antisocial, paranoid, and schizoid disorders are more common in men; histrionic disorder is more common in women; and borderline is seen equally in men and women.

6. b. Schizotypal personality disorder includes bizarre, schizophrenia-type symptoms, such as ideas of reference and depersonalization.

7. b. Though there is evidence for the influence of genetics on all of the Cluster A personality disorders, such influence is most established for schizotypal personality disorder. People with this disorder often have biological relatives with schizophrenia, physical and behavioral abnormalities similar to those in patients with schizophrenia, childhood adjustment problems similar to patients with schizophrenia, and cognitive functions and brain structures similar to patients with schizophrenia.

8. a. A defect in the capacity to form social relationships and no desire to have close relationships are characteristic of schizoid personality disorder. Patients with avoidant personality disorder do not have relationships, but they desire to have them and avoid them for fear of being criticized or embarrassed.

9. d. These symptoms are characteristic of people with paranoid personality disorder.

10. c. Cognitive-behavioral therapy is used for all of the Cluster A disorders. Group therapy is useful for treating schizoid personality disorder, social skills training is useful for schizotypal and schizoid disorders, and therapy that emphasizes

therapist/patient collaboration is useful for paranoid personality disorder.

11. d. Although people who meet the criteria for antisocial personality disorder will tend to get high scores on measures of psychopathy, this is not always the case. Furthermore, some people who score very high on measures of psychopathy do not meet the criteria for antisocial personality disorder, though there is considerable overlap.

12. d. According to your text, as is the case with all disorders, the best approach in the diagnosis of antisocial personality disorder is to use multiple sources.

13. d. The three main characteristics of people with antisocial personality disorder are inadequately motivated antisocial behavior, the absence of a conscience and sense of responsibility to others, and emotional poverty.

14. b. The correlations for MZ twins tend to be somewhat higher than those for DZ twins, but mainly for the traits measured in adulthood, indicating that environmental influences are largely responsible for the antisocial traits measured in childhood.

15. d. Inmates with psychopathic tendencies were less physiologically reactive to emotional meaning.

16. a. In general, people with antisocial personality disorder display reductions in psychophysiological responses, including low resting heart rate, reduced skin conductance response, decreases in frontal lobe activity, and decreases or failure of behavioral inhibition.

17. b. Loss of a parent through death does not make a child more likely to develop antisocial personality disorder, indicating that it is not parental loss per se that promotes antisocial behavior, but the emotional climate of the family.

18. d. Those who scored high on measures of psychopathy displayed "passive avoidance learning." In other words, they showed an inability to learn from painful experiences. One explanation for this is that those who score high on measures of psychopathy may actually seek stimulation in order to elevate arousal to an optimal level.

19. c. According to response modulation theory, individuals have less difficulty avoiding punishment if (1) avoidance is the only goal, (2) the avoidance goal is made clear in the beginning, or (3) there is an extended period of time between trials. Social disapproval does not improve avoidance learning.

20. b. Cognitive therapy techniques can be modified to improve the client's ability to process subtle cues that ongoing behavior should be inhibited.

21. c. Adolescents born to women in Group 4 had fewer episodes of running away, fewer arrests and convictions, less promiscuity, and lower rates of cigarette smoking and alcohol consumption.

22. a. It has been proposed that histrionic personality disorder and antisocial personality disorder share the same underlying causes—in particular, a lack of concern for others and a preoccupation with one's own desires. These propensities are channeled into histrionic personality disorder for women and antisocial personality disorder for men.

23. c. People with narcissistic personality disorder are self-absorbed in fantasies of unlimited success and riches. They respond to criticism with rage, shame, or humiliation. They have an exaggerated sense of entitlement, expecting the world owes them something without assuming any responsibility.

24. b. These are symptoms of borderline personality disorder.

25. d. There is no mention of maladaptive cognitions for the development of borderline personality disorder in the text. Explanations for the disorder include psychodynamic factors (the tendency to split, or dichotomize), early childhood abuse, reduced serotonin activity, brain injury, and significantly smaller frontal lobes.

26. b. Dialectical behavioral therapy is based on a motivational-skills deficit model that presumes that people with borderline personality disorder lack important interpersonal, self-regulation (including emotional regulation), and distress tolerance skills.

27. b. People with avoidant personality disorder strongly desire acceptance and affection, but avoid others for fear of appearing foolish.

28. c. People with dependent personality disorder allow others to make their major decisions, to initiate important actions, and to take responsibility for significant areas of their life. They often defer to others regarding many important aspects of living.

29. a. People with obsessive-compulsive personality disorder are perfectionists. This need to be perfect often causes them to procrastinate in important matters and get overly involved in small details. They have difficulty expressing emotion and are overly conscientious.

30. c. Therapies that have been shown to be successful in treating obsessive-compulsive personality disorder include cognitive therapy and supportive therapy.

CHAPTER 10 | The Schizophrenias

A GUIDE TO THE READING

This chapters provides a description of the *nature* of schizophrenia (including its symptoms, subtypes, and associated features), the *causes* of the disorder, and *treatments* for it. You may find it easier to retain the information by grouping it in one of these three categories.

The Nature of Schizophrenia

There are different ways of explaining the nature of schizophrenia. The DSM-IV provides distinct criteria that must be met for a diagnosis of schizophrenia. You should be familiar with these criteria. Notice that there are criteria of time, substance, and symptoms; they are explained in detail on pp. 417–418. Pay special attention to the symptoms and be sure that you can name and define these; some symptoms are probably familiar (delusions, hallucinations), while others may be new to you (disorganized speech, disorganized behavior, and negative symptoms).

There are other associated features that are not part of DSM-IV's diagnostic criteria but that are commonly experienced by people with schizophrenia and that help describe the nature of the disorder. These include a lack of insight, depression, cognitive deficits, perceptual abnormalities, motor deficits, and an inability to comprehend the emotions of others and to interact appropriately with others. Lack of insight and depression are discussed in detail on pp. 424–25. Note that they are inversely related; that is, improvements in insight may lead to a deepening of depression, perhaps because greater insight makes the patient more aware of his or her difficult condition. The other associated features are discussed on pp. 429–35. Hallmark cognitive deficits include lower IQ scores, deficits in short-term memory, difficulties with abstract reasoning, an inability to plan ahead, difficulties in paying attention, and an inability to inhibit response to sensory input. This last cognitive deficit is explained in some detail on pp. 432–33 in which experiments employing prepulse inhibition are discussed. The hallmark perceptual abnormality is a sensory processing deficit. This is explained on p. 434 in which experiments on backward masking tasks are discussed. These experiments indicate that the neurons in the sensory systems do not function normally. Hallmark motor deficits include problems with movement, such as unusual posturing (see photographs on p. 445), and poor performance on tests of coordination. A final important associated feature is an inability to understand the emotions and social motives of others.

The nature of schizophrenia may be further understood by the use of subtypes. The DSM-IV distinguishes the paranoid, disorganized, catatonic, undifferentiated, and residual subtypes (see pp. 425–27 for detailed explanations). Other possible subtypes are acute versus chronic and Type I versus Type II. Acute and chronic schizophrenia are differentiated by how quickly the patient's symptoms develop and how long they have been present. Patients diagnosed as having Type I schizophrenia display a predominance of positive symptoms (e.g., hallucinations and delusions), whereas those diagnosed with Type II schizophrenia display a predominance of negative symptoms (e.g., negative affect, alogia, avolition).

Finally, it is important to note that the development of schizophrenia is related to age, gender, and social factors. A person is more likely to be diagnosed with schizophrenia if he is male, in late adolescence or early adulthood, and poor. See pp. 428–29 for more detailed epidemiological information.

The Causes of Schizophrenia

A good way to understand the causes of this disorder is to use the diathesis-stress model. According to this model, genetic and biological factors make some people vulnerable to schizophrenia. The vulnerable may or may not develop the disorder; whether they do depends on the level of environmental stress to which they are exposed. It is easier to understand the various findings supporting both a genetic/biological model and an environmental model of the etiology of schizophrenia with the diathesis-stress model in mind.

Twin, family, and adoption studies all provide evidence for a genetic component to schizophrenia. Although there is some controversy about the numbers (see Table 10-2 for a summary), it is clear that identical twins have a higher concordance rate than do fraternal twins and that siblings and children born to parents with schizophrenia have a higher rate of the disorder than the overall population. In addition, children of parents with schizophrenia who are raised in adoptive homes are still much more likely to develop the disorder than are controls. These studies provide considerable, although not complete, support for a genetic cause.

There is also ample evidence that genetics alone cannot account for schizophrenia. First, the concordance rate among identical twins is nowhere near 100 percent and the majority of people with schizophrenia have no immediate family members with the disorder. Second, there is evidence that a disordered environment contributes to the development of the disorder. Exposure to a viral infection during the second trimester of gestation may contribute to a vulnerability to schizophrenia, which would explain why so many individuals diagnosed with schizophrenia were born in early spring. And maternal exposure to stress and problems during delivery have also been shown to be related to schizophrenia. In fact, there is quite of bit of evidence that mothers who have schizophrenia experience many more complications during pregnancy and in giving birth than do normals.

Additional evidence points to a biological basis for schizophrenia; this includes differences in neurochemistry, brain structure, and brain functioning in people with schizophrenia. These biological abnormalities give us more clues about possible causes of schizophrenia and are described in detail on pp. 446–52. Biological abnormalities that have been observed across many studies include excessive dopamine activity, enlarged ventricles, reductions in the size of many brain regions, and lower levels of brain activity when completing tasks.

The search for causes has also revealed a number of developmental precursors to schizophrenia. Children who go on to be diagnosed with schizophrenia in late adolescence or adulthood show signs of abnormality in motor, interpersonal, and cognitive behavior. In fact, the range of behaviors shown by these children looks very similar to schizotypal personality disorder, which researchers suspect may be a risk factor for schizophrenia (see p. 446 for detailed discussion). High-risk children also have more difficulty adjusting to adolescence, and their level of risk is related to the severity of these developmental precursors.

Although schizophrenia clearly has a biological basis, there are several familial and social factors that may affect the course of the disease. The level of "expressed emotion" (hostility and overinvolvement with the patient) is related to the risk of relapse. There is also a relationship between the rate of schizophrenia and social class. A higher proportion of people with schizophrenia are found among those in the lower classes than among those in the middle and upper classes. This is most likely due to "social drift," that is, those with the disorder tend to drift downwards to the lower social classes. Membership in the lower classes, in turn, is likely to affect the course of the disorder, probably mostly due to the considerable stress associated with poverty. Although stress alone (without a predisposition) does not cause schizophrenia, it is often the trigger for psychotic episodes. The course and expression of schizophrenia is also influenced by culture (review p. 455 for specifics).

The Treatment of Schizophrenia

The text emphasizes the biological treatment of schizophrenia through medication. The use of antipsychotic drugs has revolutionized treatment and has dramatically reduced the hospital stays of those diagnosed with the disorder. Adherence to medication regimens may be the most important factor affecting the course of the disorder. There are two types of antipsychotics: the early antipsychotics and the atypical antipsychotics. The early antipsychotics bind to dopamine receptors and are quite successful at eliminating the positive symptoms of schizophrenia. Side effects are a problem, however, with the most serious being the development of *tardive dyskinesia,* strange movements of the mouth and tongue. The atypical antipsychotics block fewer dopamine receptors and also block certain types of serotonin receptor. These drugs have fewer side effects and are more effective in combating the negative symptoms of schizophrenia.

In addition to medication, a number of psychosocial and cognitive treatments have been developed to help with rehabilitation. Treatments for cognitive rehabilitation have had mixed results. Some promising cognitive treatments have resulted in increases in attention, memory, accuracy in identifying social cues, and actual changes in the pattern of brain activity, while others, such as training to improve executive functions, have been disappointing. Psychodynamic therapy has not been successful in treating patients with schizophrenia, but a number of social and familial approaches seem beneficial, including social-skills training, family therapy, and comprehensive programs that help patients with schizophrenia to rejoin the community (see pp. 464–65 for a detailed description of one of these programs).

TESTING YOUR UNDERSTANDING

Test your understanding of what you have read by working through the following tasks with a classmate.

1. Explain to a friend what the typical symptoms of schizophrenia are. Include examples of positive and negative symptoms.

2. Explain why insight may lead to depression for patients with schizophrenia.

3. Describe the characteristics of each of the following subtypes: paranoid, disorganized, undifferentiated, residual.

4. Imagine that your friend tells you his cousin has recently been diagnosed with schizophrenia. He wants to know how likely she is to recover. What would you tell him are the signs of a positive prognosis?

5. Describe some of the typical cognitive, perceptual, and motor deficits that accompany schizophrenia.

6. Your friend doesn't understand why his cousin developed schizophrenia when so many others around her did not. Explain what might have caused her to develop the disorder.

7. Explain three ways that the brain of an individual diagnosed with schizophrenia may differ from the norm.

8. Are social environment and the culture related to the expression of schizophrenia? If so, in what ways?

9. What kinds of treatment might your friend expect his cousin to receive?

Multiple-Choice Questions

1. The symptoms of schizophrenia vary a great deal, thus leading experts to believe that there is more than one type of schizophrenia and that the various types have several different causes. All patients with schizophrenia share one thing in common, however, which is:
   a. a similar response to antipsychotic medications.
   b. the presence of one or more psychotic symptoms.
   c. serious motor disturbance.
   d. extreme cognitive abnormalities.

2. Early psychologists had varying views on the causes and appropriate treatments of schizophrenia. Which of the following correctly summarizes the viewpoints of the psychologists listed?

   a. Kraepelin and Bleuler, biological; Meyer, individual maladjustment
   b. Kraepelin, biological; Bleuler and Meyer, individual maladjustment
   c. Kraepelin and Bleuler, individual maladjustment; Meyer, biological
   d. Kraepelin, individual maladjustment; Meyer and Bleuler, biological

3. Which of the following is NOT one of the DSM-IV criteria for schizophrenia?
   a. hallucinations
   b. delusions
   c. dysphoric mood
   d. disorganized speech

4. The text quotes one of Bleuler's patients as writing: "I wish you then a good, happy, joyful, healthy, blessed and fruitful year, and many good wine-years to come, as well as a healthy and good apple-year, and sauerkraut and cabbage and squash and seed year." This is an example of:
   a. word salad.
   b. derailment.
   c. neologism.
   d. loose association.

5. All of the following are examples of disorganized behavior discussed in the text EXCEPT:
   a. poor hygiene.
   b. inappropriate clothing.
   c. catatonia.
   d. missing appointments.

6. All of the following are negative symptoms of schizophrenia EXCEPT:
   a. significant decrease in speech.
   b. depression.
   c. lack of energy or interest.
   d. flat affect.

7. Which of the following BEST describes the role of insight and depression in schizophrenia?
   a. Impaired insight is a hallmark of schizophrenia; patients become depressed when they show improvement in insight.
   b. Impaired insight is a hallmark of schizophrenia; patients become depressed when their level of insight deteriorates.
   c. Impaired insight is quite common, but depression is relatively rare.
   d. Depression is quite common, but impaired insight is relatively rare.

8. A patient is very silly and incoherent, and bursts into laughter at odd times. He experiences delusions, but they tend to be very disorganized, and he has particularly poor grooming. He would most likely be classified as suffering from which of the following subtypes?
   a. paranoid

b. undifferentiated
c. disorganized
d. residual

9. Which of the following patients has the best prognosis?
   a. Tina, who had a sudden onset, poor premorbid functioning and a predominance of positive symptoms
   b. Tony, who had a sudden onset, good premorbid functioning, and predominantly positive symptoms
   c. Kaz, who had a gradual onset, good premorbid functioning, and predominantly positive symptoms
   d. Maya, who had a sudden onset, good premorbid functioning, and predominantly negative symptoms

10. Which of the following is TRUE regarding the risk of developing schizophrenia?
    a. The first episode of schizophrenia is most likely to occur in middle adulthood.
    b. Women tend to have their first episode at a younger age than do men.
    c. More women than men are diagnosed with the disorder.
    d. The long-term prognosis is better for women than it is for men.

11. Which of the following is FALSE regarding the cognitive deficits usually experienced by individuals with schizophrenia?
    a. They tend to have higher IQ scores than the general population.
    b. They are "overinclusive" because they have an impaired capacity to resist distracting information.
    c. Of the cognitive deficits they experience, attentional difficulties are the most distressing.
    d. They experience memory impairment, specifically impaired short-term and explicit memory.

12. Several studies of the cognitive deficits associated with schizophrenia have been done. Which of the following is NOT consistent with those studies?
    a. Patients with schizophrenia make more errors on the continuous performance test (CPT). This provides evidence that they are unable to filter out distractions.
    b. Patients with schizophrenia require a longer time period between the presentation of the target and the mask on backward masking tasks. This indicates that they have some abnormality in sensory processing.
    c. People with schizophrenia exhibit impaired prepulse inhibition; that is, they are less likely to experience a reduced startle response following a prepulse. This suggests that patients with schizophrenia have difficulty inhibiting responses to sensory input.
    d. Mice who were missing a gene for a certain type of serotonin receptor showed an increase in pre-pulse inhibition. This suggests that serotonin is involved in the impaired prepulse inhibition experienced by patients with schizophrenia.

13. Although virtually every study shows a higher concordance rate for schizophrenia among monozygotic (identical) than dizygotic (fraternal) twins, the estimates vary quite a bit. Which of the following is the most likely explanation for these findings?
    a. Environment also accounts for a significant part of the variance in who develops schizophrenia.
    b. The makeup of participants differs from study to study: some studies include more women and some more men.
    c. The makeup of participants differs from study to study: some studies employ patients with more severe cases of schizophrenia than do others.
    d. all of the above

14. Which of the following is NOT included in the evidence for the role of environmental factors in the development of schizophrenia?
    a. When both parents have schizophrenia, their children have a 46 percent chance of developing the disorder.
    b. Of the individuals diagnosed with schizophrenia, 89 percent have no known relatives with the disorder.
    c. Concordance rates among monozygotic twins are not 100 percent.
    d. Monozygotic (identical) twins may share more similar environmental experiences than do dizygotic (fraternal) twins.

15. More individuals who develop schizophrenia are born in certain months of the year. What explanation do researchers offer to account for this?
    a. The cold weather during the winter months make the babies more vulnerable to "catching" schizophrenia.
    b. Parents with a vulnerability toward schizophrenia have irregular mating patterns.
    c. The availability of certain neurotransmitters varies with the seasons.
    d. Pregnant women are more likely to get the flu during the winter months.

16. Which of the following is FALSE regarding the impact of pregnancy and birth complications on the development of schizophrenia?
    a. Maternal exposure to stress during pregnancy is related to schizophrenia.
    b. Reduced levels of oxygen to the baby during delivery are related to schizophrenia.
    c. Even if a child is not genetically vulnerable, complications during delivery can create a vulnerability to the disorder.
    d. Monozygotic twins who are discordant for schizophrenia experience a higher than average rate of obstetrical complications.

17. Based on high-risk, retrospective, and follow-back studies, all of the following are true regarding the developmental precursors of schizophrenia EXCEPT that:
    a. early signs of risk fall into several domains of behavior: motor, interpersonal, and cognitive.
    b. most children who go on to develop schizophrenia experience some form of hallucination in childhood.
    c. the most pronounced adjustment problems occur in adolescence.
    d. the more severe the childhood problems, the more severe the illness.

18. In a recent prospective study, adolescents diagnosed with schizotypal personality disorder (SPD) showed more involuntary movements, more abnormalities in their fingertips, more physical anomalies, and had higher levels of cortisol compared to control groups of healthy adolescents and adolescents with other personality disorders. From this, you can conclude that:
    a. there is a genetic factor in the development of SPD.
    b. SPD, like schizophrenia, may be related to prenatal complications.
    c. neither a nor b are correct.
    d. both a and b are correct.

19. With the advent of more sophisticated strategies for assessing the brain, several pieces of evidence have emerged that support the dopamine hypothesis. Which of the following is NOT one of those pieces of evidence?
    a. Postmortem examinations of brains of people diagnosed with schizophrenia reveal a relatively low number of dopamine receptors.
    b. The drugs that were initially successful in treating schizophrenia worked by blocking the activity of dopamine.
    c. There is a greater release of dopamine by neurons in the striatum in individuals with schizophrenia.
    d. Large doses of drugs that increase dopamine (e.g., L-Dopa, cocaine) can create psychosis.

20. Which of the following is NOT a neurotransmitter that may be implicated in schizophrenia?
    a. GABA
    b. noradrenaline
    c. glutamate
    d. serotonin

21. Individuals with schizophrenia show a number of structural anomalies in their brains, including enlarged ventricles and reduced frontal and temporal lobes. The BEST conclusion that can be drawn about the cause of these abnormalities is that:
    a. they are the result of schizophrenia, rather than the cause.
    b. they are due to damage that occurred prenatally.
    c. they are due to genetic factors.
    d. b and c

22. The brains of individuals who have schizophrenia function differently than do the brains of those considered normal. The specific functional abnormality most likely to cause schizophrenia is:
    a. general overactivity of the brain.
    b. reduced activity in frontal lobes when performing cognitive tasks.
    c. reduced activity in temporal lobes when asked to identify odors.
    d. impairment in the connections among various regions of the brain.

23. The characteristics of the family that seem most closely related to the course of schizophrenia are:
    a. the infant-mother relationship.
    b. the level of expressed emotion.
    c. abuse during childhood.
    d. apathy toward the patient.

24. Which of the following is the BEST explanation for the relationship between schizophrenia and low social class?
    a. People who have schizophrenia tend to drift downward as a result of their illness.
    b. The stress of poverty leads to the onset of schizophrenia.
    c. The parents of an individual with schizophrenia are more likely to be ill and therefore more likely to be a member of a low social class.
    d. Low social class is associated with environmental risk factors, such as exposure to toxins.

25. Culture has been shown to have an effect on schizophrenia. Which of the following is NOT an example of the effect of culture on schizophrenia?
    a. Culture affects the expression of schizophrenia.
    b. Culture affects the rate of schizophrenia.
    c. Culture affects the course of schizophrenia.
    d. Culture affects the content of psychotic symptoms.

26. What is the factor that has the greatest influence on the course of schizophrenia?
    a. stress
    b. premorbid functioning
    c. gender
    d. adherence to medication regimens.

27. All of the following are side effects of early antipsychotic medications EXCEPT:
    a. flattened affect.
    b. tardive dyskinesia.
    c. weight gain or loss.
    d. extrapyramidal movements.

28. Although the amount of time spent in the hospital has declined radically since the advent of antipsychotic medications, readmission rates have soared. All of the following are reasons for this "revolving door" phenomenon EXCEPT:
    a. the high rate of unemployment among people who have schizophrenia.
    b. the fact that only very few pills can be given to the patient at any one time.
    c. inadequate follow-up services.
    d. lack of adherence to medications.

29. Which of the following is the MOST accurate statement regarding cognitive rehabilitation for patients with schizophrenia?
    a. Cognitive treatments have been very successful in treating patients with schizophrenia.
    b. When properly implemented, cognitive treatments can replace medication.
    c. The results of cognitive treatments have been disappointing for the most part.
    d. The results of cognitive treatments have been mixed.

30. Which of the following BEST represents the results of a study comparing a biopsychosocial treatment (ACT) with brokered case management (HMO) of schizophrenia?
    a. Both treatments worked very well in helping patients with schizophrenia make the transition from a hospital to the community.
    b. The HMO treatment was superior.
    c. The ACT treatment was superior.
    d. Neither treatment proved successful.

Fill in the Blank

1. _____ _____ is a phrase coined by Emil Kraeplin, the first to advance a widely accepted classification system to describe what we now call *schizophrenia*. The phrase literally means "early, or premature, deterioration."

   Dementia praecox

2. Delusions of _____ are characterized by the belief that one is an especially important figure, such as Jesus Christ or the president of the United States.

   grandeur

3. Individuals exhibiting delusions of _____ believe that someone is controlling their thoughts or behaviors.

   control

4. People who believe that others have malevolent intentions or are "out to get" them may be exhibiting delusions of _____.

   persecution

5. Delusions of _____ are characterized by the unfounded belief that certain events or people have special significance for the person.

   reference

6. _____ delusions are characterized by the unverified belief that something is drastically wrong with one's body.

   Somatic

7. _____ hallucinations are the most common form of hallucination experienced by individuals with schizophrenia.

   Auditory

8. An individual with schizophrenia who shifts from one unconnected topic of conversation to another is exhibiting _____.

   derailment

9. _____ associations are produced by the rhyming of words.

   Clang

10. A person exhibiting _____ _____ shows no discernible signs of emotion, no emotional expression.

    flat affect

11. _____ is characterized by a marked decrease in the amount of speech produced.

    Alogia

12. _____ is characterized by an apparent lack of energy or interest in activities.

    Avolition

13. Hallucinations, delusions, and disorganized thoughts and behaviors are examples of _____ symptoms.

    positive

14. Flat affect, alogia, and avolition are examples of _____ symptoms.

    negative

15. The index case or twin who is first seen at a psychological clinic is called the _____.

    proband

16. _____ disorders are influenced by multiple genes.

    Polygenic

17. _____-_____ technology is used to evaluate the occurrence of a familial disorder alongside a genetic marker.

    Linkage-analysis

18. _____ is the neurotransmitter that has been most implicated in schizophrenia.

    Dopamine

19. Families that tend toward hostility and overinvolvement are said to display _____ _____.

    expressed emotion

20. _____ _____ is a side effect of some antipsychotic medications that involves involuntary smacking of the mouth and tongue.

    Tardive dyskinesia

LEVELS OF ANALYSIS: EXAMINING THE CHAPTER'S THEMES

Three themes are addressed explicitly in relation to schizophrenia: biological and psychological levels of analysis, the development of the disease, and the treatment of choice.

Biological and Psychological Levels of Analysis

Both of these levels of analysis were present in early studies of schizophrenia. Eugene Bleuler and Emil Kraepelin, two of the earliest psychiatrists to define and study the disorder, were convinced that the causes of schizophrenia were biological. They laid the groundwork for the biological analysis of the causes of and treatments for the disease. At about the same time, Adolf Meyer, a brain pathologist, was convinced that there were no biological differences between patients with schizophrenia and normals. He proposed that individual maladjustment lay at the root of the disorder and instigated an analysis of the interpersonal and learning experiences involved in schizophrenia. Twin, family, and adoption studies conducted since then have confirmed that there is both a genetic and an environmental component to the disorder.

These two levels of analysis are integrated in the diathesis-stress model in which a diathesis, or vulnerability, to schizophrenia is a necessary but not sufficient cause for the development of the disorder. Vulnerability to schizophrenia is most likely genetic, although there is some evidence that prenatal exposure to a virus and complications during delivery can contribute as well. For people with a vulnerability to schizophrenia, a sufficient level of environmental stress is necessary to develop the disorder.

Social factors, while not necessarily causal, have been shown to be related to the clinical course of schizophrenia. The higher prevalence of the disorder among the poor seems to be due primarily to downward social drift; however, there is some evidence that the stress of poverty may lead to a relapse and a generally poorer prognosis. Familial factors, particularly high emotional expression in the family, is also related to higher risk of a relapse. Finally, culture affects the clinical expression and course of the illness. The content of delusions and hallucinations clearly shows a cultural flavor. Patients with schizophrenia from developing nations fare far better than do patients in developed nations, probably due to the family's response to the illness.

Development

Schizophrenia is clearly related to human development. The first schizophrenic episode usually occurs in late adolescence or early adulthood. It rarely occurs in children or in adults over age thirty-five.

Treatment of Choice

For schizophrenia, the treatment of choice is clearly psychotropic medication. These medications are highly successful in relieving the positive symptoms of schizophrenia and the newer, atypical, medications show promise in alleviating the negative symptoms as well. Adherence to medication regimines is the most influential variable in predicting the clinical course of schizophrenia. Patients on medication are less likely to suffer a relapse, and the earlier patients start medication, the better their long-term prognosis.

There is little evidence that psychodynamic therapies are useful for treating schizophrenia. Cognitive rehabilitation, social-skills training, and family therapy, however, may contribute to recovery when used in conjunction with medications.

ANSWER KEY

MULTIPLE-CHOICE QUESTIONS

1. b. All individuals who have schizophrenia experience one or more psychotic symptoms. Response to medications and cognitive and motor abnormalities vary a great deal among patients.

2. a. Kraepelin was the first to classify severe psychological disorders; he believed that schizophrenia was caused by a chemical imbalance that interfered with the nervous system. Bleuler coined the term *schizophrenia* and believed that brain disease caused the disorder. Meyer believed schizophrenia was the result of inadequate early learning that led to individual maladjustment.

3. c. The DSM-IV criteria for schizophrenia include hallucinations, delusions, disorganized speech, disorganized or catatonic behavior, and negative symptoms (alogia, avolition, and flat affect). In addition, patients must have experienced symptoms for at least six months and have had a marked deterioration of functioning (temporal criteria) as well as a gross impairment of reality testing; more than one psychological process must also be affected (e.g., thought, perception, emotion, etc.; substantive criteria).

4. d. *Loose association* refers to subtle irregularities in the connections patients make. Here, the word "fruitful" leads to some uncommon associations (e.g., wine, apple, squash). *Word salad* is speech that is so disorganized that it makes no sense. *Derailment* refers to speech that shifts from one topic to another with no apparent connection. *Neologisms* are new words that, in this context, have only private meaning.

5. d. Poor hygiene, inappropriate clothing, and catatonia are all classic examples of disorganized behavior.

6. b. Depression is an associated feature of schizophrenia but is not one of the negative symptoms.

7. a. Both lack of insight and depression are very common among people with schizophrenia; there is an inverse relationship between insight and depression.

8. c. This is a good description of disorganized schizophrenia. Patients diagnosed with paranoid schizophrenia fabricate systematized and complex delusions; patients with undifferentiated schizophrenia do not meet criteria for other subtypes but show psychotic symptoms; patients with residual schizophrenia have an absence of prominent symptoms but have two or more distressing but minor symptoms (e.g., withdrawal, peculiar behavior, flat affect, etc.)

9. b. Patients who experience a sudden onset of symptoms, who had good premorbid functioning, and who experience mostly positive symptoms have the best prognosis.

10. d. Prognosis is better for women, perhaps because of their social skills or because of the effects of estrogen on neurotransmitters. The age of first episode is usually late adolescence or early adulthood, and men are more likely to be diagnosed and diagnosed at a younger age.

11. a. Individuals with schizophrenia actually score lower than the general population on IQ tests. All the other answers are accurate descriptions of cognitive impairments.

12. b. All of the experiments and their implications are described correctly; however, option b refers to a sensory processing difficulty, not a cognitive impairment. Option c refers to a cognitive deficit in response to sensory input. For a good example of problems in basic sensory processing, see the case study on p. 434.

13. c. Option c is the best choice because the concordance rate is higher for the twins of severely disturbed patients. Option a is true but is not the best explanation for this particular phenomena.

14. a. The evidence in option a supports the importance of genetic factors in schizophrenia.

15. d. Maternal exposure to viral infections during the fourth through sixth months (the second trimester) of pregnancy is related to increased risk of developing schizophrenia.

16. c. It is not yet known whether obstetrical complications alone can create a vulnerability to schizophrenia. Some believe that genetics and obstetrical complications interact to produce schizophrenia.

17. b. Children rarely experience hallucinations. All the other responses are true.

18. d. These anomalies are indicative of both genetic factors and prenatal complications.

19. a. Individuals with schizophrenia have a much higher number of dopamine receptors than do normals. This is consistent with the hypothesis that it is an increase in dopamine activity that causes schizophrenia.

20. b. All but noradrenaline have been implicated in schizophrenia.

21. d. There is evidence to implicate both prenatal damage and a genetic component in schizophrenia. Again, one plausible explanation is that an inherited predisposition makes some fetuses more sensitive to obstetrical complications.

22. d. Options b and c are found in the brains of individuals with other disorders as well; it is impairment rather than excessive activity that seems to be the key functional abnormality for individuals with schizophrenia.

23. b. High levels of expressed emotion are related to a risk of relapse; childhood experiences have not been shown to be related to the course of schizophrenia.

24. a. The greatest support has been garnered for option a, the social drift hypothesis.

25. b. The rate of schizophrenia is about the same worldwide.

26. d. All of these affect the course, but adherence to medication regimines has the greatest effect.

27. a. Although the early antipsychotics did not effectively treat the negative symptoms of schizophrenia, they did not cause them.

28. b. Patients do not need to be hospitalized in order to get medications. The other three responses are the top reasons for patients returning to the hospital.

29. d. Some treatments have proven successful (for example, training in attention and memory), while others have been disappointing (for example, training to improve executive functions). Cognitive rehabilitation is always used as an adjunct to medication therapy.

30. c. Compared to patients in HMO treatment, those in ACT programs experienced greater reductions in symptoms and were more satisfied with their treatment.

CHAPTER 11 | Late-Onset Disorders

A GUIDE TO THE READING

This chapter discusses the physical and psychological vulnerabilities to the disorders of aging, the characteristics of late-onset disorders such as dementia, and the causes and treatments of late-onset depression, anxiety, substance abuse, and psychotic disorders.

Vulnerability to the Disorders of Aging

The incidence of mental illness for those over the age of sixty-five has been about 13 percent over the past years. An aging person's vulnerability to psychological problems is very much related to their mental health and adjustment level earlier in life. People who were healthy tend to remain healthy. However, some vulnerabilities increase with age. Biological changes include declines in each of the following areas: the ability of cells to synthesize proteins, immune functioning, sensory acuity, the structure and function of the brain, and sex hormones (see pp. 472–74 for a detailed description of these declines). There are also psychological declines in cognitive skills, particularly in the ability to store new information and the reaction time for visual and auditory stimuli. Negative life events prior to age sixty-five, a history of depression, and decreased social contacts all contribute to vulnerability for those over age sixty-five. In contrast, good emotional health prior to age sixty-five and life skills in coping serve to decrease psychological vulnerability.

Dementia and Delirium

Dementia is a gradual decline in cognitive functioning that includes impairment in memory as well as impairment in at least one of the following areas: language, motor skills,

identification of familiar objects, the ability to plan ahead, and the ability to inhibit inappropriate behavior (see pp. 477, 483, and 486 for DSM-IV criteria). Delirium, in contrast, is a cognitive disturbance due to a medical condition or substance intoxication that has a rapid onset, fluctuates over time, and usually responds rapidly to treatment (see p. 487 for DSM-IV criteria). Dementia has a high rate of comorbidity with psychotic and depressive symptoms. There are many types of dementia, but the two most common are Alzheimer's disease and vascular dementia. Be familiar with the symptom profile of each. Alzheimer's is described in detail on pages 477–79; vascular dementia on pages 483–85. Though the cause of Alzheimer's is not known, it can be definitively diagnosed in an autopsy by the presence of *neurofibrillary tangles,* an accumulation of protein between neurons, and *senile plaques,* a loss of cells. Hypotheses about causes are being generated based on biological correlates to the disease, such as the presence of beta amyloid in the cerebral spinal fluid, abnormally low levels of acetylcholine, increases in aluminum in the body, and the heightened risk of developing the disorder in relatives of those with Alzheimer's. There are currently no effective treatments for Alzheimer's, but many potential treatments are being explored (for example, acetylcholine agonists; review pages 481–83 and Box 11-2 for a summary of this research). Vascular dementia is caused by a stroke, or a series of strokes, that result in areas of dead brain tissue. The onset is much quicker than that of Alzheimer's and mental health is more impaired.

Other forms of dementia involve degeneration in different areas of the brain. *Frontal lobe dementia* involves marked changes in personality and language problems, and *dementia due to Parkinson's disease* involves the dopamine neurons in subcortical regions of the brain. Patients with Parkinson's disease experience memory loss and deficits in executive functions, such as planning and organizing (see p. 486 for DSM-IV criteria).

Mood and Anxiety Disorders in the Elderly

Generally, rates of depression and anxiety decline as people age; those over the age of sixty-five have the lowest rate of clinical depression. There is, however, a sharp increase in depression in those over eighty and depression is the most common psychological disorder among the elderly. Those who experience physical illness and disability are the most at risk for developing depression, and depression in the elderly is often accompanied by cognitive deficits and suicide. Depression in the elderly is treated in much the same way as depression in younger people, though age biases on the part of the patient or the therapist may interfere with therapy. See the case of Mr. B for a good example of depression and treatment for an older person (pp. 490–91 and 491–92).

Anxiety in the elderly is caused by the same factors that cause anxiety in younger people. However, the elderly are especially inclined to experience anxiety about death and anxiety about the prospect of becoming very ill and dependent. Cognitive-behavioral therapy, biofeedback, and exercise have proven effective for treating anxiety in the elderly. Drug treatments are also useful, but the side effects (such as impaired cognitive functioning) and potential interactions with other drugs must be carefully weighed before prescribing antianxiety drugs for those over sixty-five.

Substance Abuse and Psychosis in the Elderly

The use of alcohol and drugs declines with age, but the consequences of use can be much more severe. Abuse of prescription medications is a common substance abuse problem among the elderly (see case study on pp. 493–94 for an illustration). There is also concern that substance abuse will increase as the baby boom generation become senior citizens, therefore researchers are calling for new approaches to treating addicts who are elderly. *Delusional disorder* involves a nonbizarre delusion (that is, something that could actually happen, such as someone poisoning your food) that occurs for at least one month (see p. 495 for DSM-IV criteria). It is usually first diagnosed in middle or late adulthood. The most common type of delusion is the persecutory type (people plotting against you), though there are many types (review p. 495 for a list and examples). The cause of this disorder is unknown, but it may stem from the same genetic causes as schizophrenia. Insufficient social contact and sensory deficits may also contribute to the disorder (see the case of Alice on p. 496 for an illustration). It is usually treated by antipsychotic drugs, though side effects include loss of emo-

tion and decreased motivation. Psychotherapy is also beneficial in many cases.

The first onset of schizophrenia usually occurs before age forty, however 4 percent of males and 18 percent of females with the disorder experience their first onset after age sixty-five (see Figure 11-4 for a graph of ages of onset for men and women). Late onset appears to be influenced by the protective effect of estrogen, hereditary factors, and the loss of social support. As with delusional disorder, antipsychotic medications are used to treat late-onset schizophrenia, but special care must be taken to monitor side effects.

TESTING YOUR UNDERSTANDING

Test your understanding of what you have read by working through the following tasks with a classmate.

1. Your father has begun to make comments about his age. He seems to be afraid of getting older and sometimes mentions that he expects to be depressed and maybe even "crazy" when he becomes a senior citizen. Explain to your father why that is very unlikely, and what his biases are that make him think that the elderly have high rates of mental illness.

2. Though the rates of most mental disorders decrease with age, those over age sixty-five do have increased biological vulnerabilities to certain mental disorders. List those vulnerabilities, and how psychological factors can protect or increase vulnerability in the elderly.

3. Your aunt is concerned about your grandmother's memory. She is not sure if your grandmother is experiencing "normal" changes in memory or is developing Alzheimer's disease. How would you help your aunt diagnose your grandmother?

4. If your grandmother does appear to be suffering from Alzheimer's, explain to your aunt what caused it and what she can do to help.

5. Distinguish between Alzheimer's disease, vascular dementia, and delirium.

6. What major risk factors for depression, anxiety, and suicide are specific to the elderly?

7. Explain why late-onset schizophrenia is more common in women than in men.

Multiple-Choice Questions

1. Demographers predict that there will be an increase of at least ____ percent in the population over age 65 by 2020.
   a. 20

b. 30
c. 50
d. 60

2. Though personality styles tend to remain the same, there are some developmental trends that result in changing personality styles with age. Which of the following is NOT a change that occurs as people age?
   a. Older adults have less of a preference for routines.
   b. Older adults are less impulsive.
   c. Older adults are more suspicious.
   d. Older adults are more introverted.

3. About what percent of those over age sixty-five will have suffered from a mental illness, other than a cognitive disorder, during the previous year?
   a. 4 percent
   b. 8 percent
   c. 13 percent
   d. 21 percent

4. In general, which model provides the most useful framework for understanding the causes of mental illness in the elderly?
   a. the biological model
   b. the psychological model
   c. the diathesis-stress model
   d. the social model

5. Which of the following is NOT one of the explanations given for why there is a 10 percent reduction in weight and volume of the brain by the age of eighty?
   a. loss of neurons in the substantia nigra and the temporal region
   b. loss of neurons in the brain stem
   c. decrease in the size of neurons
   d. decline in the number of synapses among the neurons

6. There are reductions in several hormonal systems that play a role in the loss of abilities that occur with advanced age. Supplements for which of the following hormones have been linked to the maintenance of youthful characteristics such as higher muscle mass in laboratory animals?
   a. thyroid stimulating hormone
   b. growth hormone
   c. sex hormones
   d. DHEA

7. Joon has just turned seventy. Which of the following cognitive skills is the most likely to be intact?
   a. the ability to store new information
   b. the speed of her reaction to visual stimuli
   c. her vocabulary
   d. the speed of her reaction to auditory stimuli

8. Which of the following helps reduce the likelihood that a person over the age of sixty-five will develop depression?
   a. fewer negative life events before the age of sixty-five
   b. no history of depression in the family
   c. maintaining social contacts
   d. all of the above

9. Which of the following is NOT a symptom of dementia?
   a. a decline in autonomic functions such as breathing
   b. a decline in motor skills
   c. deterioration in the ability to communicate with language
   d. a decline in the ability to inhibit inappropriate behavior

10. Will is seventy-two years old. He seems to have become more and more forgetful over the last few years. He also has had difficulty with simple household tasks, such as cooking. This also seems to have become worse over the past two years. He tends to get disoriented easily and is losing his ability to write even simple letters. Will would best be diagnosed as having:
    a. Alzheimer's disease.
    b. vascular dementia.
    c. frontal lobe dementia.
    d. dementia due to Parkinson's.

11. Natasha is eighty-two years old. People were always talking about how alert and aware she was, and how she seemed just as sharp as she was at thirty. Then, very suddenly, she seemed to lose some speech ability, became very forgetful, and had a lot of trouble performing even the simplest tasks. Natasha would best be diagnosed as having:
    a. Alzheimer's disease.
    b. vascular dementia.
    c. frontal lobe dementia.
    d. dementia due to Parkinson's.

12. Matilda is seventy-five years old. Her family takes her to a psychologist because they have noticed changes in her. They explain to the psychologist that she "just doesn't seem like herself." Always a shy person, she is now loud and sometimes embarrassing in public. She shows little evidence of memory impairment. Matilda would best be diagnosed with:
    a. Alzheimer's disease.
    b. vascular dementia.
    c. frontal lobe dementia.
    d. dementia due to Parkinson's.

13. John, who is sixty-six, has been disturbed by his increasing forgetfulness. At first he thought it was just "old age," but now he is also noticing trouble using language and doing his gardening, which he loves. In

fact, when he tried to garden the other day he noticed a disturbing tremor in both his arms. John would best be diagnosed with:
   a. Alzheimer's disease.
   b. vascular dementia.
   c. frontal lobe dementia.
   d. dementia due to Parkinson's.

14. Which of the following best describes the rates of Alzheimer's disease as people age?
   a. The rates increase steadily as people age.
   b. The rates decrease steadily as people age.
   c. The rates increase as people age, but disproportionately, with less of an increase after age eighty-five.
   d. The rates increase as people age, but disproportionately, with more of an increase after age eighty-five.

15. In his study of ninety-three elderly nuns, Snowdon examined the autobiographies they wrote in their early twenties. He divided the nuns into those with a high density of ideas in their autobiography (the number of ideas conveyed per sentence) and those with low density of ideas. The nuns that went on to develop Alzheimer's disease had:
   a. low idea density.
   b. high idea density.
   c. There was no difference between the groups.
   d. There were insufficient cases of Alzheimer's to test.

16. Alzheimer's disease is associated with two types of neural anomalies, neurofibrillary tangles and senile plaques. Which of the following is NOT a hypothesis for the cause of these anomalies?
   a. The accumulation of beta amyloid in the cerebral spinal fluid.
   b. An increase in aluminum in the body.
   c. The accumulation of artificial sweeteners in the cerebral spinal fluid.
   d. A defective gene on chromosome 21.

17. Which of the following does NOT appear to have beneficial effects in the treatment of Alzheimer's disease?
   a. nicotine
   b. drugs that increase the neurotransmitter acetylcholine
   c. estrogen
   d. antidepressant medication

18. Which of the following is NOT a risk factor for vascular dementia?
   a. being female
   b. a stroke
   c. lesions in the white matter surrounding the ventricles
   d. cardiovascular disease risk factors

19. Up to what percent of patients with Parkinson's disease show dementia?
   a. 40 percent
   b. 60 percent
   c. 80 percent
   d. 99 percent

20. Why is delirium more common among the elderly?
   a. Age-related changes in the brain make the elderly more vulnerable to delirium.
   b. There is a greater accumulation of neurofibrillary tangles and senile plaques after age sixty-five.
   c. Medical conditions that can produce delirium are more common in the elderly.
   d. The gene that causes delirium does not express itself until later in life.

21. Gallo and his colleagues conducted longitudinal research to determine whether the decrease in self-reported symptoms of negative mood associated with aging was real or due to a "cohort effect." They compared reports of sadness of 1,651 adults to their reports of sadness thirteen years later. There was a decrease in self-reported sadness with age. This indicates that changes in sadness are due to:
   a. a clear age effect.
   b. a clear cohort effect.
   c. It is impossible to tell using this type of research design.
   d. a combination of a cohort effect and an age effect.

22. Which of the following best describes the pattern of depression in the elderly?
   a. Depression decreases with age, but begins to increase again after age eighty.
   b. Depression decreases with age.
   c. Depression decreases with age, but begins to increase again after age sixty-five.
   d. Depression increases with age.

23. What is the most common psychological disorder among older adults?
   a. depression
   b. anxiety
   c. substance abuse
   d. schizophrenia

24. Which of the following is NOT a major risk factor for depression for older adults given in the text?
   a. health problems
   b. rumination
   c. vascular disorders of the brain
   d. death or illness of a loved one

25. Which of the following is true regarding the treatment of depression in the elderly?
   a. The treatment approach required is entirely different than the one used to treat depression in young people.

b. Unlike with young people, the best approach for the elderly involves a psychodynamic approach.

c. Antidepressants are more effective, probably because the elderly are more suspicious of therapy.

d. There is no difference in treating the elderly compared to treating younger people.

26. All of the following were treatments mentioned in the text for elderly patients with anxiety EXCEPT:
    a. interpersonal therapy.
    b. cognitive-behavioral therapy.
    c. biofeedback.
    d. exercise.

27. Why is substance abuse in the elderly a cause for concern?
    a. Substance abuse increases with age.
    b. Substance abuse in the elderly is much more difficult to treat.
    c. The consequences of drug abuse in the elderly are more significant.
    d. all of the above

28. Scott has recently begun to refuse his meals at the convalescent hospital where he lives. He proclaims that the staff is trying to poison him, and he will only eat food brought in by his daughter. Aside from his refusal to eat food prepared at the hospital, Scott's functioning appears not to be affected. He would best be diagnosed with what subtype of delusional disorder?
    a. erotomanic
    b. persecutory
    c. somatic
    d. grandiose

29. Which of the following is true regarding the gender differences in the rates of schizophrenia?
    a. Women are more likely to receive the diagnosis.
    b. Men are more likely to receive the diagnosis.
    c. Women are more likely to receive the diagnosis before age twenty-five; men are more likely to receive the diagnosis after age thirty-six.
    d. Men are more likely to receive the diagnosis before age twenty-five; women are more likely to receive the diagnosis after age thirty-six.

30. Which of the following is NOT true regarding late-onset schizophrenia, compared to earlier-onset schizophrenia?
    a. Hereditary factors play a larger role.
    b. Sensory deficits are much more common.
    c. Patients experience more delusions and hallucinations.
    d. Cognitive deterioration is more common.

Fill in the Blank

1. Deterioration in the ability to communicate with language is called _____.   aphasia

2. A decline in motor skills is called _____.   apraxia

3. _____ is the failure to identify familiar objects or people.   Agnosia

4. Loss of _____ abilities includes loss of the abilities to plan ahead and to inhibit inappropriate behavior.   executive

5. Two characteristic neural abnormalities found in people with Alzheimer's disease are

    _____ _____, an accumulation of proteins between neurons, and   neurofibrillary tangles

    _____ _____, a loss of cells.   senile plaques

6. _____ dementia is caused by a stroke and typically has a sudden onset.   Vascular

7. An _____ is an area of dead or dying brain tissue.   infarct

8. _____ _____ dementia, or Pick's disease, involves mild memory deficits and marked changes in personality.   Frontal lobe

9. _____ disease is a disorder that is the result of degeneration of dopamine neurons in subcortical regions of the brain.   Parkinson's

10. _____ is a cognitive disturbance that has a rapid onset, fluctuates over time, and usually responds rapidly to treatment.   Delirium

11. _____ disorder is a type of psychotic disorder in which the person experiences nonbizarre delusions for at least one month.   Delusional

12. A(n) _____ delusion involves the belief that another person is in love with oneself.   erotomanic

13. _____ delusions involve inflated worth, power, knowledge, identity, or special relationships to a deity or famous person.   Grandiose

14. _____ delusions involve the belief that an individual's sexual partner is unfaithful.   Jealous

15. _____ delusions involve the belief that a person is malevolently treated in some way.   Persecutory

16. _____ delusions involve a belief in the existence of some physical defect or general medical condition.   Somatic

17. _____ is another word for late-onset schizophrenia.   Paraphrenia

18. _____ is the general, progressive deterioration of cognitive functioning that is often accompanied by changes in psychological and emotional states such as depression, agitation, aggression, and apathy.   Dementia

LEVELS OF ANALYSIS: EXAMINING THE CHAPTER'S THEMES

Three themes are particularly relevant to psychological disorders in older adults: biological and psychological levels of analysis, development, and treatment of choice. Also, be sure to read the "science and practice" Box 11-2 for a discussion of cutting edge research that may lead to genetic therapy for Alzheimer's disease.

Biological and Psychological Levels of Analysis

As with younger adults and children, the diathesis-stress model provides a useful framework for understanding the causes of mental disorders in older adults. Biological and psychological vulnerability can increase with age. For example, older adults experiences decreases in the weight and volume of the brain and declines in IQ scores. Psychological vulnerabilities may also decrease with age, due to the life skills that have been acquired to help older adults cope with stress. This ability to cope, along with a decrease in actual stressors (for instance, work stress, child rearing) contribute to an overall decrease in psychology vulnerability with age and therefore a decrease in mental disorders.

Development

Overall, personality and mental health remain fairly stable throughout adult life. However, there appear to be some developmental trends that result in changes in personality and in vulnerability to psychological disorders. With regard to personality, older adults have a greater preference for routines, and they are less impulsive, less aggressive, more suspicious, and more introverted. Physical vulnerabilities include a decrease in the ability of cells to synthesize proteins, a decline in immune functioning, muscle mass, bone density, sensory acuity, weight and volume of the brain, number and size of neurons, and hormone levels, and an increase in the proportion of body fat. These physical vulnerabilities contribute to the higher rates of dementia and delirium in older adults. Psychological vulnerability includes declines in the ability to store new information and in the speed of the individual's reactions to visual and auditory treatments. Overall, though, as mentioned above, psychological vulnerability tends to reduce with age. This lower level of vulnerability contributes to a decrease in rates of all psychological disorders other than cognitive disorders.

Treatment of Choice

Treatments for psychological disorders in the elderly tend to be very similar to those used with younger adults. Some issues of concern are the side effects of medications, which can have more serious consequences for older adults, and age-related biases on the part of the therapists and older patients, which may have an impact on the therapeutic relationship.

ANSWER KEY

MULTIPLE-CHOICE QUESTIONS

1. d. Future projections to 2020 estimate that the population over age sixty-five will increase at least 60 percent.

2. a. Older adults have more of a preference for routines.

3. c. According to community screening studies, the incidence rate of mental illness, excluding cognitive disturbance, in the elderly is about 13 percent (see Table 11-1 for a summary).

4. c. Like the psychological disorders that occur in younger adults and children, the disorders that occur in older adults are the result of multiple etiological factors.

5. b. Neurons in the brain stem, which plays a major role in reflexes such as respiration, are less likely to decline with age.

6. d. In laboratory animals, DHEA has been linked to the maintenance of youthful characteristics such as higher muscle mass. However, it has not yet been established that DHEA, or any other drug, retards or reverses the aging process in humans.

7. c. Vocabulary changes little with age. The ability to store new information and the reaction speed to visual and auditory stimuli are the two most pronounced changes in cognitive ability.

8. d. Negative life events prior to age sixty-five, a family history of depression, and the loss of social contacts are all risk factors for psychological disorders in the elderly.

9. a. People with dementia do not typically experience a decline in autonomic functions such as breathing; see pp. 475–77 for a list of symptoms associated with dementia.

10. a. Alzheimer's disease is characterized by gradual onset, forgetfulness, impaired ability to perform certain motor tasks, and impaired ability to use language to communicate (see pp. 478–79 for a list of symptoms associated with Alzheimer's disease).

11. b. Vascular dementia involves the same cognitive symptoms as Alzheimer's disease (forgetfulness, impaired ability to perform certain motor tasks, and impaired ability to use language to communicate), but can be differentiated by its sudden onset (usually as the result of a stroke).

12. c. Frontal lobe dementia is characterized by marked changes in personality, disinhibition, unconcern, language problems, and socially inappropriate behavior. It typically involves only mild memory deficits and no visuo-spatial impairment.

13. d. Dementia due to Parkinson's disease involves the same cognitive deficits that are seen in Alzheimer's disease. John's tremor is an indication that he is suffering from Parkinson's, and that his symptoms of dementia are due to this.

14. c. Before age sixty-five, rates triple for every five-year increase in age. The rates double between ages sixty-five and seventy-five. The rate of increase drops down to 1.5 around age eighty-five.

15. a. All those who had Alzheimer's had low idea density early in life, indicating that the vulnerability to Alzheimer's disease exists in young adulthood for some individuals.

16. c. Beta amyloid and aluminum have been hypothesized to be linked to the formation of neurofibrillary tangles and senile plaques, and a defective gene on chromosome 21 is involved in forming amyloid. There is no evidence that artificial sweeteners cause the neural anomalies.

17. d. Nicotine and other drugs that increase the neurotransmitter acetylcholine can improve cognitive functioning and performance of everyday skills, though they have severe side effects. Estrogen, anti-inflammatory drugs, nerve growth factors, and antioxidant vitamins are also being studied as potential preventative treatments.

18. a. Vascular dementia tends to occur more frequently in males than in females.

19. b. Somewhere between 20 and 60 percent of patients with Parkinson's disease also show dementia.

20. c. Delirium is a cognitive disturbance that has a rapid onset, fluctuates over time, and usually responds rapidly to treatment. It occurs in response to a general medical condition or to substance intoxication. It is not attributable to genes or changes in the brain, and neurofibrillary tangles and senile plaques are associated with dementia, not delirium.

21. a. A "cohort effect" occurs when a group of individuals born during a particular time period differ in their tendencies to report negative feelings compared to groups born during a different time period. If the results were due to a cohort effect, the reports of sadness would have been the same over time. These results show a clear age effect on self-reported sadness.

22. a. Depression rates in young adults are about 10 percent, in middle-aged adults about 6–8 percent, and in those over sixty-five, between 1 and 3 percent. There is a sharp rise in rates, however, after age eighty.

23. a. Though rates of depression tend to decrease with age, so do the rates of other mental disorders. Depression is the most common psychological disorder among older adults.

24. b. The main factors that contribute to late-life depression differ from those that cause depression in young adulthood. Major risk factors include health problems (including vascular disorders of the brain) and social factors, such as the death or illness of a loved one.

25. d. Though an elderly depressed patient may view a younger therapist with suspicion, studies indicate that cognitive-behavioral therapy and medication work equally well for treating late-life depression. The same findings were found with younger patients.

26. a. Cognitive-behavioral therapy, biofeedback, and exercise are all innovative treatments used to treat anxiety in older people.

27. c. There is a general decline in the use of alcohol and drugs in the elderly, but when substance abuse does occur, there are more immediate life-threatening consequences for older people.

28. b. Those with delusional disorder, persecutory type, believe they are being malevolently treated in some way. See p. 495 for a description of all the subtypes.

29. d. The rates of schizophrenia by gender change with age. Men are more likely to receive the diagnosis before age twenty-five; women are more likely to receive the diagnosis after age thirty-six.

30. a. Hereditary factors appear to play a smaller role in late-onset schizophrenia.

CHAPTER 12 | Psychological Factors and Physical Disorders

A GUIDE TO THE READING

The cognitive disorders discussed in Chapter 11 are disorders in which the condition of the body influences and even triggers a disorder of the mind. This chapter presents evidence that what we think and how we feel can change our physical health. The general mechanisms by which our psychological states affect our physical well-being will be discussed, as well as specific diseases that clearly have a psychological component: coronary heart disease, peptic ulcers, AIDS, cancer, and asthma.

Interaction of Mind and Body

Patients are diagnosed with a *psychological factor affecting a general medical condition* when there is a disorder of known physical pathology present and psychologically meaningful events are judged to have contributed to the onset or worsening of the disorder. Psychological factors also affect healing; be sure to review Box 12-1 on *placebo effects* for a discussion of these healing factors. The impact of psychological factors on physical health is consistent with the diathesis-stress model, wherein a psychological disturbance triggers pathology in someone who is biologically vulnerable (see Figure 12-1 for an illustration). Biological processes are discussed in some detail in this chapter and may seem difficult to understand. Keep in mind that psychological factors exacerbate physical disorders in two physical systems: the HPA axis and the immune system. Coronary heart disease and peptic ulcers involve the HPA axis; cancer, AIDS, and asthma involve the immune system.

The HPA axis. Physical problems can result from prolonged exposure to stress and prolonged activation of the HPA axis. The relationship between exposure to stress and physical health problems is described using Hans Selye's classic theory of stress, which involves the "general adaptation syndrome" and a modern revision of this theory based on more recent research. The excellent summary of the general adaptation syndrome in Figure 12-2 should make it easy to understand. The modern theory of stress is more specific and is illustrated in Figure 12-3 and described in detail on pages 506–8. Classic stress theory assumes that the body always tries to maintain a state of *homeostasis,* the maintenance of an ideal set point for each bodily state (for example, blood pressure). Be sure to review pages 506–7 for reasons why this theory is inadequate. Modern stress theory, in contrast, proposes *allostasis,* the adaptation of many bodily states simultaneously across many life circumstances. *Stress mediators,* like the glucocorticoids and the catecholamines help us to adapt to stress in the short run, but can exacerbate disease in the long run. Frequent or repeated stress, accompanied by overexposure to the stress mediators creates a high *allostatic load,* which leads to stress-related diseases. Figure 12-4 illustrates allostasis and allostatic load; it should help you to understand these processes.

The immune system. Personality, emotion, and cognition can all alter the body's immune responses and thereby alter the risk for contracting infectious diseases, allergies, cancer, etc. To understand how this happens, it is important to understand how the immune system works. *Antigens,* foreign invaders such as bacteria, are recognized and destroyed by *macrophages* (white blood cells), and *lymphocytes* (B cells, T cells, and, in the case of cancer, natural killer cells). Figure 12-5 provides a summary of how each of these cells works and a helpful illustration. Once the immune system has encountered a specific antigen, it can recognize it (immunologic memory) and fight it (immunocompetence) more quickly (see p. 511 for methods for assessing immunocompetence).

Psychological moderating factors. Psychological factors play a role in causing and alleviating physical diseases. Specific moderating factors include life events, poverty, classical conditioning, and voluntary behavior. The more stressful life events a person experiences, the more likely he or she is to get sick (see p. 512 for a list of research findings supporting this hypotheses; see Table 12-1 for a list of the most stressful life events). Repetitive daily hassles and life events that are uncontrollable may have even more devastating effects on physical health. People who are hardy or optimistic in the face of life events resist disease much better than those who are pessimistic. Classical conditioning may also contribute to psychosomatic illness; see the case study on page 514 for an illustration of how this might take place. Finally, voluntary behaviors such as smoking, inadequate exercise, alcohol, sexual behavior, etc., can influence a person's susceptibility to physical illness.

Coronary Heart Disease (CHD)

Coronary heart disease is the number one cause of death in the Western world. There are a number of physical and behavior risk factors (see p. 515) and one psychological risk factor—having a *Type A* personality. A person with a Type A personality is competitive, ambitious, aggressive, hostile, and has an exaggerated sense of time urgency. Review pages 516–17 for a list of research findings indicating that Type A personality and hostility specifically lead to CHD. Helplessness, depression, and hopelessness have all been shown to increase risk for CHD as well, perhaps reflecting desperate efforts to control the environment, which sometimes proves uncontrollable (see Figure 12-6 for a graph). Finally, many studies have demonstrated a link between stress and CHD; review pages 519–21 for examples of these studies and their findings.

Peptic Ulcers

A *peptic ulcer* is a hole in the mucous membrane or the *duodenum*, the upper portion of the small intestine. Peptic ulcers are triggered by a bacterium called *h. pylori*, which can enlarge a break in the mucous membrane. However, 90 percent of those infected with *h. pylori* don't have ulcers, indicating that stress is involved in the development of an ulcer. Inherited biological vulnerabilities, such as excess acid in the

stomach or weak mucous defense against acid, may make some people more susceptible than others. There is also ample evidence that emotional states, exposure to stress, and the inability to predict or control the environment are related to the development of ulcers. Be sure to review the various studies on pages 524–26. Also, be sure to read the last paragraph on page 526 for an excellent overall summary of peptic ulcers.

Immune System Disorders

Depression, helplessness, hopelessness, and stressful life events have all been linked to changes in the immune system. For example, in one study, pessimists were about twice as likely as optimists to contract infectious diseases. T cell functioning and natural killer (NK) cell functioning have both been demonstrated to be suppressed by these psychological factors. Be sure to review these studies on pages 527–28.

AIDS. Psychological factors have been shown to suppress T cells and NK cells in HIV-positive men, and HIV infection and AIDS can, in turn, affect psychological functioning. Perhaps the most profound effect is the development of HIV-related dementia. Subcortical areas and eventually the frontal lobes are affected, impairing verbal memory, psychomotor ability, and problem-solving ability. Taking care of a patient who suffers from HIV-related dementia is very stressful, and the immune systems of caregivers may also be compromised.

Cancer. Hopelessness and depression also appear to play a role in the susceptibility to cancer and survival rates of cancer patients. In fact, factors such as lack of meaning in one's life, job instability, and no plans for the future predict who will have lung cancer better than does the amount of smoking. Writing about or discussing emotionally troubling topics has been shown to increase immune activity and can be protective. For example, women who had been diagnosed with breast cancer who were in a psychotherapy group lived twice as long as women who were not in the psychotherapy group.

Asthma. Asthma can be caused by infection, allergy, or psychological factors. It is estimated that up to 70 percent of all cases involve psychological factors such as anxiety, dependency needs, and troubled relationships between the parent and the asthmatic child. This was demonstrated in one study in which separation from parents was shown to have beneficial effects on the asthma of children for whom emotional factors were judged to be involved, but not for children for whom emotional factors were not judged to be involved in their asthma.

TESTING YOUR UNDERSTANDING

Test your understanding of what you have read by working through the following tasks with a classmate.

1. Imagine you have a friend who is diagnosed with a peptic ulcer. She is confused because the doctor prescribed an antibiotic but also recommended that she see a therapist for relaxation training and supportive counseling. She can't understand if she has a biological problem or if the ulcer is due to being "too stressed out." Explain to her how ulcers develop and why the doctor's advice makes sense.

2. You and your friends tend to get your worst colds and flus right after finals time. Explain to your friends why this happens. Describe the general adaptation theory and the specific findings regarding the HPA axis. Explain the concept of allostasis and how this is related to their postfinals colds.

3. Your sister-in-law has always been reluctant to treat her children's colds with medicine because she wants them to have confidence that their bodies can "heal themselves." Explain to your nephew how our bodies heal themselves.

4. Explain the moderating factors that can affect a person's health.

5. Think of someone you know who fits the description of the Type A personality. Imagine describing to him or her the link between this type of personality and coronary heart disease. How exactly do these personality traits affect the risk for CHD?

6. Explain why it is very good advice to tell someone suffering from cancer or AIDS to remain hopeful and optimistic and to talk about his or her feelings.

Multiple-Choice Questions

1. Why does the DSM-IV now describe what used to be called psychosomatic disorders as "psychological factors affecting a general medical condition?"
   a. Psychosomatic is an outdated term.
   b. Evidence now suggests that many physical disorders, not just a limited set, are influenced by the mind.
   c. Evidence now suggests that bodily disorders can influence the mind *and* psychological factors can influence physical health.
   d. all of the above

2. Up to what percent of patients diagnosed with physical illnesses such as heart disease and Parkinson's disease show real improvements after taking placebos?
   a. 20 percent
   b. 40 percent
   c. 50 percent
   d. 70 percent

3. According to the classic theory of stress, psychological factors influence physical disease through the stress caused by:
   a. the general adaptation syndrome.
   b. maladaptive cognitions.
   c. unhealthy behavioral patterns.
   d. physical vulnerability.

4. Modern theories of stress identify specific actions that initiate the stress response. Which of the following initiates the stress response?
   a. The hypothalamus stimulates the sympathetic nervous system.
   b. The adrenal cortex secretes cortisol.
   c. The hypothalamus releases corticotropin-releasing hormone.
   d. both a and c

5. Which of the following is NOT an effect of cortisol?
   a. It protects the body against a stressor.
   b. It reduces the number of receptors in the thalamus.
   c. It can lead to deficient problem solving.
   d. It can lead to susceptibility to and poor recovery from disease.

6. Which of the following is NOT one of the three inadequacies of the classic homeostatic theory of stress, according to the text?
   a. The ideal set-point varies depending on what type of activity you are engaged in.
   b. Maintaining any particular set-point can affect the balance of many other set-points.
   c. The body does not always try to regulate our internal states.
   d. Our bodies regulate their internal states based on both present and future events.

7. Allostatic load is elevated by:
   a. frequent stress.
   b. repeated stress.
   c. inability to efficiently shut off the stress mediators.
   d. all of the above

8. There are many diseases involving the immune system that can be exacerbated by psychological factors. Which of the following is NOT one of those diseases?
   a. carpal tunnel syndrome
   b. infectious diseases
   c. allergies
   d. autoimmune diseases

9. Which of the following is a lymphocyte?
   a. macrophage
   b. T cell
   c. T cell and B cell
   d. all of the above

10. Antigens are destroyed in four main ways. Which of the following surround and digest antigens?
    a. macrophages
    b. T cells
    c. B cells
    d. natural killer cells

11. Which of the following should NOT happen with high immunocompetence?
    a. The amount of immunoglobin (antibodies formed by B cells) is higher in the blood.
    b. T cells are reduced when the antigen is introduced.
    c. Natural killer (NK) cells are able to kill tumors.
    d. The skin reddens and swells when injected with an antigen.

12. There are a number of factors that moderate the influence of psychological factors on physical health. Which of the following is NOT a moderator discussed in the book?
    a. operant conditioning
    b. classical conditioning
    c. life events
    d. voluntary behavior

13. Which of the following is the MOST stressful event, according to Holmes and Rahe's Social Readjustment Rating Scale?
    a. trouble with boss
    b. minor violations of the law
    c. large mortgage
    d. marriage

14. Though George has not experienced many huge life events lately, he definitely has experienced a lot of repetitive daily hassles, such as losing his wallet and having to cope with rises in gas prices. Stacey's day-to-day life has been very smooth lately, but she has experienced a number of important stressful life events lately. She was recently married, and she and her spouse have bought a new home. According to the research, who is more likely to experience negative effects on physical health?
    a. George
    b. Stacey
    c. the effects will be about the same
    d. impossible to tell with the information given

15. Several laboratory experiments have demonstrated that classical conditioning can be used to make a previously neutral stimulus cause a physical reaction, such as an asthma attack. What conclusion can be made based on this research?
    a. A great many cases of psychosomatic illness can be accounted for using the classical conditioning model.
    b. Classical conditioning can be used to induce psychosomatic illness outside the laboratory just as well as in the laboratory.
    c. Only some patients can be conditioned and only in the laboratory.

    d. Only some patients can be conditioned, but equally well both in and out of the laboratory.

16. Which of the following voluntary behaviors accounts for the most deaths?
    a. poor diet and exercise
    b. smoking
    c. alcohol
    d. sexual behavior

17. Which of the following is NOT one of the seven major risk factors for coronary heart disease (CHD)?
    a. growing old
    b. being female
    c. high serum cholesterol
    d. genetics

18. Denise is having a difficult morning and has missed her train to work. Rather than get all worked up, she tells herself not to worry and goes to get a cup of tea while she waits for the next train. Denise probably has what type of personality?
    a. Type A
    b. Type B
    c. Type C
    d. Type D

19. Based on the studies presented in the text, how much higher is the risk for coronary heart disease (CHD) among people with Type A personalities compared to people with Type B personalities?
    a. about 1.5 times higher
    b. 2 to 3 times higher
    c. 4 to 5 times higher
    d. 8 to 9 times higher

20. A person with a Type A personality has a high potential for anger and a competitive need for control. When he or she is thwarted, the high potential for anger leads to _____, and the competitive need for control leads to _____, which both contribute to risk for coronary heart disease.
    a. frustration; a prolonged emergency reaction
    b. helplessness; frustration
    c. hostility; helplessness
    d. a prolonged emergency reaction; hostility

21. In a longitudinal study of seventy-eight Harvard juniors, the men who showed signs of hypertensive pathology were those with _____ as measured by the TAT.
    a. a high need for power and high inhibition
    b. a high need for power and low inhibition
    c. a low need for power and high inhibition
    d. a high need for power and low inhibition

22. Which of the following is at the greatest risk for heart disease?
    a. Jim, who is the head of his division, responsible for making all the decisions, and has a very demanding job

b. Jeffrey, who runs a daycare in his home and who finds his job pretty easy

c. John, who works on a factory line, has little decision-making responsibility and finds his job only moderating demanding

d. Joshua, who is a middle manager given very little responsibility, and who finds his job very demanding

23. Researchers have found that one of the reasons frequent stress contributes to heart disease is because it causes the heart to beat faster, using up the lifetime capacity of the heart more quickly. Why, then, does exercise, which increases heart rate, lower the risk of heart disease?

a. It is the combination of increased heart rate with other stress responses that increases risk; increased heart rate alone is not enough to increase risk

b. Although exercise temporarily raises heart rate, its long-term consequences are to lower heart rate.

c. both of the above

d. neither of the above

24. Peptic ulcers are primarily caused by:

a. bacteria.

b. stress.

c. an injury.

d. a virus.

25. Which of the following is NOT one of the stressful situations that has been shown to heighten the risk of ulcers in rats?

a. conflict

b. unpredictability

c. uncontrollability

d. difficulty

26. What do studies of rats reveal about the relationship of *h. pylori* and stress in the development of ulcers?

a. Rats who experience stress in the absence of *h. pylori* never developed ulcers.

b. Rats with *h. pylori* always developed ulcers, regardless of the level of stress.

c. Although most rats who developed ulcers had *h. pylori* in their system, under sufficient amounts of stress, rats without *h. pylori* also developed ulcers.

d. Sufficient amounts of stress lead to ulcers, regardless of the presence of *h. pylori*.

27. When people with ulcers are treated both with antibiotics that kill *h. pylori* along and with acid reducers, the recurrence rate of ulcers is between:

a. 3 and 8 percent

b. 8 and 15 percent

c. 15 and 25 percent

d. 25 and 33 percent

28. The parts of the brain that appear to be affected in AIDS-related dementia are the subcortical regions and the _____ lobes.

a. temporal

b. parietal

c. frontal

d. occipital

29. Which of the following is true regarding the role of psychological factors in cancer?

a. Cancer is purely biological and is not impacted by psychological factors.

b. Psychological factors such as hopelessness can affect susceptibility and survival rates.

c. Psychological factors affect survival rates, but cannot be used to predict who will get cancer.

d. The cause of cancer is primarily psychological.

30. Which of the following is NOT one of the three causes of asthma mentioned in your text?

a. infection

b. allergy

c. psychological factors

d. genetics

Fill in the Blank

1. A(n) _____ disorder occurs when a bodily disorder influences a mental disorder, such as in Alzheimer's disease.

    organic

2. _____ effects occur when pretend treatments have effects on physical health.

    Placebo

3. _____ refers to the constitutional weaknesses that underlie physical pathology.

    Diathesis

4. A _____ is an event that threatens the individual's balance or homeostasis.

    stressor

5. The _____ _____ syndrome is a sequence of three stages that a person goes through when he or she encounters stressor.

    general adaptation

6. The first stage in the classic theory of stress is the _____ _____, wherein physiological arousal prepares the body to fight or flee the stressor.

    alarm reaction

7. The second state in the classic theory of stress is called _____, in which defense and adaptation are sustained and optimal.

    resistance or adaptation

8. The final stage in the classic theory of stress, _____ occurs when the stressor persists and the adaptive response ceases. Illness or death then follows.

    exhaustion

9. _____ refers to the adaptation of many bodily states simultaneously across many life circumstances.

    Allostasis

10. High _____ _____ occurs when there is frequent stress, repeated stress, or the inability to shut off the stress mediators efficiently in response to stress when they aroused.

    allostatic load

11. The inactivation of the body's protective immune system is called _____.

    immunosuppression

12. _____ are foreign invaders such as bacteria, viruses, and cancer cells.

    Antigens

13. _____ are white blood cells whereas _____ cells come from bone marrow and _____ cells come from the thymus.

    Macrophages; B

    T

14. B cells and T cells are _____.

    lymphocytes

15. The immune system does it better job of destroying a specific invader the second time that it sees it. This is called _____ memory.

    immunologic

16. _____ psychology studies the causes, the cure, and prevention of physical illnesses that involve behaviors we can choose.

    Health

17. _____ _____ _____ kills more people than any other disease in the Western world.

    Coronary heart disease

18. _____ _____ personality involves an exaggerated sense of time urgency, competitiveness and ambition, and aggressiveness and hostility.

    Type A

19. _____ is the belief that one's present helplessness will continue into the far future and undermine all one's endeavors.

    Hopelessness

20. A(n) _____ is a hole, or erosion, in the wall of an organ.

    ulcer

21. An event is _____ when no response an individual can make will change the probability of the event.

    uncontrollable

LEVELS OF ANALYSIS: EXAMINING THE CHAPTER'S THEMES

The most important theme in this chapter is the biological and psychological levels of analysis theme. Researchers have shown that what we think and how we feel can trigger or exacerbate many physical health problems providing evidence that our psychological state and our physical state are very much interrelated. Therefore, in order to understand a psychological or physical problem, we must consider both the psychological and physical state of the individual.

Biological and Psychological Levels of Analysis

The diathesis-stress model is very useful for understanding the diagnosis of "psychological factor affecting a general medical condition." Psychological factors can trigger or worsen a physical condition for which a person has a biological predisposition. These psychological factors can affect a large number of organ systems, and the process by which psychological factors affect physical conditions is similar across systems. The reason why one person facing stress develops heart problems and another a peptic ulcer is because each person has different biological vulnerabilities. The mechanisms through which psychological stress affects the body appear to involve the release of the glucocorticoids and catecholamines in response to stress. These hormones are helpful in combating stress in the short run, but can damage the body when levels are sustained over a long period of time. In addition, exposure to stress weakens the immune system, making the body more vulnerable to infectious disease. Psychological factors also clearly play a role in the treatment of physical disorders. The experience of being treated alone, whether with a medication or with a placebo (pretend treatment) has a notable effect on recovery. Increasing hopefulness, decreasing helplessness, and talking about one's difficulties are a few examples of psychological interventions that have been shown to have a positive impact on the treatment and survival rate of a number of serious medical conditions.

Treatment of Choice

Treatment for the patient's particular physical condition is, of course, always called for. However, evidence suggests that psychological treatments can have a significant impact on recovery. For example, women diagnosed with breast cancer who were randomly assigned to a therapy group lived twice as long as women in the control group, who did not receive psychotherapy. Cognitive and behavioral therapy and specific techniques such as relaxation, stress management, and social problem solving can all increase recovery rates for patients who receive these treatments.

ANSWER KEY

MULTIPLE-CHOICE QUESTIONS

1. b. Disorders in which the mind influences bodily disorders were formerly called psychosomatic or psychophysiological disorders because it was believed that only certain mental disorders had both psychological and physiological components. Given the mounting evidence that many physical disorders, not just a limited set, are influenced by the mind, the DSM-IV now uses the term "psychological factors affecting a general medical condition."

2. d. Up to 70 percent of patients diagnosed with physical illnesses, such as heart disease and Parkinson's disease, show real improvements after taking placebos (Box 12-1).

3. a. The classic theory of stress postulates that psychological factors influence physical disease by means of the stress caused by the general adaptation syndrome.

4. d. When a person is exposed to a stressor, the hypothalamus simultaneously stimulates the sympathetic nervous system and releases corticotropin-releasing hormone (CRH). CRH travels to the pituitary gland, which secretes ACTH, which in turn activates the adrenal cortex to secrete cortisol.

5. b. In the short run, cortisol protects the body against a stressor. Continued release of cortisol can have damaging effects, including reducing the number of receptors in the *hippocampus*, deficient problem solving, and susceptibility to and poor recovery from disease.

6. c. Answers a, b, and d are all inadequacies of the classic theory according to the text.

7. d. Allostatic load is the continued wear and tear on the body in response to continuous or frequent stress accompanied by the overexposure to stress mediators, such as catecholamines (adrenaline and noradrenaline) and glucocorticoids (cortisol). See Figure 12-4.

8. a. Carpal tunnel syndrome is not mentioned as one of the diseases that can be exacerbated by psychological factors.

9. c. T cells and B cells are lymphocytes. Macrophages are white blood cells.

10. a. Macrophages, literally "big eaters," surround and digest antigens, spitting them out onto their surface and summoning helper T cells (which signal B cells) and killer T cells to take action.

11. b. Immunocompetence refers to how well the immune system responds when confronted with an antigen it has seen before. Immunoglobin, T cells, the efficacy of NK cells should increase with high immunocompetence. Reddening and swelling of the skin in response to the antigen also indicates that the immune system is working well.

12. a. The specific moderating factors that have been identified in research include life events, poverty, classical conditioning, and voluntary behavior.

13. d. Keep in mind that positive life events can be very stressful, even though they are positive.

14. a. Research indicates that repetitive daily hassles are better predictors of illness than major life events. In addition, the life events Sally has experienced are controllable; research has shown that it might be uncontrollable life events (such as a death or being laid off from work) that precede illness, not just life events in general.

15. c. Classical conditioning to induce psychosomatic illness has only been demonstrated under limited laboratory conditions and only some patients can be so conditioned.

16. b. Of the 2.15 million deaths in 1990 in the United States, tobacco accounted for 400,000 of them; poor diet and exercise, 300,000; alcohol, 100,000; and sexual behavior, 30,000.

seven major risk factors for CHD are: growing old, being male, smoking cigarettes, having high blood pressure, having high serum cholesterol, physical inactivity, and genetics.

b. People with Type B personalities are relaxed, serene, and have no sense of time urgency. People with Type A personalities have an exaggerated sense of time urgency and are competitive and aggressive. There are no Type C or D personalities.

19. b. Across three different studies, the risk for CHD among those with Type A personalities was 1.9 to 3 times the risk compared to those with Type B personalities.

20. c. In people with Type A personalities their potential for anger leads to hostility, their competitive need for control leads to helplessness, ambition leads to frustration, and time urgency leads to a prolonged emergency reaction (see Figure 12-6).

21. a. The need for power combined with its inhibition led to a greater risk for severe high blood pressure. This inhibited need for power may be viewed as a sign of the repeated helplessness in these individual's lives.

22. d. Karasek et al. found that people with high job demands and low decision latitude had the highest risk for coronary heart disease (Figure 12-8).

23. b. While exercise increases heart rate temporarily, its long-term consequences are to lower heart rate.

24. a. Ulcers are almost always triggered by a common

bacterium called *h. pylori*. There is ample evidence that stress can increase risk for or exacerbate an ulcer, however, in 90 percent of the cases, *h. pylori* is present.

25. d. The three stressful situations that heighten emotionality and increase the risk of ulcers are conflict, a psychological state that produces anxiety; unpredictability, when noxious events are preceded by a signal; and uncontrollability, a situation in which no response an individual can make will change the outcome of an event.

26. a. Studies of rats show that stress, in the absence of *h. pylori,* does not seem to produce ulcers, but it does in the presence of *h. pylori*.

27. b. Now that antibiotics are used in addition to acid reducers, the recurrence rate of ulcers is between 8 and 15 percent.

28. c. The frontal lobes appear to be affected, as evidenced by behavioral symptoms such as impaired problem-solving ability.

29. b. Psychological factors can increase susceptibility, increase survival rate, and predict who will get cancer, perhaps even better than amount of smoking.

30. d. It has been estimated that infection, allergy, and psychological factors each play the dominant role in about a third of the cases. Other estimates suggest that 70 percent of all cases involve psychosocial factors such as anxiety, dependency needs, and troubled relations with a parent.

CHAPTER 13 | Sexual Disorders

A GUIDE TO THE READING

Many disorders are covered in this chapter, making it a bit challenging. Use the model of the five layers of erotic life to help you learn the disorders. See pages 536–37 for a helpful summary of these layers. The majority of the disorders are related to Layer V (sexual performance); here memory can be aided by learning the disorders as they relate to the stages of the normal human sexual response. Keep in mind that what is considered "normal" sexual behavior varies across time and across cultures. What is considered a "disorder" will also vary. For example, in the United States, homosexuality was until recently considered a mental disorder, but is no longer. The criterion that is currently used for abnormality in the sexual realm is the gross impairment of affectionate, erotic relations between human beings.

Layer I: Gender Identity

Gender identity is the deepest layer and thus the most difficult to change. At this layer, there is one disorder, gender identity disorder. Those with the disorder are called *transsexuals;* they experience a strong and persistent cross-gender identification and a discomfort or even disgust with their own sex (see p. 538 for DSM-IV criteria). It is a rare disorder (about 1 in every 100,000 are diagnosed) and it is chronic and probably unchangeable. It is hypothesized to be caused by exposure to sex hormones during the second and fourth month of pregnancy. Male-to-female transsexuals are produced when chromosomal male fetuses are exposed to too little masculinizing hormones and female-to-male transsexuals are produced when chromosomal female fetuses are accidentally exposed to masculinizing hormones. Be sure to review pages 539–40 for a detailed explanation of the

process. The only successful treatment for transsexuals is sex reassignment surgery. Results indicate up to 97 percent of patients have a satisfactory outcome after surgery.

Layer II: Sexual Orientation

There are both homosexual and heterosexual sexual orientations, with a continuum of bisexuality in between. There are no disorders at this layer, but you should be familiar with the causes of homosexuality and heterosexuality. There is evidence that a strong predisposition to homosexuality or heterosexuality results from the process of neurochemical events during the second and fourth months of pregnancy. This predisposition may then be activated by hormonal changes at the onset of puberty or by rearing, role models, genes, and early sexual experiences. Biologically, male homosexuals have been shown to have a much smaller medial anterior hypothalamus compared to heterosexual men. Homosexuality appears to be heritable based on twin studies. For the most part, efforts to change sexual orientation are unsuccessful, though behavioral therapy does sometimes lead to changes in bisexual men.

Layer III: Sexual Preferences

Sexual preferences and interests are acquired during the first fifteen years of life and are fairly stable throughout life. Disorders at this layer are the *paraphilias,* disorders in which sexual arousal is limited to unusual objects and situations. Many people may experience arousal by these unusual objects or situations, but those with paraphilias can only be aroused by those objects or situations, and they repeatedly and intentionally engage in these situations. Paraphilias that involve a preference for nonhuman objects include fetishes and transvestism. A fetish typically accompanies early erotic play and grows in strength through repeatedly fantasizing paired with orgasm (see p. 546 for DSM-IV criteria). Transvestism occurs when a man persistently dresses in women's clothes to achieve sexual arousal (see p. 548 for DSM-IV criteria). Cross-dressing typically appears in childhood and transvestites are no more likely to be homosexual compared to those without transvestism. Paraphilias that involve a preference for situations that involve suffering and humiliation includes sadism and masochism. The sadist is aroused by inflicting pain and humiliation and the masochist by receiving pain and humiliation (see pp. 550 and 551 for DSM-IV criteria). Paraphilias that involve sexual arousal with nonconsenting partners includes exhibitionism, voyeurism, and pedophilia. Exhibitionism involves exposing the genitals to unwitting strangers (see p. 551 for DSM-IV criteria). It is the most common sexual crime in the U.S., and appears rarely outside the U.S. and Europe. Voyeurism involves observing unsuspecting people (see p. 552 for DSM-IV criteria). Pedophilia involves sexual relations with a child (see p. 553 for DSM-IV criteria). About 30 percent of all convictions for sex offenses are for child molesting. Most pedophiles are known to the child they molest.

The psychodynamic view explains paraphilias as a *cathexis,* the charging of a neutral object with psychical energy. This view is consistent with the evidence that paraphilias begin in childhood, are resistant to change, and are persistent. The behavioral view provides an explanation of how the paraphilias develop. The object of sexual pleasure is a conditioned stimulus, resulting from a pairing of the object with early sexual pleasure. When the person masturbates to the object (or the fantasy of it), he or she is provided with additional acquisition trials. As with phobias, only a limited set of objects can actually become paraphilic, which is consistent with the preparedness theory (see Chapter 5). Sexual preferences do not extinguish themselves on their own, but there are treatments that have been successful in altering sexual preferences (see Treatment Table 13-2 for a summary of treatment outcomes). Cognitive-behavioral approaches are somewhat helpful; see pages 555–56 for descriptions of particular techniques. Chemical castration, though illegal in the U.S., has been shown to be very effective, with reoffense rates dropping from 70 percent to 3 percent for those who are chemically castrated in Europe.

Layer IV: Sex Role

Sex role is the public expression of gender identity—what one says and what one does to indicate being a man or a woman. There are no disorders of sex role, but you should be familiar with the research on what underlies sex roles; review pages 557–59.. There is clear evidence that prenatal hormones influence sex role development and that parenting and socialization do not seem to influence sex role as much as was previously thought, at least not in the short run.

Layer V: Sexual Performance

An easy way to remember the many disorders at this layer is to learn the human sexual response. The disorders of sexual functioning are linked to each stage of normal functioning. The human sexual response is described on pages 559–60. There is also a helpful table that describes each of the disorders in stages (Table 13-3). Dysfunction in the first stage, the *sexual desire disorders*, may take the form of *hypoactive sexual disorder,* a lack of desire for sexual activity, or *sexual aversion disorder,* an actual aversion to sex. Dysfunction in the second stage, the *sexual arousal disorders*, in men is termed *male erectile disorder*, which is a persistent inability to achieve or maintain an erection, and in females is termed *female sexual arousal disorder*, which is a persistent inability to achieve or maintain vaginal lubrication and swelling. Dysfunction in the third stage, the *sexual orgasmic disorders*, can occur in men as either *premature ejaculation*, ejaculation after brief stimulation and before the person wished it, or *retarded ejaculation*, delayed ejaculation after prolonged stimulation. In women, *female orgasmic disorder* is the persistent absence of orgasm after stimulation. There are also two *sexual pain disorders*, *dyspareunia*, extreme pain associated with intercourse, and *vaginismus*, involuntary muscle spasms at the entrance to the vagina that prevent intercourse. The process of sexual arousal is similar in men and women; excitement stimulates the parasympathetic nerves in the spinal cord, which widen the blood vessels in the genitals, causing arousal. Orgasm is controlled by the sympathetic nervous system (see pages 559–60 for a complete description of male and female arousal). Female orgasmic disorder is the most common sexual dysfunction in women, with about 10 to 25 percent of adult women who have never had an orgasm. Premature ejaculation and erectile disorder are the most common sexual dysfunctions in men. Be sure to review the boxes in this section for the DSM-IV criteria for each of these disorders.

Sexual dysfunction may be caused by biomedical or psychological problems. Drugs such as alcohol and cocaine, medications such as antihypertensives and tranquilizers, and diseases such as diabetes can reduce sexual desire. Poor circulation, low testosterone, and disorders of the pituitary-hypothalamic-gonadal axis may be responsible for some erectile disorders. Psychological problems such as negative emotional states, unconscious conflicts, fear of pregnancy, marital problems, early traumatic sexual experiences, and inhibiting cognitions also contribute to sexual dysfunction (see Table 13-4 for psychodynamic, behavioral, cognitive and biological views of orgasmic disorder).

Sexual disorders are typically treated with direct sexual therapy or medications, such as Viagra. See pages 567–68 for a description of direct sexual therapy and *sensate focus,* the major strategy of direct sexual therapy. Only about 25 percent of patients fail to improve with sensate focus for female sexual unresponsiveness; guided masturbation is the treatment of choice for women who have never experienced an orgasm. Viagra is now the treatment of choice for male erectile dysfunction; 73 percent of men taking Viagra benefited compared to half as many given a placebo. Be sure to review Table 13-5 for detailed information about treatment success for direct sexual therapy and Viagra.

TESTING YOUR UNDERSTANDING

Test your understanding of what you have read by working through the following tasks with a classmate.

1. Describe the five layers of erotic life and the extent to which humans are changeable at each of these layers.

2. Many people are confused about transsexualism and are unsure how it is different from transvestism and homosexuality. Explain these differences to a friend.

3. A few decades ago, homosexuals were labeled abnormal and psychologists made attempts to change homosexuals to heterosexuals. Explain why this is no longer the case.

4. Your friend confesses to you that he has had dreams about women's shoes that really turn him on. He's a little worried that there may be something wrong with him. What questions would you ask him to determine if he actually has a sexual disorder?

5. Little girls may prefer dolls and little boys, trucks. They may tease children who do not follow these sexual stereotypes. Explain why this happens, and why children get more flexible about sex role stereotypes as they age.

6. Describe the human sexual response and the disorders that can accompany each stage.

7. Imagine that your roommate confides in you that he or she has been having trouble getting aroused enough for sex with a partner. What are the possible causes of this problem, and what can be done to help your roommate?

Multiple-Choice Questions

1. What is the criterion for abnormality in the sexual realm, according to the text?
   a. harmful to self or others
   b. inability to perform sexually
   c. impairment of affectionate, erotic relations between human beings
   d. deviant behavior

2. Which layer of erotic life is deeper than sexual orientation?
   a. gender identity
   b. sexual interest
   c. sex role
   d. sexual performance

3. Ed always felt very uncomfortable in his body. As a child, he was much more interested in dolls and playing house than in guns and trucks. When he reached adolescence, he started dating men and he described himself as a woman stuck in a man's body. Ed would best be described as a:
   a. transvestite.
   b. transsexual.
   c. homosexual.
   d. paraphiliac.

4. What is the most likely cause of transsexualism, according to your text?
   a. inappropriate parenting
   b. early childhood sexual abuse
   c. an undersized medial anterior hypothalamus
   d. inappropriate exposure to masculinizing hormones during pregnancy

5. When a 46XX fetus (chromosomally female) is exposed to massive amounts of masculinizing hormones, both male sex organs and a male sexual identity ensue. This process is known as:
   a. adrenogenital syndrome (AGS).
   b. androgen insensitivity syndrome (AIS).
   c. transsexualism.
   d. transvestism.

6. Psychotherapy with the goal of making a transsexual person "normal" is:
   a. quite successful in most cases.
   b. often successful.
   c. moderately successful.
   d. pretty much useless.

7. Evidence suggests that the etiology of homosexuality involves:
   a. a disruption of the hormonal processes between the second and fourth month of pregnancy.
   b. a smaller medial anterior hypothalamus.
   c. genetics.
   d. all of the above

8. Which of the following is true about homosexuality and the DSM-IV?
   a. Homosexuality is listed as one of the sexual disorders; specifically, it is a paraphilia.
   b. Homosexuality is not included in the DSM-IV.
   c. Homosexuality is not included, but ego-dystonic homosexuality is.
   d. none of the above

9. What is the hallmark for crossing the line from normal fantasy to paraphilia?
   a. when the person acts on it
   b. when the object becomes necessary for arousal
   c. when the person is markedly distressed by his or her actions
   d. any of the above

10. In the case study of Leo discussed in the text, Leo is extremely aroused by women's shoes and can only have sex with his wife if he is looking at, touching, or thinking about her shoes at the same time. Which term best describes Leo's disorder?
    a. fetish
    b. necrophilia
    c. voyeurism
    d. pedophilia

11. Transvestism occurs exclusively in men. Men with transvestism are aroused by dressing as a woman. What is the relationship between transvestism and male homosexuality?
    a. All transvestites are homosexual.
    b. Most transvestites are homosexual.
    c. Transvestites are no more likely to be homosexual than the average American man.
    d. Transvestites are never homosexual.

12. Researchers have argued about whether _____ should be classified as disorders.
    a. fetishism and transvestism
    b. masochism and voyeurism
    c. transvestism and masochism
    d. fetishism and voyeurism

13. _____ involves touching and rubbing against a nonconsenting person.
    a. Exhibitionism
    b. Frotteurism
    c. Telephone scatologia
    d. Voyeurism

14. Which is the most common sexual crime in the United States?
    a. exhibitionism
    b. frotteurism
    c. telephone scatologia
    d. voyeurism

15. When a child is sexually molested by a pedophile, who among the choices below is most likely to be the perpetrator?
    a. a relative
    b. a stranger
    c. a teacher
    d. another child

16. The psychodynamic view explains the paraphilias as a result of a cathexis, the charging of a neutral object with psychical energy. Cathected paraphilias have three properties that are consistent with paraphilias. Which one of the following is NOT one of those properties?
    a. They have their beginnings in childhood experience.
    b. They are a result of unconscious conflict.
    c. They resist change.
    d. They last and last—usually for a lifetime.

17. According to the behavioral view, a paraphilia is created by the pairing of an object with early sexual pleasure and the reinforcement of this pleasure through acquisition trials. This mechanism is:
    a. operant conditioning.
    b. classical conditioning.
    c. covert sensitization.
    d. maladaptive cognitions.

18. Which of the following is NOT one of the cognitive-behavioral techniques used to treat people with paraphilias?
    a. electric shock
    b. orgasmic reconditioning
    c. chemical castration
    d. masturbatory satiation

19. For which of the following layers of erotic life are there no mental disorders?
    a. gender identity
    b. sexual interest
    c. sex role
    d. sexual performance

20. The conclusion that sex roles are biologically deep and unchangeable is untenable because of which of the following reasons?
    a. Parents who attempt to raise their children androgynously usually succeed.
    b. The etiology of sex role is clearly psychological, not biological.
    c. Sex-role stereotypes weaken as children grow up.
    d. Actually, sex roles do appear to be deep and unchangeable.

21. Which nerves control the blood vessels of the genitals and thus play a role in sexual excitement?
    a. the parasympathetic nerves
    b. the sympathetic nerves
    c. the somatic nerves
    d. the autonomic nerves

22. Jennifer has noticed recently that when she and her partner are engaged in foreplay, she doesn't get as lubricated as she used to and her lack of lubrication is making intercourse difficult. Jennifer would best fit into which category of sexual dysfunctions?
    a. sexual desire disorders
    b. sexual arousal disorders
    c. sexual orgasmic disorders
    d. sexual pain disorders

23. Dyspareunia is which type of sexual disorder?
    a. sexual desire disorder
    b. sexual arousal disorder
    c. sexual orgasmic disorder
    d. sexual pain disorder

23. Women are most likely to be diagnosed with a _____ disorder, whereas men are more likely to be diagnosed with a _____ disorder.
    a. sexual desire; sexual arousal
    b. sexual arousal; sexual desire
    c. sexual orgasmic; sexual arousal
    d. sexual arousal; sexual orgasmic

24. Which stage of sleep is almost invariably accompanied by penile erection?
    a. Stage 1
    b. Stage 2
    c. Stage 3
    d. REM sleep

25. Nonorgasmic women:
    a. have little or no sex drive.
    b. have less desire for sex compared to the average woman.
    c. can enjoy foreplay and intercourse itself.
    d. have arousal disorders by definition.

26. The definition of a sexual dysfunction, both orgasmic and arousal-related, is:
    a. based on absolute criteria.
    b. relative to the culture.
    c. relative to the expectations of the couple.
    d. relative to the person.

27. Which of the following is NOT one of the biological causes of sexual dysfunction listed in your text?
    a. prenatal hormones
    b. poor circulation
    c. use of drugs
    d. disorders of the pituitary-hypothalamic-gonadal axis

28. The idea that men and women who become "orgasm watchers" are more likely to develop an orgasmic disorder is consistent with which model?
    a. psychodynamic
    b. behavioral
    c. cognitive
    d. biological

29. Which of the following is NOT one of the phases of the sensate focus strategy for treating sexual dysfunction?
    a. masturbation
    b. pleasuring
    c. genital stimulation
    d. nondemand intercourse

30. About what percent of men benefit from Viagra?
    a. 52 percent
    b. 63 percent
    c. 73 percent
    d. 90 percent

Fill in the Blank

1. _____ _____ is the deepest layer of erotic life and the most difficult to change.

   Gender identity

2. _____ _____ is the layer of our erotic life that involves the types of persons, parts of the body, and situations that are the objects of our sexual fantasies and arousal.

   Sexual interest

3. _____ _____ is the public expression of gender identity, what individual says or does to indicate that he is a man or she is a woman.

   Sex role

4. _____ _____ disorder occurs when a person's sense of what gender he or she is different than the gender of his or her body.

   Gender identity

5. _____ involve sexual arousal and preference for nonhuman objects, unusual situations, and nonconsenting partners.

   Paraphilias

6. To have a _____ is to be sexually aroused by a nonliving object.

   fetish

7. _____ occurs when a man persistently dresses in women's clothes to achieve sexual arousal.

   Transvestism

8. The _____ becomes sexually aroused by inflicting suffering or humiliation on another human being, whereas the _____ becomes sexually aroused by having suffering or humiliation inflicted on him or her.

    sadist

    masochist

9. _____ involves exposing the genitals to unwitting, and usually unwilling, strangers.

    Exhibitionism

10. _____ involves observing the naked body, the disrobing, or the sexual activity of an unsuspecting victim.

    Voyeurism

11. _____ _____ consists of recurrent and intense sexual urges to make obscene calls to a nonconsenting individual.

    Telephone scatologia

12. _____ involves touching and rubbing against a nonconsenting person, usually in a crowded places.

    Frotteurism

13. _____ involves sexual relations with prepubescent children.

    Pedophilia

14. _____ refers to the charging of a neutral object with psychical energy.

    Cathexis

15. _____ _____ is used to treat paraphilias by using imagined sexual stimuli followed by the use of aversive unconditioned stimuli.

    Covert sensitization

16. The substitution of a more acceptable scene when a man masturbates to climax is known as _____ _____.

    orgasmic reconditioning

17. _____ is one of the sexual pain disorders in which the muscles of the vagina spasm involuntarily when intercourse is attempted.

    Vaginismus

18. _____ is a sexual pain disorder in which severe pain occurs during intercourse.

    Dyspareunia

19. _____ _____ consists of great difficulty in reaching orgasm during sexual intercourse for men.

    Retarded ejaculation

20. William Masters and Virginia Johnson created _____ _____ therapy to treat sexually dysfunctional patients.

    direct sexual

21. _____ _____ is a major psychotherapy strategy for impaired excitement in females and erectile dysfunction in males.

    Sensate focus

LEVELS OF ANALYSIS: EXAMINING THE CHAPTER'S THEMES

Two important and interrelated themes emerge in this chapter: biological and psychological levels of analysis and treatment of choice.

Biological and Psychological Levels of Analysis

The extent to which the sexual disorders can be explained biologically and psychologically varies across the layers of sexuality. The deepest layers, gender identity and sexual orientation, clearly have a biological basis. It has been hypothesized that the etiology of both identity and orientation is based in the prenatal hormones that the fetus is exposed to during the second to fourth month of pregnancy. Perhaps because of these biological roots, gender identity is almost impossible to change and sexual orientation is very difficult to change. As we move up the layers, closer to the surface, the importance of the psychological level of analysis increases. Though there is plenty of evidence for a biological basis of sexual orientation (prenatal hormones, anatomical differences in the brain, genetics) there do also appear to be psychological factors that affect sexual orientation, such as rearing, role models, content of play, etc. Sexual preferences appear to be best explained psychologically, with psychodynamic and behavioral theories providing the best explanations for the development of paraphilias. Sex roles clearly require both biological and psychological explanations to account for the rigidity of adherence to sex roles in young children and the increasing acceptance of androgyny as children age. Finally, sexual performance can be impaired by either psychological or biological causes or both. Biological treatments such as Viagra and psychological treatments such as direct sexual therapy have been successful in treating the sexual dysfunctions.

Treatment of Choice

The treatment of choice for the sexual disorders is usually based on whether the particular disorder that is being treated is primarily biological or psychological. The treatment of choice for gender identity disorder is sex reassignment surgery, because it is a biologically rooted disorder that does not respond to psychological treatment. Although sexual orientation is no longer viewed as a disorder, previous attempts to change orientation proved less than successful. The paraphilias can be changed with cognitive-behavioral treatment, though change is difficult and success rates are not perfect. Because of this, some countries have adopted chemical castration as the treatment of choice for criminal paraphiliacs. The treatment of choice for many of the sexual dysfunctions is direct sexual therapy, though the high success rates of Viagra for treating male erectile disorder have made it the treatment of choice for that disorder.

ANSWER KEY

MULTIPLE-CHOICE QUESTIONS

1. c. The overall criterion for abnormality in the sexual realm is the gross impairment of affectionate, erotic relations between human beings.

2. a. The layers of erotic life, from base to surface, are gender identity, sexual orientation, sexual interest, sex role, and sexual performance.

3. b. A man who feels he is a woman trapped in a male body is a transsexual. Transvestites are men who become aroused by dressing as women.

4. d. Gender identity, both normal and abnormal, is hypothesized to come from the hormonal process in the second to fourth month of pregnancy. Transsexualism is hypothesized to result when chromosomal males are exposed to insufficient levels of masculinizing hormones or when chromosomal females are exposed to small amounts of masculinizing hormones.

5. a. AGS involves the exposure of 46XX fetuses to masculinizing hormones; AIS occurs when 46XY (chromosomally masculine) fetuses are completely insensitive to masculinizing hormones. These children are born with female sex organs and female gender identity. Transsexuals are born with the sex organs of one gender, but the gender identity of the other.

6. d. Psychotherapy to help transsexuals feel comfortable with their bodies is almost useless. The treatment of choice for transsexualism is sex reassignment surgery (Table 13-1).

7. d. Sexual orientation is affected by genetics, prenatal hormones, and brain structure.

8. b. Neither homosexuality nor ego-dystonic homosexuality is included in the DSM-IV.

9. d. Normal fantasies become paraphilias when the person acts on it, when the object becomes necessary for arousal, when the person is markedly distressed by his or her actions, or when the object displaces the human partner.

10. a. Leo has a fetish, a sexual preference for a nonhuman object. Necrophilia is a rare from of paraphilia when a person is aroused by dead bodies. A voyeur is someone who is aroused by watching others engage in sexual activity. A pedophile is someone who is aroused by prepubescent children.

11. c. Three quarters of transvestites are married and have children, and on average they have had less homosexual experience than the average American man. Homosexuals may occasionally dress in female clothes in order to attract another men, but they are not aroused by cross-dressing.

12. c. There has been debate recently whether masochism and transvestism are actually mental disorders. Some suggest that they represent "deviance without pathology."

13. b. Frotteurism involves touching and rubbing against a nonconsenting person.

14. a. Exhibitionism is the most common sexual crime in the U.S., where it constitutes roughly one-third of arrests for sexual offenses.

15. a. Most acts of convicted pedophiles take place between a child and a family acquaintance, neighbor, or relative.

16. b. The three properties of cathetected paraphilias are (1) they have their beginnings in childhood experience, (2) they resist change, and (3) they last and last—usually for a lifetime.

17. b. The behavioral model proposes that paraphilias develop as a result of classical conditioning, whereby a fetishistic object is paired with erotic stimulation, and this pairing is strengthened by continual pairing of the object, or fantasy of the object, with masturbation.

18. c. Chemical castration refers to the use of drugs to neutralize the hormone that the testicles produce, making sex impossible. It is not a cognitive-behavioral approach, nor is it currently used in the United States. It is, however, the most effective treatment for people with paraphilias.

19. c. Sex role is the public expression of gender identity—what one says and what one does to indicate being a man or a woman. There are no disorders of sex role.

20. c. Sex role does appear to be at least partly determined by fetal hormones, and programs to raise children androgynously have enjoyed little success. However, children do appear to "grow out" of their sex-role stereotypes as they age.

21. a. The parasympathetic nerves in the spinal cord control the blood vessel of the genitals. The sympathetic nerves play a role in orgasm.

22. b. Jennifer appears to be having problems becoming adequately aroused; this would be diagnosed as a female sexual arousal disorder (Table 13-3).

23. d. Dyspareunia, extreme pain associated with intercourse, and vaginismus, involuntary muscle spasms at the entrance to the vagina, are categorized as sexual pain disorders (Table 13-3).

23. c. Women are most likely to be diagnosed with female orgasmic disorder, whereas men are more likely to be diagnosed with male erectile disorder or premature ejaculation, both arousal disorders.

24. d. REM sleep is almost invariably accompanied by penile erection; measuring nocturnal erections is therefore used with men with erectile problems to determine whether their problems are psychologically or physically caused.

25. c. Women with orgasmic disorder may have strong sex drives and enjoy sexual activity a great deal.

26. c. According to the text, the definition of a sexual dysfunction, both orgasmic and arousal-related, is relative to the expectations of the couple.

27. a. Biological causes of sexual dysfunction include: use of drugs, aging, poor circulation, low testosterone, disorders of the pituitary-hypothalamic-gonadal axis, and neurological disease. Prenatal hormones are not related to the development of sexual dysfunction.

28. c. Orgasm watchers have thoughts such as "I wonder if I'll climax this time," and "This is taking much too long. He must think I'm frigid." This can lead to orgasmic dysfunction, according to the cognitive model.

29. a. Although guided masturbation is sometimes used in sex therapy, it is not one of the three phases of sensate focus, which is an exercise for couples.

30. c. According to double-blind, placebo-controlled studies sponsored by the manufacturer, 73 percent of men taking Viagra benefited compared to half as many given a placebo.

CHAPTER 14   Substance Use Disorders

A GUIDE TO THE READING

Perhaps the most challenging aspect of this chapter is the many drugs that are covered. You'll need to know the diagnostic criteria, the short-term and long-term effects, the treatments of choice, and the medical and social complications of each drug. Fortunately, there is much in common among the drugs. The DSM-IV criteria are quite similar, as are some of the biological correlates and the complications of the drugs. The first section of the chapter, "Drug Use and Abuse" is a helpful summary of these commonalties; be sure to read it carefully. Also, use the exercises below as an aid to learning the details for each drug class. The last section of the chapter discusses options for preventing drug dependence; be sure to know the pros and cons of each option.

Drug Use and Abuse

It is important to know the difference between substance dependence and substance abuse (see DSM-IV boxes on page 578). Use the "three C's" of *substance dependence* to help you remember its characteristics: loss of **C**ontrol, **C**ontinued used despite adverse circumstances, and **C**ompulsive need for the drug. *Substance abuse* is a maladaptive, harmful pattern of drug use without the physical dependence. Be sure to review the World Health Organization's definition of dependence syndrome as well (p. 579). The route of administration determines how quickly the drug affects the brain: smoking and direct injection are quick, oral ingestion takes longer. Drugs that are *lipid (fat) soluble* pass through membranes more easily and are absorbed more quickly. The effects of drugs are principally based on their interaction with neurotransmitters and neurotransmitter receptor sites (see p.

582 for various ways in which drugs and neurotransmit[ters] interact).

There are a number of models of drug dependence, all [of] which contribute to our understanding. Be familiar wi[th] each of the models presented on pages 583–89. Psycholog[i]cal models focus on the high rate of comorbidity with othe[r] mental disorders and suggest that drugs are used to reduce symptoms of other disorders or as a defense mechanism against internal conflict. The genetic vulnerability model focuses on the evidence for a genetic transmission of alcoholism. Opponent-process theory explains why people continue to use drugs after the positive effects wear off (see Figure 14-3 for a summary and illustration). Positive reinforcement models focus on the pleasurable feelings induced by the drug as the primary explanation for drug use. Many of the systems that are known to mediate natural rewards are those affected by reinforcing drugs, particularly the *nucleus accumbens*, which is affected by almost every drug discussed in this chapter. Dopamine systems and endogenous opioids play an important role in drug use as well. Conditioning and learning models recognize the pairing of drug use with environmental cues and are thus able to account for the high rate of relapse among substance abusers.

Alcohol

Alcoholism is second only to cigarette smoking as the most serious drug problem in the United States. Risks for alcoholism include being in the 10- to 24-year-old age range, being male, and being white. Low doses produce feelings of relaxation and mild euphoria, high doses are associated with depressant effects and impairment of sensory functions, motor functions, and memory. Alcohol reduces neural

e neurotransmitters norepinephrine,
act nd GABA. Long-term use can lead to
do al symptoms when the substance is
t clearly heritable (see pp. 594–96 for
biological mechanisms). Stress early
e biological risk as well. Psychologi-
isocial personality disorder, and the
tion in response to stress. Treatment
and prevention of relapse, which can
e-behavioral therapy (see Figure 14-6
gram) or with drug treatment (review
s of drugs used to treat alcoholism).
oholics recover. Alcoholism costs the
100,000 deaths and $100 billion

opiate use does lead to lower blood pressure, decreased sex drive, respiratory depression, a high degree of tolerance, and intense withdrawal effects (see pp. 614–15 for a description). Factors that may contribute to opiate dependence include family conflict, drug availability, and psychological state. The primary treatment for opiate addiction is pharmacological. Oral synthetic opiates, usually methadone, are substituted for the drug. Review pp. 615–17 and Box 14-2 for the advantages and disadvantages of methadone treatment. The costs of opiate addiction include increased rates of AIDS and other sexually transmitted diseases (because sex is exchanged for the drug) and crimes such as robbery and prostitution (for procurement of the drug).

Hallucinogens

Hallucinogens are distinguished as a class of drugs by their ability to alter sensory perception, awareness, and thoughts. The rates of use of drugs such as LSD (a synthetic drug), mescaline (from the cactus plant peyote), and psilocybin (found in several species of mushrooms), are relatively low in the United States. People do not usually use these drugs chronically, nor do they become addicted to them. Psychological effects vary from person to person; be sure to review pages 619–20 for a description. The drugs appear to affect the serotonin and norepinephrine systems. LSD also affects glutamate and dopamine and causes pronounced changes in the limbic circuits of the brain. These drugs have few medical and social complications, though a "bad trip" can cause severe panic and flashbacks, and perceptual alterations may cause suicide. PCP and MDMA (Ecstasy) are synthetic drugs that have hallucinatory effects and much more serious physical effects, including violence, brain damage, and suicide (see pp. 621–22).

ers

of
th

most widely used psychoactive drug.
einated beverages and nonprescription
iost commonly used illegal stimulants are
nd methamphetamines, synthetic drugs de-
wentieth century. Cocaine, prepared from the
oca plant, is associated with the most medical
the most addiction among the stimulant drugs.
ivates the sympathetic nervous system and the
system; release of dopamine in the nucleus ac-
s linked to the rewarding properties of this drug.
m effects include feelings of stimulation and eu-
enhanced alertness, increased sexuality, and deepen-
emotions. Chronic use leads to reductions in mental
notor abilities, changes in the neural structure in the
n, psychosis, paranoia, and sudden death. Treatments in-
de antidepressants or dopamine agonists during the with-
awal phase, behavioral approaches to increase motivation
o stay abstinent, and extinction of conditioned craving using learning techniques for relapse avoidance. Costs of cocaine use include rises in violent crime (to get money to procure the drug), pregnancy in addicted women (when sex is exchanged for the drug), and medical complications (such as AIDS) from shared needles.

The Opiates

Also called narcotics, the opiate drugs are compounds extracted from the poppy plant, including opium, morphine, codeine, and synthetic derivatives such as heroin and meperidine (Demerol). The drugs are named "opiates" because they interact with opiate receptors in the brain (see pp. 613–14 for details on how this happens). Short term effects include pain relief, general feelings of well-being, and calmness. There are few toxic effects from long-term use, though

Marijuana

Marijuana is made from the hemp plant and is the most commonly used illicit drug in the United States. Short-term effects include feelings of well-being, euphoria, tranquillity, and exaggerated emotions. In very high doses, hallucinations and paranoia may occur. Negative effects include deficits in short-term memory, distortions in the sense of time, and genetic damage. Tolerance can occur, but physical dependence is very unlikely. Psychological dependence is more common. The drug is extremely lipid soluble and is absorbed by all tissues, thus it affects nearly all biological systems. There is evidence that it affects the nucleus accumbens, regions in the limbic system, and acetycholine. Costs include effects on the lungs, suppression of immune responses, and changes in a person's lifestyle, personality, and ambitions.

Tobacco

Tobacco is derived from the tobacco plant, and nicotine is the active and addictive ingredient. It is one of the most widely consumed psychoactive drugs in the world and kills nearly twenty times as many people per year as all illegal drugs combined. Smoking is the most common method of intake and provides rapid entry into the brain. It stimulates cholinergic receptors in the autonomic nervous system and induces the release of catecholamines. The effects are complex; review pages 626–27 for a description. It is the most addictive drug and it has a distinct withdrawal syndrome (see p. 628). Theories as to why people smoke include social factors, the positive reinforcing effects of nicotine, stress reduction and coping, and optimizing mental performance. Most smokers quit without psychotherapy or pharmacotherapy, though behavioral therapy, group counseling, and physician advice can be useful, especially in conjunction with nicotine replacement therapy. The costs of smoking to society are huge, with about 450,000 smoking-related deaths per year and a cost of about $70 billion dollars a year in the U.S. Smoking is implicated in lung cancer, heart disease, hypertension, and emphysema, and it shortens the lifespan.

Barbiturates and Benzodiazepines

The principal effect of these drugs is to depress the activity of the central nervous system. The effects are similar to the effects of alcohol. Benzodiazepines are safer than barbiturates and more widely used; they include Xanax, Valium, and Librium. These drugs affect the GABA system, enhancing the inhibitory effect of GABA. Tolerance and withdrawal can develop, and treatment consists of management of the withdrawal syndrome combined with supportive psychotherapy.

TESTING YOUR UNDERSTANDING

Test your understanding of what you have read by working through the following tasks with a classmate.

1. College students often wonder how to tell whether a person is an alcoholic, or just drinks a lot. Based on the DSM-IV criteria and the World Health Organization's definition, how would you explain the distinction to a friend?

2. In general, how do drugs have the affect that they do? Why do some affect the brain more quickly than others?

3. Think of someone you know who is an alcoholic. How would you explain to this person's family why he or she became an alcoholic?

4. Imagine a friend is planning to try a drug at a party tonight and asks you what will happen and how dangerous it will be. Explain the effects of each of the major drugs.

5. Your cousin is concerned about her friend, who is in treatment for substance dependence. She is very concerned because her friend recently had a relapse. Explain to your cousin about relapse and why this is fairly normal in the recovery process.

6. Imagine you are asked to talk with students in a local junior high school about drug use. What would you say to discourage them from using drugs?

7. What would you recommend we do as a country to combat drug use? Why did you choose that strategy?

Multiple-Choice Questions

1. Jerry has always been a heavy drinker. Lately his friends have noticed that he seems to drink more and more alcohol in order to get drunk. He has been showing up to work very late or not at all and has had two DUIs (driving under the influence), which have cost him jail time and thousands of dollars. He continues to drink, however, even more than ever before. Jerry would best be diagnosed with:
   a. substance abuse.
   b. substance dependence.
   c. neither
   d. both

2. About what percent of people relapse after receiving treatment for a substance disorder?
   a. 30 percent
   b. 45 percent
   c. 65 percent
   d. 80 percent

3. Which route of administration takes the longest for the drug to reach the brain?
   a. oral administration
   b. administration through smoking
   c. direct injection into a vein
   d. The route of administration does not effect how long it will take for the drug to reach the brain, though the type of drug does.

4. What is the most common coexisting mental disorder among male substance abusers?
   a. depression
   b. anxiety
   c. antisocial personality disorder
   d. schizophrenia

5. Studies have shown that children of alcoholics are ___ times more likely to become alcohol dependent compared to people in the general population.
   a. two
   b. four
   c. eight
   d. fifteen

6. Which theory best accounts for why people continue to take drugs even when the pleasure derived from taking the drug is gone?
   a. the psychological model
   b. the genetic model
   c. the opponent-process model
   d. the positive reinforcement model

7. Which drug is involved in the most serious drug problem in the United States?
   a. alcohol
   b. nicotine
   c. heroin
   d. cocaine

8. Denise is at a party and has taken a heavy dose of a drug. She is experiencing difficulty walking, everything looks blurry, and her reflexes are very slow. She is having difficulty remembering conversations she has had just a few moments ago. What drug did Denise most likely ingest?
   a. alcohol
   b. nicotine
   c. morphine
   d. marijuana

9. What is one of the biological differences reported for sons of alcoholics compared to sons from families with no alcoholism?
   a. Sons of alcoholics only need a little alcohol to start feeling the effects.
   b. Sons of alcoholics need more alcohol to start feeling the effects.
   c. Sons of alcoholics have elevated levels of dopamine.
   d. Sons of alcoholics have lowered levels of dopamine.

10. Treatment for alcoholism focuses on:
    a. detoxification.
    b. personality change.
    c. relapse prevention.
    d. family change.

11. Teaching the patient with alcohol dependence to identify and cope effectively with high-risk situations and to view relapse as a single, independent event rather than a disaster that can never be undone best describes what type of therapy?
    a. cognitive-behavioral
    b. Alcoholics Anonymous (AA)
    c. interpersonal therapy
    d. humanistic therapy

12. About how many alcoholics recover?
    a. one-fourth
    b. one-third
    c. one-half
    d. three-fourths

13. About how many people die each year in the U.S. from causes that are traced to alcohol abuse?
    a. 10,000
    b. 50,000
    c. 100,000
    d. 500,000

14. Which of the following drugs is NOT a stimulant?
    a. heroin
    b. amphetamine
    c. cocaine
    d. caffeine

15. Theo has just taken a drug. He is feeling very well, almost euphoric. He is very alert, sexually excited, and has lots of energy. His perceptual processes seem intact. What drug has Theo probably just taken?
    a. Xanax
    b. nicotine
    c. morphine
    d. cocaine

16. Which drug is the most reinforcing?
    a. alcohol
    b. heroin
    c. cocaine
    d. marijuana

17. The primary pharmacological effect of cocaine is the activation of the _____ system.
    a. serotonin
    b. dopamine
    c. norepinephrine
    d. acetylcholine

18. Sandra, a cocaine addict, is undergoing outpatient treatment. She is given a voucher, which she can use to get retail items, every time she checks in with a cocaine-negative urine sample. Sandra is being treated with:
    a. cognitive therapy.
    b. learning-based therapy.
    c. contingency management.
    d. group therapy.

19. Which of the following classes of drugs is used to relieve pain and suffering?
    a. stimulants
    b. opiates
    c. hallucinogens
    d. barbiturates

20. Which of the following drugs is most likely to lead to sudden death?
    a. heroin
    b. marijuana
    c. nicotine
    d. cocaine

21. Which of the following is the most problematic regarding the use of the opiate drugs?
    a. the toxic effects on the body

b. the time spent and behaviors engaged in to procure the drug

c. the risk of death from use of the drug

d. none of the above

22. Rudy is in detox, withdrawing from a drug. He is experiencing irritability, loss of appetite, tremors, insomnia, violent yawning, and excessive tearing and sneezing. His muscles are weak and he has cramps and diarrhea. Rudy is probably withdrawing from what drug?
    a. alcohol
    b. marijuana
    c. heroin
    d. cocaine

23. For which of the following drug classes is treatment primarily pharmacological?
    a. alcohol
    b. hallucinogenic
    c. stimulant
    d. opiates

24. Animals will press a lever, sometimes thousands of times, to self-administer each of the following drugs EXCEPT:
    a. stimulants.
    b. opiates.
    c. barbiturates.
    d. hallucinogens.

25. Which of the following is not a negative consequence of hallucinogenic drugs?
    a. toxic effects on the body
    b. acute psychotic reactions
    c. perceptual alterations that may cause suicide
    d. flashbacks

26. Which is the most commonly used illegal drug in the U.S.?
    a. cocaine
    b. heroin
    c. marijuana
    d. nicotine

27. Keith has just taken a drug at a party. He is experiencing feelings of well-being and mild euphoria. He then starts to feel very relaxed and dreamy. He notices that his music sounds *really* good, and he's not really sure how long he's been at this party. Keith is probably using:
    a. barbiturates.
    b. opiates.
    c. marijuana.
    d. alcohol.

28. Which of the following is the most addictive drug?
    a. amphetamines
    b. barbiturates
    c. alcohol
    d. nicotine

29. Sod has recently stopped taking a drug that he has taken for many years. He is experiencing irritability, anxiety, restlessness, impaired concentration, and strong cravings for the drug. He has headaches and is unable to sleep well. His appetite is huge, and he tends to be hostile. He is most likely withdrawing from what drug?
    a. alcohol
    b. nicotine
    c. heroin
    d. cocaine

30. Mary has just taken a heavy dose of a drug. She is having difficulty thinking, her speech is slurred, her comprehension and memory are impaired. She acts aggressively, but then she loses consciousness and her breathing is very slow. When drug did Mary just take?
    a. a barbiturate
    b. a stimulant
    c. an opiate
    d. marijuana

Fill in the Blank

1. _____ _____ involves loss of control over drug use, continued use of a drug despite adverse circumstances, and physical or emotional dependence.

   Substance dependence

2. _____ _____ involves a maladaptive, harmful pattern of drug use that does not include physical dependence.

   Drug abuse

3. _____ occurs when the constant presence of a drug somehow induces long-lasting changes in the brain.

   Neuroadaptation

4. _____ drugs are those that affect brain function, mood, and behavior.

   Psychoactive

5. _____ refers to the amount of a drug that must be given in order to obtain a particular response.

    Potency

6. The _____-_____ barrier is composed of specialized cells that prevent particular compounds in the circulatory system from entering the brain.

    blood-brain

7. _____ refers to a state of decreased response to a drug following prior or repeated exposure to that drug.

    Tolerance

8. _____ dependence is characterized by the need for the drug in order to function normally, and by the appearance of a withdrawal syndrome upon cessation of the drug.

    Physical

9. _____-_____ theory is based on the idea that systems react and adapt to stimuli by opposing their initial effects.

    Opponent-process

10. The _____ _____ brain region is located deep in the basal forebrain and appears to be critical for the reinforcing effects of many drugs.

    nucleus accumbens

11. _____ _____ are the brain's own morphinelike substances, such as enkephalins, endorphins, and dynorphins.

    Endogenous opioids

12. _____ _____ alcoholism affects both males and females, has an onset after twenty-five, and is associated with personality traits characteristic of persons with passive-dependent personalities; _____ _____ alcoholism occurs only in males and is typified by low reward dependence, low harm avoidance, and high novelty seeking.

    Type 1

    Type 2

13. The _____ drugs, also known as narcotics, relieve pain and suffering.

    opiate

14. _____ have a marked ability to alter sensory perception, awareness, and thoughts.

    Hallucinogens

15. _____ involves the transposition of one mode of sensory sensations for another.

    Synesthesia

16. Symptoms that appear in chronic marijuana users, such as dullness, apathy, cognitive and memory impairments, and loss of interest in personal appearance and conventional goals, are collectively called _____ _____.

    amotivational syndrome

Additional Exercise: Drug Characteristics

Give examples of specific drugs in each drug class, how these drugs affect the brain, and the medical and social complications associated with the drugs.

Drug class	Specific drugs	Effects on brain	Medical and social complications
Alcohol	N/A		
Stimulants			
Opiates			
Hallucinogens			
Marijuana	N/A		
Tobacco			
Barbiturates/ Benzodiazepines			

LEVELS OF ANALYSIS: EXAMINING THE CHAPTER'S THEMES

Two important themes that emerge in this chapter are biological and psychological levels of analysis and treatment of choice.

Biological and Psychological Levels of Analysis

Biological and psychological factors interact in causing substance addiction, in determining the short-term and long-term effects of a drug, and in effectively treating addiction. Drugs affect the brain in multiple ways, for example, by mimicking the action of neurotransmitters, by changing the structure and function of neurons in the brain, and by affecting brain systems. The effect and use of drugs is also determined by environmental cues and psychological addiction. Building evidence for the role of stress in drug use has highlighted the importance of the diathesis-stress model in explaining why some people become addicted to substances and others do not. The specific biological and psychological correlates vary somewhat from drug to drug, but the important thing to remember is that substance dependence is a complex phenomenon that results from the interaction of many factors.

Treatment of Choice

Because there is such a high rate of relapse in people suffering from substance dependence and abuse, the focus of treatment is relapse prevention. Relapse prevention is accomplished through biological and psychological treatment, depending on the drug that the person is addicted to and the availability of pharmacological treatments for that drug. In the case of heroin addiction, methadone is used to suppress cravings and to help prevent relapse. For alcohol addiction, both psychological and pharmacological treatments are used. To treat those addicted to cocaine, an incredibly reinforcing drug, other types of reinforcement are used to help keep addicts from using the drug (such as earning "points" for staying clean, which can later be exchanged for retail goods). Keep in mind that pharmacological treatments for substance dependence are controversial, with some taking the view that one addiction is being substituted for another. Be sure to read Box 14-2 for a description of this controversy.

ANSWER KEY

MULTIPLE-CHOICE QUESTIONS

1. b. Tolerance, impairment in daily functioning, and continued use of the substance are symptoms of substance dependence. Substance abuse is a maladaptive, harmful pattern of drug use that does not include physical dependence.

2. d. Nearly 80 percent of people relapse after receiving treatment. Some of those people go on to recover in the long run, but relapses are an integral part of the recovery process.

3. a. If a drug is taken orally, it must pass through the gastrointestinal tract and be absorbed by the liver. Thus, drugs taken orally often reach the brain slowly and in relatively low concentrations.

4. c. Antisocial personality disorder is the most common coexisting mental disorder among male substance abusers. The prevalence of antisocial personality disorder is 2 to 3 percent in the general population, and about 16 to 49 percent among substance abusers.

5. b. Studies have shown that children of alcoholics are four times more likely to become alcohol dependent compared to people in the general population, even for children who were adopted away from alcoholic families into families with no alcoholism.

6. c. According to opponent-process theory, systems react and adapt to stimuli by opposing their initial effects. In the case of drug use, the pleasurable state induced by drugs diminishes over time and is replaced by a negative, unpleasant state (withdrawal). Drugs continue to be used in order to compensate for the unpleasant state in order to achieve at least a neutral state.

7. b. Alcoholism is outweighed only by smoking as the most serious drug problem in the U.S.

8. a. Heavy doses of alcohol are associated with depressant effects and considerable impairment of sensory and motor functions, including decreases in visual acuity and sensitivity to taste and smell. Reflexes are slowed and movement and speech may be sluggish. Memory processes are also disrupted.

9. b. Sons of alcoholics may need to drink more alcohol to experience the same subjective effects as people without a family history of alcoholism. They show discrepancies in the serotonin and GABA systems.

10. c. Though detoxification is usually a necessary first step, relapse prevention is the main goal of treatment.

11. a. This is a description of the cognitive-behavioral approach developed and tested by G. Alan Marlatt.

12. b. By age sixty-five, about one-third of alcoholics are dead or in awful shape, about one-third are abstinent or drinking socially, and about one-third are still trying to quit.

13. c. About 100,000 people die each year in the U.S. from deaths that are traced to alcohol abuse.

14. a. Heroin is an opiate drug; all the others are stimulants.

15. d. Cocaine produces feelings of stimulation, well-being, vigor, euphoria, enhanced alertness, increased sexuality, heightened energy, and deepened emotions.

16. c. Cocaine may well be the most reinforcing drug. Monkeys will make up to 6,000 lever presses to obtain one infusion of cocaine.

17. b. The primary pharmacological effect of cocaine is the activation of the dopamine system. Moreover, the release of dopamine in the nucleus accumbens appears to be directly linked to the rewarding properties of the drug.

18. c. Incentives for improvement are the major technique for contingency management.

19. b. The opiates, such as morphine, codeine, and opium, have been used to relieve pain for thousands of years.

20. d. Unlike the other drugs on the list, cocaine can lead to sudden death.

21. b. The main focus in the lives of opiate addicts is how to get more of the drug. They engage in high-risk behaviors to accomplish this, such as crime, prostitution, and sharing of drug paraphernalia.

22. c. These are the classic symptoms of opiate withdrawal.

23. d. The treatment of choice for opiate addiction is the substitution of an oral synthetic opiate, usually methadone.

24. d. Animals cannot be taught to self-administer hallucinogens. The drugs themselves do not affect the brain reward system nor do people become addicted to them.

25. a. Hallucinogens have very few toxic effects on the body.

26. c. About one-third of the population has used marijuana at least once. Nicotine is used more than marijuana, but it is a legal drug.

27. c. The symptoms are typical of marijuana use.

28. d. Nicotine is among the most addictive of drugs. It is rated the highest in terms of dependence (Table 14-4).

29. b. These are classic symptoms of nicotine withdrawal.

30. a. The effects of barbiturates are similar to those of alcohol. The symptoms described above are typical of heavy doses of barbiturates.

ADDITIONAL EXERCISES

Drug class	Specific drugs	Effects on brain	Medical and social complications
Alcohol	N/A	Reduces neural activity Affects norepinephrine, dopamine, serotonin, and GABA	Cirrhosis of the liver Damage to the nervous system Damage to heart Cancer Fetal alcohol syndrome
Stimulants	Amphetamine Methamphetamine Cocaine Caffeine	Activates sympathetic nervous system Releases dopamine	AIDS (from needle sharing) Psychosis, paranoia, irritability Attention and concentration problems Sleeping and eating problems Sudden death
Opiates	Opium Morphine Codeine Heroin Demerol	Stimulate opiate receptors in limbic regions of the brain	AIDS (from needle sharing) Sexually transmitted diseases/pregnancy Poor diet Lack of motivation to seek out medical care

Drug class	*Specific drugs*	*Effects on brain*	*Medical and social complications*

Hallucinogens	LSD
	Mescaline
	Psilocybin
	PCP
	MDMA (XTC)
		Affects serotonin,
		  norepinephrine,
		  glutamate, and
		  dopamine systems
		Changes limbic system
			"Bad trips" can cause severe panic
			Perceptual alterations can lead to
			  suicide
			Flashbacks
			PCP and MDMA can cause brain damage
			  and suicide

Marijuana	N/A	Effects the nucleus
		  accumbens, regions in
		  the limbic system, and
		  acetycholine
			Effects on lungs when smoked
			Suppression of immune responses
			Changes in lifestyle, personality, and
			  ambitions

Tobacco	Nicotine	Stimulates cholinergic
		  receptors in CNS,
		  induces the release of
		  catacholamines, and
		  many neurotransmitters,
		  activates frontal lobes,
		  nucleus accumbens, and
		  amygdala
			Lung cancer
			Coronary heart disease
			Hypertension
			Emphysema
			Shortens life span
			Lower birth weight in fetuses

Barbiturates/
Benzodiazepines
	Nembutal
	Seconal
	Amytal
	Xanax
	Valium
	Librium
		Depresses CNS,
		  increases the effectiveness
		  of GABA
			Tolerance and withdrawal symptoms
			For barbiturates, tremor, anxiety,
			  insomnia, delirium, and seizures
			For benzodiazepines, anxiety, sleep
			  disturbance, heightened sensitivity,
			  and EEG changes

CHAPTER 15 | Social and Legal Perspectives

A GUIDE TO THE READING

This chapter describes the impact of mental illness on individuals, families, and society. Two important areas of law for the mentally ill are discussed: involuntary and criminal commitment. It concludes by outlining some new challenges to the legal system and by discussing what happens when psychologists or lawmakers abuse mental health care. The many anecdotes in this chapter are especially useful in illustrating and explaining the legal and ethical issues encountered when working with the mentally ill.

The Impact of Mental Illness

Individuals with mental illness continue to be stigmatized, based on views that mental disorders are willful or a sign of depravity, or that psychiatric patients are dangerous. Such stigmatizing attitudes keep people from seeking treatment and interfere with community services for the mentally ill. Further, many of the mentally ill have become homeless; estimates of the proportion of the homeless with a mental illness range from 45 to 72 percent.

Mental illness also impacts the family. Family members must dramatically lower their expectations of the person with mental illness and cope with the emotional burden of worrying about and caring for a loved one with mental illness. Review the case of Jane for an excellent illustration of the impact of mental illness on the family.

Mental illness also has a considerable impact on society. Mental illness leads to losses in worker productivity, additional burdens on the criminal justice system when individuals are not treated adequately by the health care system, and additional burdens for general health care providers, be-

cause those with mental illness tend to utilize more services for physical problems. Several dramatic shifts in the delivery of care for the mentally ill have impacted their treatment profoundly. These include the proliferation of managed care systems, the shift from institutionalized care to community and outpatient care, and the dramatic increase in mental health practitioners and people utilizing mental health services in the second half of the twentieth century. Be sure to review these changes and the issues and concerns related to them on pages 645–47. To address issues of concern, patients and families have formed groups to advocate for the mentally ill. They have created a "Patients' Bill of Rights" to ensure that a patient's rights are not violated during the treatment process (see Table 15-1).

Involuntary Commitment

Involuntary or civil commitment is commitment to a psychiatric facility without the patient's consent. The decision to commit a patient is a difficult one, for it entails a substantial violation of the patient's civil rights. Be sure to review the list of rights and privileges that collectively make up "due process of law" on page 654. Criteria for civil commitment do vary from state to state, but generally laws have become more stringent, so that fewer patients are hospitalized against their will, and the duration of commitment is shorter (see the case of Mr. Mayock on pages 649–50 for an illustrative example of the difficult issues involved in involuntary commitment). Criteria that appear in all states are (1) the presence of a mental disorder, (2) dangerousness to self or others, and (3) grave disability. Be sure to read pages 651–53 carefully for a detailed discussion of issues related to these criteria. Commitment is typically initiated by families or police officers, often beginning with emergency room visits. Two doctoral-level mental health professionals and an order from a judge are usually required to commit someone. In order to civilly commit someone, the judge must have "clear and convincing proof," which means the judge should be roughly 75 percent certain that the patient requires civil commitment.

When involuntary commitment takes place, it is important to assure a right to treatment for those who are hospitalized. The idea of right to treatment was first enunciated in *Rouse* v. *Cameron*; later, minimal standards of care were stipulated in *Wyatt* v. *Stickney*. Unfortunately, the additional costs associated with these standards have resulted in some hospitals closing their doors to mental patients. A new approach that is now being used is "outpatient commitment," wherein patients must take medications and/or show up for outpatient appointments. If they do not comply, they are then hospitalized. Be sure to review the arguments for and against involuntary hospitalization on pages 656–57.

Criminal Commitment

Criminal commitment refers to the psychiatric hospitalization of people who have been accused of committing a felony, but who are not legally responsible because they lack a *mens rea*, or guilty mind. Criminal commitment can take place if someone is not competent to stand trial, or if someone is found to be legally insane. To be competent to stand trial in most states, the defendant must be aware of his or her personal identity, be oriented to time and space, and be able to understand the roles of the judge, jury, and attorneys. Defendants found incompetent to stand trial are sent to institutions until they are able to be tried. The amount of time such a patient can be hospitalized varies from state to state.

The insanity defense requires that the defendant was wholly or partially irrational when the crime took place, and that this state of mind affected his or her behavior. It is rarely used—even more rarely successful—and results in long-term incarceration that can last longer than a jail sentence. However, public perception of the insanity defense has been negative. Be sure to review pages 659–60 for examples of how some states have tried to cope with this negative perception. The standards for legal insanity vary from state to state; reviewing the three cases on pages 660–61 and Table 15-2 will help you to understand these standards and how they apply to specific cases. The M'Naghten rule states that, at the time of the crime, the person had a "defect of reason, from disease of the mind" that resulted in not knowing the "nature and quality of the act," or not knowing that what he or she was doing was wrong. Most states use this standard, either alone, or in conjunction with other rules. The Durham test is broader than the M'Naghten standard, only requiring that "the unlawful act was the product of mental disease or

mental defect." This standard is only used in one state, because states found that it relied too heavily on the expert testimony of psychiatrists and because it is so difficult to define "mental disease." The American Law Institute (ALI) rule is a compromise between the M'Naghten rule and the Durham rule. It incorporates the requirement of a mental disease, the individual's inability to know what he or she is doing is wrong, and the inability to conform to the law, and it specifies that repeated criminal and antisocial conduct cannot be used for an insanity defense (see p. 664 for the rule in its entirety). The ALI rule is used in twenty-one states.

New Challenges to the Legal System

Dissociative identity disorder and legal responsibility. Controversy about how to handle cases in which the insanity defense is based on dissociative identity disorder (DID) exists on a number of levels. Some question whether DID actually exists. If it does exist, we need to know how to distinguish real personalities from fake personalities. Finally, the question of how to punish the whole person for the acts of only one personality is quite problematic.

Accuracy of recovered memories. The idea of repressed memories, while central to psychology, also causes thorny legal problems. First, it is difficult and often impossible to verify the accuracy of a recovered memory of something that took places years or even decades ago. Second, there is a statute of limitations on most crimes, which can make it difficult to try cases based on recovered memories. Finally, it has been found that "recovered" memories can be implanted in suggestible people; be sure to read the case of Paul Ingram on pages 669–70 as an example.

The Abuse of Mental Health Care

Mental health practitioners do sometimes violate their legal and ethical responsibilities when caring for clients. Such clinical malpractice can result in the loss of their license to practice and/or legal proceedings, depending on the nature of the violation. Entering into a sexual relationship with a client and planting false memories in a client are two examples given in your text of clinical malpractice. Society can also have a negative influence on the treatment of the mentally ill. Social stereotypes can "pathologize" otherwise normal behavior (for instance, homosexuality). Governments can abuse the mental health care system to control dissidents (see p. 673 for an example). Finally, society can stigmatize those with mental illness (for example, by not hiring a person for a job, or not accepting someone into graduate school; see the case of Myra Grossman as an example).

TESTING YOUR UNDERSTANDING

Test your understanding of what you have read by working through the following tasks with a classmate.

1. Imagine someone asks you why you are studying psychology. Provide a reason based on what we know about the impact of mental illness on individuals, their families, and society.

2. Imagine you are a psychologist who is seeing a patient for the first time. You suspect the patient may need to be hospitalized involuntarily. Under what conditions may you initiate such a commitment?

3. Think of someone you know or have heard of who suffers from a mental illness. Describe this person's rights as a patient. Why are patient's rights sometimes restricted?

4. Explain the difference between being incompetent to stand trial and the insanity defense.

5. There are many media depictions of defendants who use the insanity defense, some more accurate than others. Explain what tests are actually used by the criminal justice system to measure insanity.

6. Why do dissociative identity disorder and recovered memories cause problems for the legal system?

7. List the ways that abuse of mental health care can occur, including abuse by individual practitioners and abuse by governments.

Multiple-Choice Questions

1. Which of the following is least likely to happen to someone who is seriously mentally ill in today's health care system?
   a. years of institutional care
   b. becoming homeless
   c. living in squalid conditions in the community
   d. not being hospitalized even when the patient needs it

2. What is true of mental illness in the United States today?
   a. It is not as significant a problem as it was thirty years ago.
   b. It continues to be a significant problem.
   c. There are more cases of mental illness and fewer mental health professionals.
   d. There are more mental health professionals and fewer cases of mental illness.

3. What is true regarding mental illness and dangerousness?
   a. People with serious mental illness are two to three times more likely to show aggression than nonpatients.
   b. Most individuals with mental illnesses never show aggressive behavior.
   c. The view that the mentally ill are dangerous is a misperception.
   d. all of the above

4. About what percentage of the homeless are estimated to be mentally ill?
   a. 15 percent
   b. 30 percent
   c. 60 percent
   d. 90 percent

5. Why is caring for a mentally ill child so difficult on parents?
   a. They must lower their expectations of the child.
   b. They often must support the child even as an adult.
   c. Many people with severe mental illness lack insight and refuse to accept any kind of treatment.
   d. all of the above

6. Why is it less likely that spouses will be impacted by serious mental illness compared to siblings and parents?
   a. Spouses can divorce a patient, but parents and children cannot.
   b. Parents tend to become or remain the primary caregiver, even after the patient marries.
   c. Patients with serious mental illness are much less likely to marry.
   d. all of the above

7. Why is meant by the phrase "the criminalization of mental illness?"
   a. The mentally ill are more likely to be criminals.
   b. Criminals are more likely to be mentally ill.
   c. The mentally ill are stigmatized by society.
   d. The undertreated mentally ill tend to end up in the criminal justice system.

8. What was the driving force behind the deinstitutionalization of mental patients in the mid-twentieth century?
   a. the introduction of psychotropic medications
   b. the community health movement
   c. governmental attempts to make systematic changes in the health care system
   d. both a and b

9. Of the following sources of mental health treatment support, which provides most of the funding for inpatient treatment?
   a. public money (government)
   b. managed care organizations
   c. private insurance companies
   d. both a and b

10. Which of the following best describes the status of mental health care in the managed care system
    a. Mental health care is now more easily accessible.

b. Mental health care coverage has been eliminated by a substantial number of HMOs.

c. Overall, the quality of treatment appears to be the same as before managed care.

d. Doctors are the ones who decided what and how much mental health treatment will be provided.

11. When advocacy groups seek parity for the treatment of mental illness, what are they seeking?
   a. specific coverage for mental health treatment by insurance companies
   b. legal requirements for the same coverage, treatment limitations, and financial requirements as other medical conditions
   c. equal treatment for mental illness across insurance companies
   d. equal treatment for similar mental illnesses

12. Which of the following is NOT one of the patient's rights as stated in the Patients' Bill of Rights?
   a. the right to refuse hospitalization
   b. the right to appropriate treatment
   c. the right to confidentiality of personal records
   d. the right to private conversations

13. How many patients with chronic psychotic disorders do not believe they are mentally ill, or are not sure they are mentally ill?
   a. 5 percent
   b. 15 percent
   c. 30 percent
   d. 45 percent

14. Which of the following is the most problematic today in involuntarily committing someone who is mentally ill to a hospital?
   a. people who are committed when they should not be
   b. people who are not committed when they probably should be
   c. states without rules regarding involuntary commitment
   d. states without procedures regarding involuntary commitment

15. Who are the authorities who most often initiate the process of civil commitment?
   a. the police
   b. medical doctors
   c. psychologists and psychiatrists
   d. judges

16. Which of the following is NOT one of the three elements that are included in all statutes about civil commitment?
   a. the presence of a mental disorder
   b. dangerousness to self or others
   c. child abuse
   d. grave disability

17. On what grounds are the most involuntary hospitalizations justified?
   a. the presence of a mental disorder
   b. dangerousness to self or others
   c. child abuse
   d. grave disability

18. What makes civil commitment so problematic?
   a. Liberty is traditionally deprived only after a crime is committed.
   b. It is very difficult to predict dangerousness.
   c. Judges usually overturn requests for civil commitment.
   d. both a and b

19. Which of the following is the 75 percent standard, the one used for civil commitment decisions?
   a. preponderance of evidence
   b. beyond a reasonable doubt
   c. clear and convincing proof
   d. pretty darn sure

20. The right to treatment was enunciated in response to:
   a. patients being turned away from hospitals.
   b. patients in hospitals who didn't receive adequate treatment.
   c. increases in homeless rates of the mentally ill.
   d. the rise of managed care.

21. Some, like Thomas Szasz, argue that involuntary commitment and involuntary treatment should be abolished because:
   a. the criteria for mental disorders are not precise and specific enough.
   b. certain antipsychotic drugs have adverse side effects.
   c. the guidelines for involuntary treatment are too restrictive.
   d. both a and b

22. Which of the following is NOT one of the criteria used to determine if someone is competent to stand trial?
   a. awareness of personal identity
   b. orientation to time and space
   c. comprehension of the crime for which they are accused
   d. comprehension of the roles of the judge, jury, and attorneys

23. What happens to people who are found incompetent to stand trial?
   a. Their cases are dismissed.
   b. They are sent to prison until they are able to be tried.
   c. They are sent to institutions until they are able to be tried.
   d. The judge determines the sentence, based on the evidence.

24. About how often is the insanity defense used in homicide cases?
    a. one in four cases
    b. one in forty cases
    c. one in four hundred cases
    d. one in four thousand cases

25. Which of the following standards for insanity is focused exclusively on the individual's cognitions, specifically the knowledge between right and wrong?
    a. the M'Naghten standard
    b. the Durham standard
    c. the American Law Institute (ALI) rule
    d. the Insanity Defense Reform Act (IDRA)

26. Which of the following standards for insanity is the broadest, based only on whether the crime was the product of a mental disease or defect?
    a. the M'Naghten standard
    b. the Durham standard
    c. the American Law Institute (ALI) rule
    d. the Insanity Defense Reform Act (IDRA)

27. Which standard is used in the most states?
    a. the M'Naghten standard
    b. the Durham standard
    c. the American Law Institute (ALI) rule
    d. the Insanity Defense Reform Act (IDRA)

28. Why is the use of dissociative identity disorder (DID) as a defense so difficult to deal with from a legal perspective?
    a. Some believe that DID does not actually exist.
    b. DID can be faked.
    c. It is impossible to punish only the personality that committed the crime.
    d. all of the above

29. Why are cases based on recovered memories so difficult to deal with in a court of law?
    a. The memory often cannot be corroborated.
    b. Memories of crimes committed long ago may exceed the statute of limitations.
    c. Memories can be "planted" in susceptible people.
    d. all of the above

30. What are the consequences of malpractice for mental health practitioners?
    a. The practitioner loses his or her professional license.
    b. The practitioner is barred from membership in professional organizations.
    c. There may be legal proceedings against the practitioner.
    d. All of the above are possible consequences.

Fill in the Blank

1. The view of mental disorders as willful or as a sign of depravity reflect the _____ of mental illness.   stigma

2. The fact that the criminal justice system bears a substantial burden for the care of people with mental illness is referred to as the _____ of mental illness.   criminalization

3. _____ occurs when individuals remain in state hospitals for extended periods of time and lose their independent living skills.   Institutionalization

4. The introduction of psychotropic drugs and the community mental health movement led to the _____ of mental patients.   deinstitutionalization

5. The _____ _____ phenomenon refers to patients experiencing repeated brief hospitalizations with the goal of stabilizing symptoms rather than rehabilitation.   revolving door

6. _____ refers to equal requirements for treatment for people who are mentally ill and people who are suffering from other medical disorders.   Parity

7. _____ commitment is commitment to a psychiatric facility without the patient's consent.   Civil or involuntary

8. _____ prediction of violence draws on the professional's experience with varied cases, whereas _____ prediction is based upon mathematical formulas and specific, objective data on the patient.

        Clinical

        actuarial

9. The _____ _____ _____ standard requires just enough proof to shift the weight of evidence to one side.

        preponderance of evidence

10. _____ _____ _____ _____ is the most severe standard of proof and requires that the evidence be so compelling as to convince a reasonable listener beyond a reasonable doubt.

        Beyond a reasonable doubt

11. _____ _____ _____ proof is an intermediate standard, requiring about 75 percent certainty.

        Clear and convincing

12. _____ commitment refers to the psychiatric hospitalization of people who have been accused of committing a felony, but who are not legally responsible for reasons of insanity.

        Criminal

13. The _____ _____ requires that the defendant was wholly or partially irrational when the crime took place, and that this state of mind affected his or her behavior.

        insanity defense

14. The _____ _____ rule stated that mental disease may impair self-control even when reasoning ability remains intact.

        irresistible impulse

ANSWER KEY

Multiple-Choice Questions

1. a. In the past twenty years, the emphasis in mental health care has shifted away from institutionalization and toward community treatment. With the advent of managed care and concern about patients' rights, patients are more likely to be undertreated than to be hospitalized for years.

2. b. Prevalence rates indicate that mental illness continues to be a significant problem in the United States. There are more mental health professionals and more people seeking mental health services than before.

3. d. Though people with serious mental illness are two to three times more likely to show aggression than nonpatients, most individuals with mental illnesses never show aggressive behavior. The view of the mentally ill as dangerous is a misperception, fueled in part by media depictions.

4. c. The percentage of the homeless with a DSM-IV mental illness, including substance abuse disorder, is estimated to be between 45 and 72 percent.

5. d. All of the options mentioned impact the parents of the mentally ill.

6. c. The rate of marriage among patients with serious mental illness is much lower than it is among the general population.

7. d. The criminal justice system currently bears a substantial burden in caring for those with mental illness. This is because those with untreated mental illness sometimes engage in aberrant public behavior that results in their incarceration.

8. d. The removal of the mentally ill from long-term hospitalization to community mental health centers was the result of the community health movement and the introduction of psychotropic medications. Governmental attempts to make systematic changes in the health care system in the 1990s contributed to the trend toward managed care.

9. a. Although governmental support of inpatient mental health services has declined since 1950, the government still provides most of the funding for inpatient treatment.

10. b. A substantial number of HMOs and insurance companies have eliminated coverage for mental health services.

11. b. Parity for treatment of mental illness refers to legal requirements for equal coverage of mental illness and general medical illnesses by HMOs and insurance companies.

12. a. Patients can be hospitalized against their wishes under certain conditions.

13. d. About 19 percent of patients with chronic psychotic disorders do not believe they are mentally ill, about 25 percent are not sure they are mentally ill.

14. b. In recent years, the laws governing involuntary commitment have become more stringent, so that fewer patients are hospitalized against their will. Thus, there are many more controversial cases about failure to hospitalize than the reverse. States rules and procedures for civil commitment do vary somewhat, but every state has such rules and procedures.

15. a. Police officers are the authorities who most often initiate the process of civil commitment.

16. c. Child abuse is a reportable offense, but does not lead to civil commitment. The state department of children's services is informed and conducts an investigation.

17. b. Roughly 60 percent of those committed are dangerous to themselves, about 49 percent are dangerous to others, and about 32 percent are gravely disabled.

18. d. The legal problem is that Western legal traditions generally mandate the deprivation of liberty only after a crime has been committed. The scientific problem is that it is very difficult to accurately predict dangerousness.

19. c. The preponderance of evidence standard is the 51 percent standard, the beyond a reasonable doubt standard is the 90 or 99 percent standard, and the clear and convincing proof standard is the 75 percent standard.

20. b. The right to treatment was enunciated in response to hospitalization without adequate treatment. Judge Bazelon wrote, in *Rouse* v. *Cameron,* that "the purpose of hospitalization is treatment, not punishment . . . absent treatment, the hospital is transformed into a penitentiary where one could be held indefinitely for no convicted reason."

21. d. Answers a and b are reasons put forward by those who argue that involuntary commitment and involuntary treatment should be abolished. Those who argue that the guidelines are too strict are concerned that patients who need to be committed are not, and thus not receiving the care they need.

22. c. In most states, competency to stand trial is assumed if the defendant is aware of his of her personal identity, is oriented to time and space, and can understand the roles of the judge, jury, and attorneys.

23. c. Defendants found incompetent to stand trial are sent to institutions until they are able to be tried.

24. c. The insanity defense is invoked in fewer than one in four hundred homicide cases and is successful in many fewer cases than that.

25. a. The M'Naghten standard is focused exclusively on the individual's cognitions, specifically the knowledge between right and wrong.

26. b. In the Durham test, incapacitating conditions, such as the inability to tell right from wrong, are not specified. One goes directly from "mental disease" to the act.

27. a. Nearly half the states use the M'Naghten rule alone as the yardstick for insanity, while other states use the M'Naghten rule in conjunction with other rules.

28. d. All three of the above problems make DID very difficult to deal with in a court of law.

29. d. All of the reasons given above make cases based on recovered memories difficult to deal with in a court of law.

30. d. Depending on the nature of the ethical and/or legal violation, a practitioner may suffer any one or all of these consequences.

CHAPTER 16 | Future Directions

A GUIDE TO THE READING

The authors conclude the text by discussing four future directions for psychology, based on the four themes of the book. The biopsychology of murder is examined in relation to the levels of analysis theme. *Rampage murders,* in particular, such as those that took place at Columbine High School, are looked at in great detail. In the science and practice theme, the effectiveness and economics of psychotherapy is discussed. The prevention of depression, anxiety, and aggression is explored in the development theme. Finally, positive psychology is discussed as an alternative approach to determining the treatment of choice for mental disorders.

Biological and Psychological Levels of Analysis: The Biopsychology of Murder

Violence and aggression are not categories in the DSM-IV. Most people with mental illness are not violent, and the inclusion of violence in the DSM-IV might serve to further stigmatize the mentally ill. The recent rash of "rampage murders" requires an explanation, however, and it appears, at least in some cases, that there are psychological and biological issues involved, in addition to social issues such as media violence and access to guns. The case of Michael Carneal, presented on pages 679–81, is an example of a case with psychological factors. Be sure to review this case and the evidence for psychological problems that may have led to the shootings. Michael appeared to have symptoms of depression and schizophrenia, which he kept to himself, fearing the stigma of mental illness. This case, and others like it, have led some to encourage the inclusion of violence in the DSM-V, so that much-needed research can be conducted to help us understand and prevent these violent acts.

Rampage murders differ from murders that are committed in the heat of passion or during armed robbery or gang warfare. Rampage murders seem senseless. The perpetrator does not flee and is quite likely to kill him- or herself or let him- or herself be killed. Rampage killers are better educated, less deprived, and more likely to be white than other killers. At least half of the 102 rampage killers in the last fifty years had a history of serious mental disorders and histories of violence. They will sometimes describe very precisely the details of the planned murder spree. There is also evidence of biological differences in the brains of murderers, including reduced activation of the prefrontal cortex, the corpus callosum, the left amygdala, hippocampus, and thalamus (see p. 683 for brain scans of a normal control and a convicted murderer). Cold-blooded killers, who plan their actions, have the same pattern, but they have more prefrontal activity than impulsive murderers. See the paragraph that begins on p. 683 and continues on p. 684 for an excellent summary of the findings regarding rampage murderers.

Science and Practice: Effectiveness and Economics of Psychotherapy

It is often difficult for practitioners to translate research findings into treatments for particular clients. Important reasons for this difficulty are the limitations of the two types of outcome research: efficacy research and effectiveness research. Be sure to know the differences between these two approaches, which are outlined on pages 684–88. Efficacy studies are controlled laboratory studies of therapy, and effectiveness studies are studies of psychotherapy as it is actually done in the real world. Carefully review the results of the *Consumer Reports* study, the largest effectiveness study to date, summarized on page 685. The study indicates that psychological treatment works very well, that it works better when it is long-term rather than short-term, and that no specific mode of therapy works better than any other. Effectiveness studies have *internal validity* problems: they do not include controls, they usually have biased sampling, diagnosis is not rigorous, and they are based on self-report and memory. Efficacy studies have *external validity* problems. Therapy is conducted in a lab, in a manner so different from therapy conducted in the community as to make it very difficult to generalize to "normal" therapy (see p. 686 for a detailed list of the differences between therapy done in a lab and therapy done in the community). Considering efficacy and effectiveness studies together, it appears that some disorders require specific curative ingredients, such as cognitive therapy for panic (see p. 686 for a list of disorders that require specific interventions), whereas others are effectively treated by nonspecific factors that occur in all modalities, such as attention from an authority figure (see p. 687 for a list of nonspecific therapy factors). To overcome the problems associated with the two different approaches, the authors suggest a combined approach, described on pp. 687–88.

With the advent of managed care, there have been dramatic changes in the economics of mental health care. The therapist, the type of therapy, and the length of therapy are all determined by a case reviewer rather than by the client or the therapist. The focus of treatment is crisis intervention and brief, problem-focused treatment. As a result, the gulf between what therapists can do and what they are allowed to do, as well as the gap between good science and good practice, has widened considerably.

Development: The Prevention Frontier

The fact that humans grow and develop throughout their lifespan suggests that early prevention may help an at-risk person avoid mental illness later in life. Promising results of prevention are discussed for depression, anxiety, and aggression. Cognitive therapy has proven effective in preventing depression in college students, high school students, and children (review these findings in detail on pp. 689–90). Cognitive, behavioral, and physiological coping strategies have been shown to help reduce future anxiety in children. Finally, a dozen or so programs are now being tested to help prevent aggression and violence in children. An example of such a program, Fast-Track, is described on p. 692 and appears promising.

Treatment of Choice: Positive Psychology

The treatment of choice for all the disorders discussed in the text has been based exclusively on the disease model. It is possible that an even more effective treatment may emerge using a strengths model, or positive psychology approach. In the early twentieth century, the field of psychology included a distinctive focus on building strengths in addition to curing mental illness earlier. However, following World War II, psychologists found that most research funding and jobs were available for those working on treatments for mental illness. The authors assert that we need to return to our roots and begin conducting research on human strength and virtue.

TESTING YOUR UNDERSTANDING

Test your understanding of what you have read by working through the following tasks with a classmate.

1. Explain to a friend why the Columbine High School shootings occurred. Include social, psychological, and biological factors.

2. What is the difference between efficacy and effectiveness studies? What are the limitations of each?

3. Why does psychotherapy work? Explain the concept of "tactics" and "nonspecific factors."

4. If a friend told you he was going to start therapy, and he has managed care insurance, what would you warn him about before he begins?

5. Why is prevention so important?

6. Imagine you go on to become a psychologist and decide to focus on positive psychology in your research. What might your research look like? What kinds of questions would you ask?

Multiple-Choice Questions

1. What are the two psychological epidemics in the United States today, according to the text?
   a. depression and anxiety
   b. depression and violence
   c. violence and substance abuse
   d. anxiety and substance abuse

2. Which is true regarding violence, aggression, and the DSM-IV?
   a. Aggression is included in the DSM-IV, but violence is not.
   b. Violence is included in the DSM-IV, but aggression is not.
   c. Neither aggression nor violence is included in the DSM-IV.
   d. Both aggression and violence are included in the DSM-IV.

3. Which theme fits with the topic of prevention?
   a. levels of analysis
   b. science and practice
   c. development
   d. treatment of choice

4. In the case of Michael, the boy who murdered three students and wounded five others at Heath High School, which psychological problems did he appear to suffer from?
   a. depression and schizophrenia
   b. depression and substance abuse
   c. schizophrenia and substance abuse
   d. There appeared to be no mental illness involved in this case.

5. Which is true of rampage murderers compared to other types of murderers?
   a. They are better educated.
   b. They are more "deprived."
   c. They are less likely to be white.
   d. They are less likely to suffer from mental illness.

6. The brain scans of cold-blooded murderers differ from the brain scans of impulsive murderers in what area?
   a. amygdala
   b. prefrontal cortex
   c. hippocampus
   d. thalamus

7. Which of the following types of outcome studies use a control group and random assignment?
   a. efficacy studies
   b. effectiveness studies
   c. both a and b
   d. neither a nor b

8. Patients in _____ studies are more likely to have multiple problems.
   a. efficacy studies
   b. effectiveness studies
   c. both a and b
   d. neither a nor b

9. Which of the following is NOT one of the methodological flaws of the *Consumer Reports* effectiveness study of psychotherapy?
   a. use of self-report data
   b. use of retrospective data
   c. lack of control groups
   d. inability to generalize

10. Which of the following is NOT one of the findings of the *Consumer Reports* effectiveness study of psychotherapy?
    a. Treatment worked very well.
    b. Long-term therapy produced much more improvement than short-term therapy.
    c. Cognitive-behavioral therapy worked best.
    d. All of the above are findings of the *Consumer Reports* study.

11. There are five properties of psychotherapy as it is practiced in the field by clinicians that are not captured by laboratory studies. Which of the following is NOT one of those properties?
    a. Psychotherapy in the field is not of fixed duration.
    b. Psychotherapy in the field is self-correcting.
    c. Patients of psychotherapy in the field actively shop for therapists.
    d. Psychotherapy in the field is concerned only with relief of specific, presenting symptoms.

12. Relaxation for phobia is an example of:
    a. a specific curative ingredient.
    b. a nonspecific tactic.
    c. a nonspecific deep strategy.
    d. building buffering strengths.

13. An example of a nonspecific tactic used in therapy is:
    a. exposure for OCD.
    b. trust.
    c. instilling hope.
    d. building optimism.

14. In the managed care system, who typically decides what treatment to use?
    a. the client
    b. the therapist
    c. the case reviewer
    d. the primary care physician

15. Which of the following treatments has been shown to be effective in preventing depression in college and high school students?
    a. antidepressant medication
    b. cognitive therapy techniques
    c. behavioral therapy techniques
    d. psychodynamic psychotherapy techniques

16. Studies of the prevention of depression in children have indicated that "booster sessions" need to be used _____ years following the intervention.
    a. two
    b. three
    c. four
    d. five

17. The Fast-Track program is designed to prevent _____ in children.
    a. depression
    b. anxiety
    c. violence
    d. substance abuse

18. Which of the following was NOT one of the distinct missions of psychology before World War II?
    a. curing mental illness
    b. making the lives of all people more productive and fulfilling
    c. identifying and nurturing high talent
    d. all of the above

19. Which of the following is NOT one of the reasons given for the focus on curing mental illness following World War II?
    a. the founding of the Veterans Administration
    b. the founding of the National Institute of Mental Health
    c. the large numbers of mentally ill following the war
    d. all of the above

20. What specific therapeutic techniques do the authors suggest we research as part of "positive psychology?"
    a. client-therapist rapport
    b. narration
    c. interpretation
    d. relaxation

Fill in the Blank

1. _____ studies are outcome studies conducted in controlled laboratories. Efficacy

2. _____ studies are treatment outcome studies of therapy as it is actually done in the real world. Effectiveness

3. _____ are nonspecific approaches, such as attention, rapport, and trust, used in all modes of therapy. Tactics

4. _____ _____, such as instilling hope and building buffering strengths, are nonspecific approaches used in all modes of therapy. Deep strategies

5. _____ _____ studies would include all the patients from a wide and representative range of modalities of treatment. Total sample

6. The _____-_____ program intervenes at school, home, and with peers to try to prevent youth violence. Fast-Track

7. _____ psychology refers to building human strengths rather than repairing pathology. Positive

ANSWER KEY

MULTIPLE-CHOICE QUESTIONS

1. b. According to the text, there is currently an epidemic of depression and of violence among young people.

2. c. Violence and aggression are not categories of mental illness in the DSM-IV.

3. c. The topic of prevention is discussed under the theme of development in the text, as the fact that humans grow and develop makes prevention possible at an earlier stage, before a disorder kicks in.

4. a. Michael's rampage appeared to be preceded by symptoms of depression and schizophrenia.

5. a. Rampage murderers are better educated, less deprived, and more likely to be white. At least half have a history of serious mental illness.

6. b. Brain scans of all murderers reveal reduced activation of the prefrontal cortex, the corpus callosum, the left amygdala, hippocampus, and thalamus. Cold-blooded killers who plan their actions have the same pattern, but they have better prefrontal activity than impulsive murderers.

7. a. Efficacy studies are conducted in laboratories under carefully controlled conditions. They employ a control group for comparison with the treatment group and random assignment to conditions.

8. b. Effectiveness studies are studies of psychotherapy as it is done in the real world. The patients typically treated by clinicians have many problems, whereas only patients with one definite problem are seen in efficacy studies.

9. d. This study, and effectiveness studies in general, are limited by the use of self-report and retrospective data and the lack of control groups. However, these studies are done in the community and thus can be generalized very well.

10. c. Results indicated that treatment worked very well, that long-term therapy produced much more improvement than short-term therapy, and that no specific modality worked better than any other.

11. d. Psychotherapy in the field is almost always concerned with improvement in the general functioning of patients, as well as with relief of specific, presenting symptoms.

12. a. Relaxation for phobia is an example of a specific curative ingredient in psychotherapy for a specific problem.

13. b. Trust, attention, rapport, etc., are all examples of nonspecific tactics used in all modalities of therapy. Exposure for OCD is a specific, curative strategy. Instilling hope and building optimism are examples of nonspecific, deeper strategies.

14. c. In managed care, the case reviewer decides what therapist a patient will see, which type of therapy the patient will receive, and how long he or she will receive treatment.

15. b. Cognitive therapy techniques have been shown to be effective in preventing depression in college and high school students.

16. a. Studies of the prevention of depression in children have indicated that "booster sessions" need to be used two years following the intervention.

17. c. The Fast-Track program is designed to prevent violence in children by intervening at school, at home, and with peers.

18. d. Psychology had three distinct missions: curing mental illness, making the lives of all people more productive and fulfilling, and identifying and nurturing high talent.

19. c. The text points to two major reasons for the focus on curing mental illness following World War II: the founding of the Veterans Administration, and the founding of the National Institute of Mental Health, both of which enable psychologists to receive money for focusing on mental illness.

20. b. Narration, or telling the story of our lives, is a powerful positive technique that is typically used in therapy but never studied.